# THE DOWNHILL HIKING CLUB

## A SHORT WALK
## ACROSS THE LEBANON

# DOM JOLY

ROBINSON

ROBINSON

First published in Great Britain in 2019 by Constable as *The Hezbollah Hiking Club*
This paperback edition published in 2021 by Robinson

1 3 5 7 9 10 8 6 4 2

A CIP catalogue record for this book
is available from the British Library.

ISBN: 978-1-47212-843-0

Typeset in Bembo by Hewer Text UK Ltd, Edinburgh
Printed and bound in Great Britain by Clays Ltd, Elcograf S.p.A.

Papers used by Robinson are from well-managed
forests and other responsible sources.

Robinson
An imprint of
Little, Brown Book Group
Carmelite House
50 Victoria Embankment
London EC4Y 0DZ

An Hachette UK Company
www.hachette.co.uk

www.littlebrown.co.uk

Praise for *The Downhill Hiking Club*:

'A total delight, from beginning to end. Immensely funny, and shot through with illuminating and telling insights into a country Joly clearly adores. I read it at a sitting and was charmed and enlightened by every page'

— **John Simpson CBE, World Affairs Editor, BBC News**

'Compelling, enlightening, funny and yet serious too. This trip through Lebanon is both journey and reportage, both intimate and informative on this complex country'

— **Simon Sebag Montefiore, *Sunday Times* bestselling author**

'Dom Joly writes travel books for people who don't usually read travel books. This is the best adventure I've had on my sofa for years. It's funny, weirdly informative and, most importantly, blister-free'

— **Jenny Eclair, *Sunday Times* bestselling author and award-winning comedian**

To Harry and Chris

'A friend is someone who knows all about you and still loves you.'

Elbert Hubbard

# Contents

'Learn to deal with the valleys, the hills will take care of themselves.'

Count Basie

# Foreword

It seems so long ago that we set off up the steps of Jezzine on our adventure. The world has changed so much since then.

As I sit in my library in Cheltenham, a place that that has been my virtual prison for the last ten months, I stare endlessly at an old map of Lebanon that I have on my wall. Oh, what I would give to be back there again, setting off on what was, without doubt, one of the most memorable adventures of my life.

If the pandemic and lockdown has taught me one thing, it's the importance of friendship. You only know how important your friends are when they are taken away from you. I am fortunate in that Harry lives near me in Cheltenham, while Chris is an almost constant Zoom presence from his feng-shui-friendly abode in Dubai. They have kept me sane through this weirdness.

It has also, of course, served to remind me of just how vital travel is to my soul. I suffer from wandermust [sic] and have been like a caged tiger even since the first reports started coming out of a place called Wuhan ...

There are constant plans being made for another, post-pandemic adventure. One idea was to follow the England Test team around Australia for an Ashes series. Another was to sail around the Black Sea in a boat (The Black Sea Sailing Club).

The latest is to take the world's longest railway journey from Lisbon to Beijing.

One day, the club will travel again.

On 4 August 2020, I was at home writing when my phone started going mad.

'Have you seen the news?'

'Turn on the news.'

'You heard the news?'

Whatever the news was, it was obviously bad. Whenever I get these sorts of messages it's never good. But I didn't automatically think of Lebanon, as I used to in the bad old days. Maybe it was another 9/11, another tsunami, another Chernobyl? I flicked to a news outlet on my phone and saw the massive explosion in Beirut and went into shock.

A massive amount of ammonium nitrate stored at Beirut Port had exploded, causing at least 204 deaths and leaving more than three hundred thousand people homeless. The ammonium had been confiscated by authorities from an abandoned ship called the MV Rhosus and then left in a warehouse without any appropriate safety measures.

Growing up, as I did, in Lebanon, you tend to get pretty used to terrible news. For such a small country, three times smaller than Belgium, it has certainly suffered way more than its fair share of horror. This explosion, however, cut me to the core. It was personal and, for once, it wasn't the result of war.

My family have been shipping agents in Beirut Port since 1900. My sister's office overlooks the port. The massive grain silo that stood right next to the explosion was so incredibly familiar to me. As a kid, I could see it out of my dad's office. I could see it from the balcony of our family home above Beirut.

To me it was the physical centrepiece of our family's history in Lebanon. In one horrific second it was blown apart, along with a massive part of Beirut. My sister, thank God, was at home but her office, like vast swathes of Beirut, was a write-off. The port, the lifeblood of this coastal nation, was utterly devastated, dealing a shattering blow to an already crippled economy.

This book was always intended to be a love letter to Lebanon. It was intended to try and change people's attitudes towards the place. Whenever Lebanon came up, people immediately associated it with war and violence. The term 'looks like Beirut' became a catchphrase for anywhere that looked beaten up or destroyed.

Lebanon was undergoing economic problems for sure, but the war was long over, and Beirut had been rebuilt. It was time for a reassessment. It was time for people to see the country as I did, as one of the most beautiful places in the world. From the ski slopes, the beaches and the pine forests to the cedars, the food and the people; so warm, so cultured, so inspiring, having kept going through everything that had been thrown at them. And then this. An accident that has left more than three hundred thousand people homeless in a country where, due to the massive influx of people fleeing the war in Syria, roughly one in four people is a refugee.

The rest of 2020 has been a shattering time for Lebanon. The economy is on the brink of collapse. COVID-19 has ravaged the population as they try to deal with the after-effects of the explosion.

Lebanon is a crucial piece in the Middle East puzzle. Instability there directly affects the whole region and, consequently, Europe and beyond. Lebanon deserves a chance to rebuild itself as a beacon of democracy and hope in a historically unstable part of the world.

It seems counter-intuitive but, if ever there was time to show support for this country, it is now. Go there, travel around, walk in the mountains, eat the food, meet the people. You will never regret it.

In the words of Khalil Gibran, one of Lebanon's most famous sons:

> 'Pity the nation that raises not its voice save when it
> walks in a funeral, boasts not except among its ruins'

**Dom Joly**
**Cheltenham, December 2020**

# BASE CAMP

England were 147 for 4.

The Lord's crowd were restless, and we were quite a few pints down when the idea formed in a slightly blurry fashion in my head.

'We should all do an adventure ...' I said, looking at Harry and Chris in what I hoped was an affectionate but enigmatic manner.

'How about you buying a round? Now *that* would be an adventure.' Harry turned his pint glass upside down to indicate his readiness for another drink.

'No ... a proper adventure. We should head off and do something big together. You know, like an extended midlife crisis sort of thing.'

The crowd roared as Joe Root waved his bat at a ball and nicked a boundary.

'ROOOOOOOOOOOOOOOOOOOOOOOOOOOOOOOO OOOOOOOOTTTTTTTT,' they roared. To anyone who didn't follow cricket it always sounded like they were booing. This applied to nobody more so than my wife, Stacey, who is Canadian. She occasionally joined me at a game only to be utterly bamboozled by the whole scene. She was not with us today. This was a boys' day out.

'I'm serious,' I continued. 'How about we do something really ... out there. How about we walk across Lebanon?'

That got their attention.

'How long would that take?' asked Chris, unconsciously adjusting the pocket square in his neatly pressed blazer.

'Oh ... I don't know ... a month?' I was totally winging it.

'Not sure my wife would let me do that,' said Chris.

'I've got work,' replied Harry to the evident surprise of the ruddy-cheeked old man in a colourful blazer sitting next to him. He had obviously assumed, from Harry's gloriously unkempt appearance, that he was on some sort of government day-release programme for ne'er-do-wells financed by some socialist council that, in his view, was responsible for the decline and fall of Western civilisation.

'Oh, come on. Are we mice or men?' I asked insistently.

'Well, I'd have to pretend that it was some sort of extended work trip,' said Chris.

'What's the food like?' said Harry. 'Is it all foreign?'

'It's the best food in the world. Hands down. You'll love it,' I said enthusiastically. 'So ... are we up for it?'

'Yes,' said Chris.

'Only if you buy that round,' said Harry, looking at his empty glass again.

And that was that. A plan was agreed and then promptly forgotten about.

The idea to walk across Lebanon was not quite as off-the-wall as it sounded. I was born in Beirut in 1967 to English parents and lived there until I was sent to boarding school in England at the age of seven. This coincided with Lebanon descending into a vicious civil war that started in 1975 and officially finished in 1990. My life morphed into a rather schizo-phrenic existence, bouncing between a posh English boarding school and life in what was then considered to be the most dangerous country in the world.

I was always rather jealous that I was just too young to have enjoyed Lebanon in her pre-war heyday when she was known as the 'Switzerland of the Middle East' and Beirut the 'Paris of the East'. Lebanon was a beautiful, sophisticated country full of culture, skiing, beaches, nightlife – an exotic playground for the international jet set. Quite why it was ever compared to Switzerland, a phenomenally dull country with a penchant for anti-multiculturalism, was beyond me. From what I knew of Lebanon, it was more a combination of the Reeperbahn and the South of France, with a skiing option.

My parents, like most non-natives to anywhere, were more evangelical about the place than the locals. They adored the country and they were both in love with the mountains in particular. They loved to hike in them. I have photos of count-less family outings there, occasionally with me bringing up the rear seated on a donkey. I think my dad was a frustrated adven-turer, duty-bound to join the family company but never happier than when on what we always called 'expeditions'. My mother adored walking, and one of the few things my parents seemed to have in common was a love of setting off on an expedition into the Lebanese mountains or further afield into Syria.

I always felt that, unlike my older half-brother, Marc-Henri, and half-sisters, Hatty and Anne-Dominique, from my parents' first marriages, I'd missed the boat in really getting to know Lebanon. The advent of war made free travel around the coun-try much more difficult and we found ourselves more and more confined within the Maronite heartland, in the hills just above Beirut where my father and his first wife, Diana, had built our house when he had taken over the family company from his father in the fifties. And then, when the war had finally ended and Lebanon started along a new, precarious path of relative peace, my parents divorced. Out of the blue, just after my eighteenth birthday, my father suddenly didn't show up for a family get-together. He had left my mother for his secretary, Cathy, a relationship that would not last long but served as a springboard for his permanent escape.

From the moment I hit my teens, my father and I had a very difficult relationship. Before this we'd got on brilliantly. We'd shared a mutual love of cricket and tennis, and I adored him. Then I committed the cardinal sin – developing opinions of my own. I started 'answering back', a crime that appeared to be on a par with treason in his eyes. Having had children of my own I can now see how annoying it is but, in the grand scheme of things, there are far worse things in the world than to be spirited and opinionated . . . being a bad father, for example.

Things rapidly went downhill. He hated the way I dressed. He disliked the music I played. He loathed my 'attitude'. To be honest, he seemed to disapprove of pretty much everything that I did. He seemed permanently disappointed in me but was unable to express why.

We were not one but two generations apart from each other. He was forty-three years old when I was born in 1967, the so-called 'Summer of Love', not that he would have been aware of that. A combination of the slightly antiquated, frozen nature of ex-pat life in Lebanon and the frenetic pace of change that Western society was undergoing in the 1960s and

1970s transported us to worlds apart. We did not communicate well. He loathed conflict but was constantly conflicted. When he had something that bothered him (which happened a lot), he would write long and painful letters. I received such a letter a couple of days after I discovered that he was leaving my mother.

'By now you will be aware of what has happened,' it read.

I wasn't.

'Know this. You will always know where I am and how to reach me.'

I never really did.

And so, I moved from a physical separation from Lebanon to an emotional one. I'd left the country to go to school for my last term and I never went home. My mother and I were extradited to England, her possessions expunged and forwarded, in a random job lot, to the pied-à-terre that we had been left in Highgate. We both hated the place. It reeked of the past, of bad memories, of holding patterns. We sold up and bought a place in Holland Park. There we remained for the next ten years or so, awkwardly clinging to each other, Levantine exiles in London.

I didn't go back to the place I called home for another twenty years. I started to block it off. I compartmentalised my life. I built a wall. Lebanon was the past. England was the present. At the age of eighteen, I pretty much started again. Year Zero. I tried not to think about Lebanon or that part of my life. The loss was too painful. I started at the University of London and attended the School of Oriental and African Studies to read first Arabic and then politics. Attended might be the wrong word. I became a goth. I had massive panic attacks. I started to go into university less and less. I became the singer in a band. I started spending lots of time with girlfriends at various provincial universities where student life was more defined and seemed a lot more fun. I was a total mess. I eventually stumbled through university and out into life. I was living in a puzzle and had lost a lot of vital pieces.

Unsure what to do next, I moved to Paris with a girlfriend and spent a year living in exile from exile. I was as rootless as it was possible to be. Then, slowly I got my life together. Having become a diplomat in Prague and a producer for ITN in Parliament, I stumbled by accident into the world of comedy. At the age of thirty I found myself. I made a show called *Trigger Happy TV* and it went global. I sold the programme to over eighty countries and it opened up the world to me. But much as I loved comedy, my real passion was writing. I started writing for the *Independent on Sunday*, travel writing for the *Sunday Times* and, in between comedy shows, sated my wanderlust by traipsing all over the globe.

But I never went back to Lebanon: it was a country that still only existed to me in the pages of my mother's photo albums. Fading photos of picnics, expeditions, boat rides, stilted parental moments all from the fifties, sixties and early seventies. It was like looking at photos of a party to which I hadn't been invited. I wanted my own photos, my own photo album. I wanted my own Lebanon.

In 2005, I dipped my toe in the water. I went to Beirut with a film crew to make a show for Sky called *Dom Joly's Excellent Adventure*. In this show I retraced the route of one of our family journeys into Syria, to the desert city of Palmyra, historically one of the favourite Joly family destinations for an expedition.

I only spent two days in Lebanon itself before heading off into Syria, but it broke the ice. Three years later I returned for a week to write a chapter about the country for my first travel book, *The Dark Tourist*. The book did very well, but I felt that the chapter on Lebanon was the weakest. My father was still alive, unspoken tensions within my family were omnipresent, and I was still tiptoeing around their lives and not making my own.

But one thing I did discover on that trip was the Lebanon Mountain Trail (LMT): a 470-kilometre-long walking trail extending from near the Israeli border in the south to the Syrian border in the north.

The LMT had been set up by a group of eco-minded enthusiasts in order to try to give Lebanon's rather stultified tourism industry a shot in the arm. It would be fair to say that it hadn't been a huge tourist draw. The trail takes you across the spine of Lebanon, along the mountain range that rises up from the Mediterranean coastal towns, before plummeting back down into the fertile Beqaa Valley and the Syrian border.

In 2009, I had met a man called Paul Khawaja who worked at the British Embassy and was an integral part of the LMT organisation. I'd arranged to meet him at the beginning of one of the stages above Tripoli in the north of the country to go for a bit of a walk and talk. The moment we met, I could feel him giving me a rather disappointed once-over. He made it very clear that he didn't think the LMT was for me. I pretended that this was no big deal, but it had rankled. I don't like being told that I can't do things, even when it is for my own good. The idea of walking across Lebanon stuck in my head. It appealed greatly. Here was a chance for me to make my own memories, find my own Lebanon.

Nine years later, I'd decided to act and, in that lubricated moment of enthusiasm, had decided to write a book about it, roping in two of my best friends to boot.

I wondered whether this was how most great adventures got started. Had Stanley, after a couple of sherbets too many in the Long Room, announced that he was off to find Livingstone and that nobody was to try to persuade him otherwise? Probably not.

The first thing I had to do was to contact Chris and Harry and gently remind them that they had agreed to walk across Lebanon with me.

I emailed them both.

'I presume you remember that we agreed to walk across Lebanon? I was thinking May?'

Chris came straight back to me.

'Excellent ... just got to get it across the line with Samar but count me in.'

There was nothing from Harry for several days. This was not surprising as communication was never his forte. Eventually I rang him.

'Harry, it's Dom. Are you up for the walk across Lebanon?'

'Yes, why not?' he replied. 'You sort it all out and let me know. I'll be there,' he continued before hanging up.

And that was that. It seemed like we were off. Now we just had to do it.

\*       \*       \*

Chris, Harry and I had been away together before. Shortly after I met Chris, he suggested that we head off to Sri Lanka to watch England play cricket. I was very tempted but a little nervous that he might have misunderstood the platonic nature of our relationship. So, I proposed that Harry join us on the trip. At the time Chris, who lived in Dubai, had a PA, Zoe, who was not only brilliant at organising stuff but happened to be a direct descendant of Mehmed V, the penultimate Ottoman Sultan and technically ninth in line to take over Turkey should the Ottoman Empire ever be resuscitated.

Chris had put Zoe in charge of the trip and it was impressive stuff. I wondered whether Zoe might be available again to help us organise the Lebanon walk? She wasn't. I think that Chris's habit of stumbling out of Sri Lankan bars at two in the morning and ringing her in Dubai to demand that she sort out a taxi had, quite rightly, made her a little wary of taking on such a task again. There was also the problem of us constantly telling her that we had a fourth person travelling with us called Sir Geoffrey Jefferson (Geoffrey with a G, Jefferson with a J) who appeared to have an inordinate number of special requests. Chris would ask Zoe to ring ahead to restaurants that we intended to visit to let them know that Sir Geoffrey was coming and that there were a number of things that he required. These included requests such as 'Nobody else in the restaurant must be wearing blue. Blue is Sir Geoffrey's colour and he will not tolerate anybody else sporting it' or that 'Sir Geoffrey will not eat at any establishment with a French chef.' Sir Geoffrey never actually joined us. He was always 'running late and would be here soon'.

Unsurprisingly Zoe resigned from her position as Chris's PA soon after the Sri Lankan trip. There was a feeling that she would have found running the Ottoman Empire a little easier. We were never sure whether she knew that Sir Geoffrey didn't actually exist. She did, however, find the number of a lady in Beirut called Caroll, whose website suggested that she might be someone who could help us organise our Lebanese adventure.

I contacted Caroll by email. She said that yes, she could set up the trip and sent through an itinerary that had us starting in the north of Lebanon, near the Syrian border, and ending up in the south, near the Israeli border. We would be following the Lebanon Mountain Trail and there were established places to stay every night that included guesthouses, monasteries and, to Chris's chagrin ... youth hostels.

I looked at the daily distances: they averaged out at about 20 kilometres a day. This didn't seem too bad as I normally walked about 10 to 15 kilometres a day with my dogs Truman and Fitzgerald in the Cotswolds. At the back of my mind, however, I was aware that the Cotswolds were very much hills rather than mountains. More worryingly, each day had a difficulty level after it. Our first three days went: *Difficult, Very Difficult, Very Difficult*. This was perhaps not the way to start, given our levels of physical fitness. So, I emailed Caroll again and told her that, as we were three unfit men who were fifty years old and with zero experience of hiking, I was a little concerned about the *Very Difficult* nature of our walk.

Caroll suggested that we flip the walk around and start in the south and head north. She said that the earlier stages were easier, and that we could 'get into our stride' that way. So, it was decided: we were to walk from Israel to Syria across the spine of Lebanon. We agreed on a date starting in the last week of April. I chose this because I didn't want it to be too hot; nor did

I want to walk through the Lebanese winter. Also, my mum told me that this was the best time for wild flowers. Now, I'm not really a wild-flower type of person but this sounded as good a reason as any other.

Chris started training on his own. By 'training', it turned out, he meant just aimlessly wandering around his gated community for half an hour or so a day walking his chihuahua, Beano, to his maximum capacity. Because Dubai is almost entirely flat, he later stepped up his training programme by joining the Dubai Polo Club so that he could use their step machine. I was already worried about Chris.

I continued walking my dogs every day and tried to find some slightly steeper hills to clamber up, without much success. Harry lives near me, in Cheltenham, and I started to hear reports that he had been spotted out walking. It turned out that he had gone for about five walks and then saw the itinerary, spotted that one of the days was only 9 kilometres long and decided not to bother training as it would be 'easy'. I worried that this was not how Ben Fogle had trained for Everest, but it was too late: flights had been booked and I'd told too many people about it to back out now.

Chris was clearly panicking. Two weeks before we were scheduled to leave I received an email from him.

Maestro. It occurs to me that we might have bitten off more than we can chew – Lebanon-wise. Before we embark on this foolhardy adventure, may I suggest an alternative course of action? I have very good connections with a wonderful five-star hotel in Thailand that would accommodate us for a very reasonable price. Might I suggest that we tell our respective other halves that we are off to Lebanon but, instead, fly to said hotel and spend three weeks in the style to which we are accustomed? You could post some stock photos of Lebanon daily on your social channels and I'm sure your imagination could conjure up a far more interesting book about our walk than reality might produce. Just a thought but I implore you to consider it seriously.

Chris

This was so Chris. And this was so tempting. After all, what was travel writing but exaggeration? An amalgamation of experiences? My duty was to do anything in pursuit of a good story, an entertaining read. I grew up in Lebanon and had a plethora of stories. I could definitely make up a book about me walking across Lebanon in which I turned out to be a naturally gifted leader and hiker. We would get into some serious scrapes – Harry would be attacked by a wild bear (even though there weren't any in Lebanon). I would bravely fight it off and save Harry without harming said bear. I would adopt the bear, call him Nigel and he would become my faithful companion. Nigel and I would go on to have many more bestselling adventures together, including: *Travels with My Bear*, *Bearly There: An Opium Journey* and *Bear with Me*.

Then there would be the hostage situation. Because Chris, a gadget freak, didn't know how to use his fancy new GPS machine we would inadvertently wander into Syria, where we would be taken prisoner by an armed gang. We would be kept hostage just as long as we could afford to stay in our Thai retreat. Occasionally I would release brave hostage videos of myself offering to sacrifice my life if they let Chris and Harry go.

Eventually we would escape and surface in Beirut (fresh off a plane from Bangkok) to international fame and acclaim, and much pampering from our wives if they hadn't already remarried and moved on.

There would certainly be no practical problem writing such a book. But I felt a curious loyalty towards Lebanon. Whenever anybody thinks about the country they equate it with war and chaos. The civil war may have officially ended in 1990 but Lebanon still has a PR problem. There was even a guy who spent his time trying to sue any news outlet that used the phrase 'looks like Beirut' to describe anywhere that was smashed to bits.

I wanted this trip to be a love letter to Lebanon. I wanted to try to avoid the usual look-at-me-I'm-a-brave-traveller-doing-brave-dangerous-things bollocks that I'd been guilty of in the past. The truth is that Lebanon is one of the most incredible countries in the world and anybody travelling there pretty much has the country to themselves. So, this was the travel writer's true quandary. When you found somewhere so beautiful, so utterly wonderful, did you share the secret with everybody else?

I hit reply to Chris. 'Tempting ... but no dice. We walk.'

It was time for me to stamp my authority on my troops. They needed to know that they had a strong and decisive leader to guide them through the weeks ahead. Unfortunately, we didn't have one. It was going to be down to me.

To cement my decision, I went shopping with Harry to get our equipment. Harry is an old-fashioned kind of man and shopping is not something that is one of his specialities. We drove to a large outdoor store that I had previously avoided like the plague, seeing as it was the haunt of those annoying middle-aged rambler types with laminated maps, walking poles and silly hats. I suddenly realised with a shudder that I was about to become one of those annoying people.

We started with a rucksack each, a kit bag, walking shirts, trousers, socks ... the pile just got bigger and bigger. I was almost convinced that we wouldn't need most of these things, but the panic was setting in and I didn't want to be without anything essential as, once we were in the High Lebanon, there wasn't going to be much in the way of shopping. I'd reached out to Twitter for help and a man called Jason, who led expeditions to Everest and such-like, had been very helpful. I'd asked him for a list of things that I might need. The things that stuck out were: toenail clippers, Vaseline and breathable underpants. Having done a bit of walking about in hot climates, I was intensely aware that the 'gentleman areas' could get extremely uncomfortable and needed to be looked after with something a little more impactful than the usual baby powder. I steered Harry towards a wall of merino wool underpants.

'We're going to need these. My guy says they are brilliant.' I pointed at the pants.

'I don't need any of those,' said Harry, as though I'd just suggested he defecate on the shop floor.

'You really do, Harry, it's going to get hot down there.' I pointed towards his crotch.

'I don't wear pants,' he said.

'What, never?'

'Never. I just don't see the point.' He started to walk towards the CamelBaks.

'Hang on, you're seriously telling me that you're going to walk across Lebanon *commando*? You're going to be in serious trouble, believe me.' I was genuinely concerned.

'No, it'll be fine,' Harry said.

He never ceased to amaze me.

Half an hour later we exited the building with a considerable hole in our bank accounts and enough equipment to stage a pretty full-on attempt at Everest, K2 and Annapurna. Our final purchase had been walking poles. Caroll had told me that they were essential, but they had always looked ludicrous to me. When ramblers strode past me in the Cotswolds with them they always had the look of skiers who'd forgotten their skis.

The final stop was at a pharmacy. We needed Vaseline, but it appeared that it was no longer available in one large tub. Only the smaller, handy-sized tubs were on offer. I had no idea how much I'd need so I bought ten tubs. Harry did the same. The pharmacist had to stifle a fit of giggles as Harry and I walked away from the counter with our lifetime supply of Vaseline. Little did she know that she had just served two of the most prominent adventurers in the Cheltenham area. To explain why we needed so much Vaseline would seem boastful and so I left her to come to her own perverted and sordid conclusions.

Preparations were complete. It was time to just do it.

# GO EAST

The last time that I had been in Lebanon had been for my father's funeral in 2011. I was in the middle of my first and only live tour of the UK – seventy dates of mostly dying on stage every night was interrupted by the news of my father's death. He'd been living with my sister Hatty and her husband Michael at the family home in Lebanon.

In the last years of his life he had become very fragile, a shadow of his former self. He'd get confused as to where he was and think everyone was stealing his money. We had been pretty much estranged since he'd left my mum when I was eighteen. We'd had something of a rapprochement late in his life, but this was with a stranger – a gentle, rather sweet version of his former complicated and internalised self. It was nice, but it felt like I was getting to know a different person. The one I knew as a distant father had already gone. I remember leaving the graveside and driving up into the mountains to the house and feeling guilty. It felt wrong leaving him down there, all alone, abandoned.

Now I was flying home for the first time without having his powerful shadow over any experience I had in Lebanon. This was very much unexplored territory for me.

Harry and I headed towards Heathrow Airport in high spirits. We would meet Chris at Beirut Airport, where he was flying in from Dubai. We would then 'acclimatise' by staying for two nights with my sister, who lived in the family house, overlooking Beirut, that I grew up in. Then we would meet Caroll and start our adventure proper.

In the car on the way, we got a message from Chris informing us that he was wearing the 'hiking blazer' that he had got his tailor to make. He also informed us that his Emirates limo had just picked him up from his house. We chose not to reply. As we approached Heathrow I got another message. This time it was from my sister, who told me that the British Embassy in Beirut had spotted my tweets about our intended trip and had got in touch with her. She said that they wanted to offer 'assistance and support' because they were nervous about what we intended to do. I sent them a message enquiring as to whether they would be able to pay for porters for the trip. Weirdly, I got nothing back.

Finally, just as we were pulling into Heathrow I received a text from Harry's Belgian wife, Virginie. It was a close-up photo of a disgusting pile of blood-specked dog poo. I assumed that she had not taken my stealing of her husband for three weeks very well. I sent quite a stern text back telling her to get a grip and to not be so possessive. It turned out that there was something wrong with their new puppy. She was worried and wanted to know whether to take him to the vet. She had sent me the photo to show Harry, as he was a devout technophobe with an old phone that did not receive photos.

We checked in and I got Harry into the British Airways lounge, where he started grumbling immediately. Harry was a man who liked things a certain way and we had crossed that uncertain line where breakfast turned into brunch and this troubled him greatly. Harry loved his breakfasts and 'brunch' was an American import that had no place in his world.

I always get in trouble at airports. They are like casinos – artificial environments where normal rules don't apply. You spend money as though it doesn't count, drink copious amounts of alcohol at times of the day that would make you an alcoholic in normal life and think nothing of having four or five meals before getting on the plane. Humans were hunter-gatherers and we are not built to withstand endless free buffets.

Someone wandered past in shorts. Shorts were now actually properly short, finishing well above the knee. Personally, I missed the meeting when this was decreed and stuck to my below-the-knee Carhartts, opting to wait for the fashion wave to flow back in my favour.

A balding man, who looked like an ageing turtle, wandered past with a black bag over his shoulder. The entire bag was covered with the word SUPERDRY in electric blue letters. I never got this. Superdry had managed to get him to pay for the privilege of walking around like some ugly human billboard advertising their business. It was nonsensical to me but hats off to the company for managing to harness the power of sheep.

I glanced to my right. A tubby man in his late forties was looking around, seemingly checking everyone out. He held a large glass of champagne and had a somewhat haughty air to him. I didn't like the look of him at all and prayed that he wouldn't engage me in conversation. Then I realised that the man in question was me. I had now started analysing my own reflection. I decided that it was probably time to give the free champagne a rest and think about the trip ahead.

We were taking a flight that I knew all too well. The BA London–Beirut trip that I had done so many times as a kid. I used to do it as a UM (Unaccompanied Minor). I would have my passport in a laminated pocket hung round my neck and would be handed over to a stewardess at check-in. I was a member of the excitingly monikered Junior Jet Club. This meant that I had a little dark blue book that I used to take up to the cockpit to get the pilots to sign. It's probably illegal now to be alone in a cockpit with a pilot, like that scene from *Airplane!* where the pilot chats to a small boy: '*You ever been in a cockpit before? You ever . . . seen a grown man naked? Do you . . . like movies about gladiators? Joey, have you ever been . . . in a Turkish prison?*'

Come to think of it, that film was made in 1980, just around the time I was making those UM flights.

It was so weird to be going 'home', returning to the house that I grew up in. The house my father built. The house that was home until it suddenly wasn't. When my dad died he had left the family house in Lebanon and our house in France to my sister Hatty, who had also taken over the family company. I had no share of my physical past. At once, I felt strangely free of his omnipresent critical scrutiny and totally disenfranchised from my own history. Before his death, I was in exile. Now I was a tourist who'd left it too late to return . . .

My dad had two daughters from his first marriage. The other, Susan, contracted leukaemia and died in 1975 when I was seven. I think, with my Freudian hat on, that this was the fault line. I think that my dad felt guilty that he'd left his first wife for my mother and that my sister had then got ill and that he somehow wasn't there for her. I think he saw me as a physical manifest-ation of it all – a living, breathing guilt boil.

The pilot announced that we were landing in Beirut. On the map on my screen I could see Beirut surrounded by places I knew so well. To the south, Tel Aviv. To the east, Damascus. Then the Syrian cities of Homs, Hama and Aleppo. Every place name brought back vivid memories.

Homs was the place that people made jokes about. 'Why did a Homsi take a car door into the desert? To wind the window down when it got too hot.'

Hama – I remembered its Roman water wheels. That was before that city was almost razed to the ground by Rifaat al-Assad, the über-violent uncle of Bashar al-Assad. But that was in another time, another conflict, earlier than the current Syrian civil war. A time when Lebanon was the war zone and when we would escape into Syria to get away from the incessant conflict. We would drive to the ruins of Palmyra and the dubious joys of the Zenobia Hotel before moving on to stay at the Baron's Hotel in Aleppo, in the footsteps of T. E. Lawrence and Freya Stark. Now everything was topsy-turvy, as it so often was in this region. Syria was the new ground zero and many of her desperate population were streaming into refugee camps in tiny Lebanon, stretching this already crowded country to the limit.

The landing was bumpy and shaky and the Lebanese on the plane applauded. When I was young, I often wondered whether it was applause for the skill of the pilot or for not having been shot at, as could happen to planes in the bad old days. The old yellow sign on top of the terminal building that used to read WELCOME TO LEB, with the rest of the letters shot up, had long gone. We passed through immigration and met up with Chris, who had landed from Dubai a couple of hours earlier.

'This is probably the only place in the world where being born in Beirut isn't a problem,' he said, laughing, as we greeted each other. He was right, of course. Although I'm British, I was born in the Lebanese capital and this condemned a traveller to hours and hours of suspicious immigration officials and overly dumb questioning.

As we exited the airport we couldn't help noticing Chris's luggage. Harry and I had two similar kit bags. Chris, however, was wheeling a silver suitcase the size of a small wardrobe. I was starting to get the feeling that he had not thought through this trip.

We exited the airport and found the smiley old taxi man that my sister Hatty always used. We got on to the airport road into Beirut. This was once the most dangerous stretch of road in the world. The visitor to Beirut would have to pass through Shia suburbs positively bristling with armed kidnappers. We passed the site where the American Marine barracks was blown up in 1983, killing 241 US service personnel and 66 others. Moments later, we whizzed past Sabra and then Chatila, the two Palestinian refugee camps that were the scenes of mass slaughter by Christian militia men in 1982. Beirut was a city of ghosts. And I was one of them.

Soon we were on a new highway that made what used to be an hour's drive into a twenty-minute affair up into the hills above Beirut. Once off the highway and on the old mountain roads, I could remember every bend of the drive home. My mind was racing. Memories flooding in.

And then we were there. We made the sharp turn onto the drive and started up the overgrown valley below the house. We reached the gatehouse. To the left was an old track that disappeared into the pine forests. I used to wander up there for hours looking for pieces of shrapnel or bullets to add to my collection. The old electronic gates slowly rolled upwards like a drawbridge on a Crusader castle. We drove past the stables on the right that were once home to our horses, Calamity Jane, Tosca, Champagne and Sappho. Now they are home to very different horsepower: a stonkingly large generator, a necessity in a country where power cuts for more than four hours a day are routine.

We drove up towards the house. It was not much different from when I'd left, over twenty years before. A little tattier perhaps, but essentially the same.

The courtyard full of dogs, the red-tiled roof, the thick, roughly hewn limestone walls, the green shutters, ancient sarcophagi 'rescued' from Syria with geraniums tumbling out of them. I got out of the car to be greeted by Hatty and her husband Michael. Dogs roared around us in glorious chaos as we headed inside for some welcoming drinks, leaving Chris to struggle behind with his ridiculously large suitcase.

As we got into the house more dogs greeted us, plus a formid-able retinue of cats. We were quickly brought up to speed about the complex peace agreement that kept all the different animals from fighting. Some dogs were only allowed out in the court-yard. Others were kept in a locked outdoor enclosure beneath the kitchen. Two top dogs were allowed access pretty much everywhere. The cats, meanwhile, also had to be separated. Two Siamese were to be kept in the drawing room and hall, while others were allowed on the terrace and on the roof of a small hut next to the kitchen above the dog enclosure, but must never meet the Siamese. Several 'rogue' cats pretty much did what they wanted but knew from bitter experience that intrusion into certain areas would get them into a lot of trouble and that, should trouble flare up, they were on their own.

It was a set-up as complicated as the Sykes–Picot Agreement of 1916 that originally split the vanquished Ottoman Empire into Western spheres of influence. It was also an animal version of the complex balance of power that has existed in Lebanon since independence with a multitude of religious factions in a series of ever-changing allegiances and quarrels. There could not have been a better physical demonstration of how Lebanon works than the animal cantons of my childhood home.

We sat on the terrace overlooking all of Beirut below us. I thought about the things I'd seen from there – the mushroom clouds of countless car bombs in Beirut, battles raging night and day, tracer fire lighting up the sky, jet fighters breaking the sound barrier low over the house as they swooped down onto Beirut like deadly birds of prey.

Now Beirut was relatively peaceful and looked both resplendent and reborn, all lit up below us. Michael had produced a splendid meal for us that we polished off despite this being our tenth or maybe even eleventh meal of the day. Behind Chris, on a counter, sat a large plate of cheese. I watched in hypnotised silence as one of the cats licked and munched its way around the selection. When the cheese was served, Harry and I, having spotted the backstage events, passed but Chris, oblivious to it all, tucked in heartily.

When the Chris cheese show was over we headed to our respective bedrooms. It had been a long day and I was drained.

# HISTORY BOY

The following morning, I stood on the balcony off my bedroom and looked down at Beirut again, so calm, so quiet. The Levantine sun was starting to warm up the flagstones and, in the pine trees, birds were singing. The Lebanese love to hunt anything that moves, and birds long ago learned that the grounds of our house were a welcome sanctuary, that rarest of things in Lebanon: a no-fire zone.

I went downstairs to see if anybody else was up. I found Chris, always an early riser, sitting alone at the breakfast table on the main terrace. He was weeping. I couldn't believe it. I knew that, of the three of us, he was probably going to find the whole thing the most difficult. He would be out of his comfort zone, slumming it and dealing with a ridiculously large suitcase, but he had cracked earlier than I thought. I presumed that the thought of us setting off the following day had broken him and now here he was weeping like a baby at the table. I readied myself to be supportive but firm. I could not have Chris becoming a burden this early on the trip. He would need to toughen up and get with the programme.

'Morning, everything all right?' I looked at Chris, trying not to appear too disappointed in him.

'Yes, maestro, I slept well but I think I'm allergic to all these cats. My eyes are streaming and it's a nightmare.' He looked up at me from behind reddened eyes.

I breathed an inner sigh of relief, went off to find him some antihistamines and thought it better not to mention the cheese incident from the night before. The pills were a miracle, and Chris soon recovered and was back on fighting form. I was glad, as a punishment beating this early on in the trip would not have helped morale. Harry joined us for breakfast and ignored the gorgeous spread of olives, labneh (a creamy yoghurt cheese), za'atar (a herby condiment), Arab bread, tomatoes and fresh fruit.

'Is there any proper food?' he asked with a panicked expression on his face.

'Like what?'

'Well ... cereal, obviously ... it's breakfast and we appear to be having a salad.' He looked shocked.

Some Coco Pops were discovered at the back of a cupboard.

After breakfast we went for a stroll around the gardens of the house but were soon out of puff. This did not bode well for the trek. As we explored, I got a call from the man from the British Embassy. He said that they were very concerned for our safety and warned us that the political situation was very tense as there was an election coming up in ten days. This was to be the first election to be held in ten years and so things might get 'hairy'. In my experience, things in Lebanon had always been tense and could probably often be described as 'hairy', but if you let things like that stop you then you would never travel anywhere even vaguely interesting. Likewise, if you didn't travel to anywhere that the Foreign Office advised you against travelling to, it would be a very dull world.

While I was not sure that there had ever been a dull time to walk across Lebanon, the fact that that we were to coincide with the election meant that we were almost certain not to be disappointed.

Lebanon has been a democracy since her independence from the French Mandate in 1943. At the time, an agreement, similar to that of my sister's animals, was set up whereby power would be shared between the various religious factions that made up the country. Working off a population census at a time in which Maronite Christians were in the majority, it was agreed that the President would always be a Maronite, the Prime Minister would be a Sunni, the Speaker of the House a Shia and so on. The problem was that the demographics were rapidly changing. Muslims tended to have more kids than Maronites and so the Maronites had refused to have another population census. Even after the civil war, this agreement had still been in place up to the last election in 2009. Since then, there had been several elections postponed or cancelled under the aegis of the security situation and so the same people had been in power for nine years and the Lebanese were understandably getting even more fed up with their politicians than usual.

We were about to walk through the country in the middle of all this. This had not been the plan; it was a coincidence that, if I was honest, rather excited me. It definitely gave our trip a little extra frisson.

I got a message from Caroll. She would be at the house the next day to drive us down to the south of Lebanon where we would start the walk. Thunderbirds were, it seemed, go ...

Hatty told me that this was a day where volunteers went to the Anglo-American cemetery in Beirut to help clean it up. It was where my father was buried, and I had not been since the day of the funeral. I hadn't even seen his gravestone. So, Harry, Hatty and I drove into Beirut to help out. Chris stayed at the house, presumably to do some last-minute tweaks to his preparation routine ...

The cemetery was not easy to find. A bit like Beijing, Beirut is a city permanently on the rebuild. In Beijing, the joke is that you could pop into a restaurant for lunch and come back out to find a new building in place. Beirut is not dissimilar. Roads are constantly being closed, blocked or built, and it took us a couple of attempts to actually locate the place. Eventually we found it and stepped out of the concrete jungle of new Beirut into an oasis of calm and bougainvillea.

The cemetery had been set up in 1913 by the then British ambassador, the Syrian Protestant College (later to become the American University of Beirut, AUB) and the American Mission as there was a dearth of places for foreign nationals to be buried. Despite its heritage, the graveyard currently received no funds, either from AUB and England or America, and relied on volunteers to look after the place. A Syrian refugee family had been moved into a small building on the site as caretakers.

When we entered there were about twenty ex-pats raking, strimming and generally clearing up the place. I found my father's gravestone and spent a couple of minutes by it.

It was curious how little emotion I felt. Here was the man who, for better or for worse, had dominated my life for forty years and yet I stood by his grave with an extraordinary sense of detachment. I wondered whether this was my inbuilt self-defence mechanism kicking in. It was similar to the out-of-body experience I'd have when my panic attacks were at their most destructive and virulent. I would suddenly be relegated to the role of an observer as opposed to a participant in my own life.

I always thought it was my mind switching to autopilot when it sensed that something was happening that was going to be too much for me to compute. In hindsight I'd been very thankful of this, but not at the time. When the terror and disorientation of panic attacks descended I would have done anything to escape. Now, however, from a position of relative stability, I felt almost cheated of some sort of authentic emotion. I stared at the gravestone willing myself to feel something substantial, but nothing came except the thought that my sister took great care of it and it was brimming with flowers.

As I stood there, a man carrying a small child introduced himself. He turned out to be the political officer at the British Embassy and knew about my walking plans. He reiterated that the election was going to be a tense time and he warned us not to wander too near the borders. I proposed that we set up a WhatsApp group with him that I would name 'Hostage Rescue Info' and agreed to keep in touch when in dodgy areas.

'That's great,' he said. 'Although, to be honest, I'm not exactly sure what I could do if you do get into trouble.'

This was not exactly reassuring, but it was nice of him to bother.

We spent a few more hours cleaning up the place and I found several more relations of mine buried there. It was odd, having so many ancestors buried in this little hidden corner of Beirut. I somehow felt that they would approve of my adventure.

But how had my ancestors come to be in Beirut? Upon my return to the UK I did a little bit of digging and, with the help of my cousin Hil, I got the basic lowdown.

The Jolys were Huguenots and had escaped France and Catholic persecution in the seventeenth century, settling in Hoxton Fields in London. They were originally from the Jura mountains of Switzerland, near a small town called Moudon.

Thomas Joly was the first Joly to go east. He ended up working in the consular services in Smyrna (now Izmir) in 1816. His son Stephen also entered the consular service there. But what was the consular service? Ages ago, my Aunt Marjorie, my father's older sister and also the family historian, had written to me explaining the family journey. Like so much of my past, I had studiously ignored it and moved on in my attempt to reinvent my life. I reread her letter with newly discovered interest, especially in my aunt's opinionated view of social history.

By the mid-sixteenth century, the Ottomans realized that they needed trade with the West if their Empire was to survive. They invited French, then English and Dutch merchants to set up trading posts in the Ottoman Empire, protected by commercial treaties known as Capitulations. These allowed them to live and trade in Ottoman territory safely, with a few privileges and the ability to retain their own nationality of origin while practicing their own religion.

Other European nations followed suit and communities popped up all over the Ottoman Empire governed by their own consuls who were backed by Consular Courts. The consuls were the socially elite of the communities, who strutted about in public in gold embroidered coats preceded by servants who thumped the ground to make way for them. Many of them were appointed from the ranks of the merchants and ran their consulates in tandem with their merchant houses.

The British Levant Company was founded in the 1580s by a group of London merchants who obtained a charter for it from Queen Elizabeth 1st. They owned a fleet of well-armed ships, capable of dealing with the pirates, which carried wool, cloth, tin and lead to Levant ports and returned with Oriental luxuries purchased in the markets.

Young factors, often at the age of 18, were sent out to the markets to negotiate on behalf of their masters, on commission. If they survived the journey out, disease and dissipation when they got there, they could make fortunes for themselves. As many of them were younger sons of squires or merchants and even of nobles, with very little expectations at home, some of them remained in the Levant. The largest European communities were in Constantinople (Istanbul), or in Smyrna (Izmir), an ancient port on the west coast of Asia Minor: it had excellent anchorage for shipping and a cool breeze in the summer as well as mines in the surrounding hills that could be exploited.

This was the place where the Joly family lived, in a cosmopolitan polyglot and sociable merchant community where by the 19th century, Europeans accounted for 20% of the population. 'The Nations' as they were called, lived in community groups governed by their consuls but they intermarried with each other and the indigenous Ionian Greeks but NEVER with the Turks.

Consequently, many of their descendants lost track of their origins in the multinational families they belonged to. They

spoke their various languages in a distinctive but not unpleasant accent much despised by the home bred British; in fact,
they regarded the Smyrniots as a breed on its own, loose
living and immoral. The wealthiest of the British Smyrniots
sent their children back to England for education so that
games and athletics would offset the danger of dissipation
when they returned home.

It must be said most of them ruled their lives by the precept
'An Englishman word is his bond' and were admired and
respected for their probity. Anyone who endangered the
reputation of the 'nation' could be severely censured by the
consul or even sent packing. For four centuries the Smyrniots
lived a prosperous life without colonial power, armies or
bloodshed of any kind. Many of them became extremely
wealthy with large mansions on the seafront which had integral warehouses and jetties for ships to load and unload. It all
came to an end in 1922.

In the aftermath of the 1st World War, Turkey, defeated
by the Allies, deposed its Sultans while the Empire was
dismantled, and the subject states parcelled out between
Britain and France. Greece saw an opportunity to recover
former Ionian Greek territory in Asia Minor. It attacked
Turkey, but its army was heavily defeated by General Kemal
Ataturk, who set light to infidel Izmir. The prevailing wind
fanned the flames until they destroyed the entire town and all
but one of the mansions on the seafront. European navies
rescued their nationals while HMS George V evacuated the
entire British colony including eleven-year-old Norman
Frederick Joly, whom you may have met as an old man
lunching with his son Gordon in the BBC canteen. A few

families who managed to safeguard their property returned to live in Turkey as Turkish citizens but most of the European communities have scattered all over the world.

But how had we got from Smyrna to Beirut? Stephen Joly's second son, Ernest, my great-grandfather, flew the coop and became a banker, working first in Istanbul and then Nicosia in Cyprus. When he lost his job in Cyprus he tried his luck in Beirut and moved there in 1891. He ended up managing a banking, insurance and shipping agency, Henry Heald & Co. In 1900 Ernest bought the company, which has been run by my family ever since, with Hatty being the current chair.

It had not been an easy tenure. In 1914, the First World War broke out. The Ottoman Empire, which ruled Lebanon at the time, allied itself with Germany. My great-grandfather Ernest, his wife, his eldest son Kenneth (my grandfather) and his twelve-year-old daughter were rounded up and taken hostage to prevent HMS *Doris*, a British warship that had appeared off the coast, from bombarding Alexandretta, a city on the Mediterranean coast of Turkey. The bombing was averted, but the hostages became internees in remote areas of Turkey; the women and children were eventually released but had a very nasty journey back to Beirut. The men, including my great-grandfather and my grandfather, stayed interned in a castle in Urfa, near the Turkish–Syrian border, until 1918 as not only the war but the Armenian massacres swirled about them. After the war, the family was reunited in Beirut. Henry Heald & Co. thrived. My great-grandfather Ernest died in 1931 and my grandfather Kenneth, now married to Gertrude, took over the company.

Unfortunately, the Second World War caused further problems. With the dissolution of the Ottoman Empire after the Great War, Lebanon had become part of the French Mandate. When war broke out in 1939, the local authorities sided with the Vichy French and therefore the Nazis. Being English, the Jolys had to move to Jerusalem, in Palestine. My grandfather, with his experience in shipping, was appointed as a temporary civil servant in Food Control, finding alternative sources of supplies and getting them to Palestine. The family, except for my dad – who was at boarding school in England and then fought in the Fleet Air Arm in the Pacific until VJ Day – stayed in Jerusalem for the duration of the war.

When the Second World War was over, my grandfather returned to Beirut to find that his staff had kept Henry Heald & Co. going through the war.

In 1947, Lebanon, four years after having rid herself of the French Mandate, became an independent republic and a far more cosmopolitan country. Henry Heald & Co. started to go from strength to strength. My dad, having gone up to Oxford, returned to Lebanon in 1951 and joined my grandfather Kenneth in the business until he retired a couple of years later.

My dad took over the company and it was then that he built the family house above Beirut. My grandfather died in Guernsey in 1957, having been awarded an OBE and the Order of the Cedar of Lebanon. My grandmother, Gertrude, retired to Cheltenham, where she died in 1987.

My dad managed to keep the company going all through the civil war that started in 1975 and through the almost endless turmoil in the country.

My father, having also been awarded an OBE, retired to his house in France and this was when my sister took over. He eventually died in Lebanon, in 2011, looked after by my sister and her husband in the house that he built and loved so.

And now here I was, the seventh generation of Levantine Jolys, returning to Lebanon and about to make a little bit of new family history in the country.

That evening we had a last supper at the house. My brother Marc-Henri, from my mother's first marriage, and his wife Mouna came, along with my oldest childhood friend, Georges, who arrived with his wife. I wished that my lovely sister Anne-Dominique, also from my mother's side, had been there: we hadn't all been together since I was eighteen.

How the hell had I become fifty? It was only minutes ago that we all used to eat in this room with the sound of gunfire resonating up from the battles in Beirut. On the walls were black-and-white photographs of my father in his Fleet Air Arm days in the Pacific during the Second World War. I looked across the table to the head where he would always sit. It was all a bit too much and part of me longed for our trip to start in order for me to get some headspace in which to sort everything out. Conversation soon turned to our impending trip. Mouna is Lebanese and a keen walker herself. I hoped that she might be reassuring. I was wrong.

'You know the mountains here are crazy steep; the walk you are going to do is very, very difficult.' She made a sign with her hands showing an almost vertical slope before shaking her head in a resigned manner, much in the way that someone might have done in the First World War upon being told that you had volunteered to go over the top the following morning. 'It will be very hard for you all, especially because you have no experience and in your physical conditions.' She looked sad for us.

I turned to my right to speak to Georges, a man I'd known since I was about six years old.

'You know, she is right,' said Georges, whom I knew for a fact had never been on a walk in his life. 'The real danger is landmines. Even if they have cleared the trail, mud and water can slip down mountains and take landmines with them. I would never do what you are doing, it is a crazy thing.'

He looked at his wife, who, despite having had quite some 'work' done to her face, was just about able to indicate her agreement.

This was really not turning out to be a very encouraging evening.

I looked over at Chris, who had been listening to what was being said. He shrugged his shoulders and we did a false bonhomie type of thing and downed our drinks. Harry didn't catch any of it as he was busy picking his way through the food trying to find elements of it that he recognised and could begin to consider eating. As he did so, Hatty regaled him with a story about her once having found a handgun stuffed under her plane seat. She was only about nine years old at the time and had waved the thing about for a while before an air hostess had taken it from her.

Possibly we had bitten off a little more than we could chew. Maybe the LMT guy I'd met ten years before who just looked me up and down and said, 'No, it's not for you' had been right. Maybe we should just get on flights to Thailand. It was too late. We were in too deep.

Before I went to bed, I stood on my balcony and took one last look at Beirut by night. Four powerful red lights flashed on top of a couple of high-rises. Somebody had illegally built two skyscrapers right on the flight path and so a solution had been found. The buildings had installed massive red lights on the roofs to warn planes on approach to Beirut Airport. It was so Lebanese.

# THE RESISTANCE MUSEUM

I awoke to two massive booms. An Israeli jet was breaking the sound barrier over Beirut in a not-so-subtle wake-up call to anybody who didn't know who was the real power in the area, letting everybody know who was boss. I wandered into Chris's room where he was doing his final packing. I couldn't help noticing a couple of peculiar items in his suitcase.

'What's this?' I asked, pointing at a black metallic device.

'It's a portable, hand-operated Nespresso machine,' said Chris proudly.

'And you intend to carry this in your backpack?'

'A man can't go without a decent espresso. You'll thank me when we're in the field.' Chris looked dead chuffed with his resourcefulness.

'And what's all this?' I asked, pointing at one of the largest medical kits I'd ever seen. It looked like what a man might take for a year's tour as a medic in Vietnam. It had everything: pills of all forms, creams, plasters, bandages, Vaseline ... so much Vaseline, even more Vaseline than Harry and me put together ... it was insane.

'You can never be too careful,' replied Chris.

'Did you just wander into the Dubai version of Boots and say I'll take everything?' I asked.

Chris nodded proudly.

This was going to be a very special trip.


Chris was that rare thing in middle-aged men: a proper new friend. You tend to get to a stage in life where your friends are your friends and not much changes. You have your childhood friends, your school friends, your university friends, your wasteland friends, your stable friends, and then your other half's mutual friends. Occasionally you make a friend because your kids are friends with another kid and, by a stroke of fortune, you actually like that kid's parents. Normally, though, even if you like one of the parents, the other is a dullard. The Holy Grail becomes a family where each of your kids is paired with a friend and both your partner and yourself get on with the respective parents. This is trickier than you might think, although my wife Stacey and I have been lucky enough to have hit the jackpot a couple of times so far. (She made me write that.)

'What does your wife do?' I asked Chris when we first met.

'This sounds very shallow, but she's a model and media personality.' It did sound very shallow, but the fact that he was aware of this and that, when I met Samar, she was clearly smarter than him made him even more annoying.

Chris is an outlier and doesn't fit into a logarithm. Living in Dubai should have been an automatic red card for friendship. He owns a big advertising agency out there. We met when I was hired by his company to direct an ad for them. The ad, which involved a man in a thick gorilla suit running around in 48 °C conditions, didn't turn out too well, but Chris and I clicked.

He is a success in advertising in a foreign land. Not only that, but he is the charming, almost old-fashioned type of gentleman that, were your daughter to bring him home and introduce him as her future husband, you might, as a parent, quietly thank the Lord.

He is a man who shares basic core values with me; a man who is sweet, funny, smart and kind but has been forced to hide these qualities in order to advance in the shallow world of advertising. We are weirdly similar.

An hour later, Caroll showed up at the house in a van. To our surprise, she was a he. Caroll was half Dutch and half Lebanese, and bore a passing resemblance to the techno-vegan Moby and so we immediately christened him as such.

I'd not really given a massive amount of thought to our plan of action. I assumed Caroll would know the logistics of the LMT and that we would dip in and out depending on what took our fancy. All that was certain was that we had to drive south to get to the beginning and I really wanted to visit the Hezbollah Museum for Resistance Tourism near the Israeli border before we started. Apart from that, everything was in play and we would take it as it came.

We took a winding road down into the valley beneath the house before starting to climb back up again. Lebanon consists of a Mediterranean coastline dotted with several cities, Tyre, Sidon, Beirut, Byblos and Tripoli. From the sea the country rises steeply up towards the mountains, separated by an interminable series of valleys. If you have been to Cannes and looked up into the hills and then to the Alpes Maritimes that rise up behind the city, you'll have a good idea of the topography.

Indeed, Los Angeles, with a similar magical sunlight and a series of canyons and hills rising up behind, is also not that different. It is no coincidence that these two places are synonymous with glitz and glamour. Unlike those two places, however, Lebanon has had to fit in the less glitzy and glamorous – the refugees, the ever-increasing poor and a multiplicity of ethnicities, religions and age-old feuds – into a finite space. There are at least seventeen different types of religious sects in Lebanon and each established their own areas or fiefdoms dotted among the mountains, which have long been a place of refuge for persecuted minorities all over the Middle East. Very often, religious or political affiliations (pretty much the same thing) change in each village you travel through. It's not hard to see why the civil war, when it finally exploded, was so vicious and harmful to this fragile little country.

The moment we lost sight of Beirut the scenery changed from the urban sprawl that covered the hills above the capital and we started to travel back in time as we drove through beautiful villages separated by thick pine forests. Gorgeous old summer villas abounded – these are the places to where Beirutis retreat in the summer when the coastal area becomes too hot and sticky. I remember once, as a six- or seven-year-old, being driven along this same road towards the summer house of a rich Sunni Muslim friend from West Beirut. I was invited to his birthday party and I was accompanied by my beloved nanny, Sylvia, who was best friends with their nanny, Brenda. When we got to the party I rapidly encountered two things I have always hated: animal cruelty and beetroot. The family had a bear, chained to a tree, that had been taught to dance when urged. The poor animal did so while surrounded by a howling gaggle of screaming children. I felt sick. I knew this was not right and longed to somehow free it from distress. I retreated indoors, into the sumptuous interior, where I was ushered onto a vast terrace laden with food. For some reason I was given a plate of beetroot and told by my nanny that I had to eat it all. Perhaps she was embarrassed at my reaction to the dancing bear and was somehow punishing me. Whatever the case, I managed two pieces of beetroot before the earthy, primal taste of the devil's root took effect and I purple vomited all over the table. I was never asked back. I still wake up in nightmares, unable to save the bear.

For a while we drove through Christian country until we entered the Shouf, an area shared between the Druze and Christians.

The Druze are possibly Lebanon's most mysterious sect. Theirs is an esoteric, monotheistic religion that was based on Islamic teachings but influenced by Eastern as well as Greek philosophy. They are very secretive; their theology is being passed on through initiation. The leading Druze family in Lebanon is the Jumblatts from Moukhtara. Posters could be seen everywhere of the family patriarch, Kamal Jumblatt, who was assassinated by the Syrians in 1977, and his successor, his son Walid. Kamal Jumblatt was something of an idealist and had harboured many ambitious ideas for his country. Among his stranger plans was one for building massive fans up in the Shouf that would blow fresh mountain air down into Beirut. He was also something of an eco-warrior, and I felt that he would have heartily approved of the LMT. A third Jumblatt, Walid's son,

Taymour, was starting to battle for poster space as he was running for his father's seat in the coming election. Politics is very much a family business in Lebanon.

We drove on, further and further south and nearer to the Israeli border. We sensed that we might be changing areas as we started spotting quite a few burnt-out houses, remnants of a not-too-distant time when whichever religion had been in the ascendant had booted out minorities from their villages.

Finally, we left the Druze area and started going through villages flying the yellow banner of Hezbollah. This was now Shia territory and images of martyrs and of their spiritual leader Hassan Nasrallah were everywhere. Below us lay the old Phoenician ports of Sidon and Tyre. Ahead of us was a thick oak forest covering an entire hill, in the middle of which fluttered an enormous Lebanese flag. This was Mleeta, site of the snappily titled Museum for Resistance Tourism, set up to honour Hezbollah's war against the Israeli occupation. This was manna from heaven for a 'Dark Tourist' like myself and I couldn't wait. I hoped that Chris and Harry would share my enthusiasm for this kind of thing.

When I'd first heard about Mleeta, I'd assumed that it was a couple of old shipping containers full of some photographs and a couple of bits of military paraphernalia. I was very wrong. Somebody had spent a fortune building this place: it was a kind of military Disneyland.

Hezbollah literally means 'the Party of God', and it was formed in the early 1980s with Iranian backing in an attempt to coordinate the various Shia armed groups operating in the south of Lebanon. At the time, they were the most economically deprived group in the country with little political clout. They were fighting the South Lebanese Army (a Christian militia supported by the Israelis) as well as the Israelis themselves, who had invaded the country in 1982. The Israelis finally pulled out of the country in 2000 and the museum had opened in 2010 on the tenth anniversary of the withdrawal. It was situated on what had been a hugely important secret base for Hezbollah, hidden in the forest.

The Israeli Army might have withdrawn from Lebanon but, as we parked in the vast car park, their jets were flying above us, flaunting Lebanese air space as they appeared to do with impunity the whole time we were to be in the country. Since we were wandering into what was essentially a massive 'fuck you' to Israel, it did make me a touch nervous.

At the entrance we were met by Ali, a tall, earnest-looking man with a thick beard and an intense stare.

'Welcome to the lands of resistance, purity and jihad,' said Ali, who was clearly not going to be big on small talk. Ali was to be our guide and he was not a man with whom one discussed the itinerary.

'First you will go to the cinema and see a movie,' he ordered.

'What if we don't want to go and see a movie?' I asked.

'You will see the movie,' replied Ali.

He marched us up a hill and into the central piazza. It was a vast complex and packed with Shia families on a day out. I took one last look at an Israeli jet that zoomed over us and then entered a large cinema. We were the only people in there. We sat down, and the film started with a fiery speech from Hassan Nasrallah, the leader of Hezbollah and a man who is in permanent hiding as he is number one on the Israeli kill list. There was then a mixture of slow-motion footage of Hezbollah fighters doing fighting things and Israeli convoys being blown up by suicide bombers, all set to some seriously dodgy music. It was definitely not the most balanced introduction to the region's complicated politics that I could provide for Harry and Chris, but it certainly got their attention.

Once the film finished in a spectacular apocalyptic orgy of fire and smoke we stumbled back out into the daylight to be met by Ali, who had presumably seen the film too many times and so had waited for us by the enormous fountain.

'Good film,' he said, more as a statement than a question.

'I felt it lacked something of a narrative arc and very much dipped in the second act, but the special effects were impressive. I'd love to have a go at curating the soundtrack however ...' I stopped as Ali wasn't listening; he was staring at another Israeli jet above us.

We stood and waited for a moment until Ali was ready.

'OK, the tour starts now. Let's go.' Ali beckoned us over to what was known as the Abyss.

This was a vast sunken area criss-crossed with pedestrian bridges. The Abyss was littered with detritus of war, all Israeli. There were downed helicopters, broken artillery pieces, mutilated jeeps and a grand centrepiece of an Israeli Merkava tank with the cannon tied into a knot. It was all very Banksy and, indeed, a sign on the fence informed the visitor that: 'This is a structural scenic art that symbolizes the destruction of the Zionist entity.' Near the tank lay a massive pile of Israeli helmets and a large sign in Hebrew on the floor.

'What does the sign say?' I asked Ali.

'It is a message to the Zionist planes that fly over here illegally.'

'And what does it say?' I pushed.

'I do not know. I do not speak Hebrew.' Ali looked me straight in the eyes as though sizing up whether I did.

We continued over the bridges where Ali was about to tell us about the Merkava tank with a knot in the gun. Then I spotted a kindle of kittens under a rusting tank, and Chris and I went all gooey and started talking to the kittens in baby voices. I couldn't help it, I'm a sucker for animals.

Growing up we had successive pairs of Rhodesian ridgebacks that slept on my bed and were closer friends to me than almost any humans could ever hope. I shared my dad's emotionally crippled nature that could only truly express itself with his uncomplicated love for animals. With dogs especially, you didn't need to hide feelings, play games – they were utterly and unquestionably devoted to you and you felt safe returning the emotion. Cats, obviously, are never to be fully trusted and always to be approached with a lot more caution, but I was still happy to bond with Ali over kittens.

Ali started telling us about his five cats and for five minutes he softened completely, and we briefly forgot all about resistance and unpleasantness. The power of animal chat is often underestimated in international diplomacy.

Cat-chat over, however, Ali snapped back into work mode and we continued our tour. He started reeling off fact after fact about ever-increasing amazing Hezbollah victories over Israel. One day, he said, they destroyed thirty-five tanks using a Kornet-E anti-tank missile. We had no idea of whether all this was true or not but, as I was about to ask, another Israeli jet buzzed over us and a group of schoolchildren turned into human anti-aircraft guns, all pointing at the sky and mock shooting.

I'd been to many places in the world like this – the Military History Museum in Hanoi, the Victorious Fatherland Liberation War Museum in Pyongyang and the Sarajevo Tunnel Museum came to mind – but none matched the scale of this place and certainly none were still in a 'hot' zone. The problem, as in all these museums, was that it was so skewed to one side's point of view and therefore no place to get a balanced view of the conflict. As an insight into the mind-set of the Resistance, however, it was fascinating.

Aware that we were probably wandering around what was undoubtedly the number-one target for Israeli bombers the next time there was any conflict, I was rather pleased when we left the open area and entered the woods. Ali was back in guide mode.

'The Resistance, they choose this hill because the oak trees released so much chlorophyll that ultra violet rays cannot penetrate through,' he told us.

'Oh right, so no sunburn ...' I smiled at Ali, who gave me a death stare.

'No, so radar cannot penetrate,' he replied, still giving me the death stare.

'Oh ... of course,' I said, looking down.

I thought this very unlikely but decided against arguing and let Ali continue. Ali did not really like questions. He took us into the middle of the forest, which was peppered with very realistic mannequins dressed as Hezbollah fighters, complete with sounds of battle coming from hidden speakers. He showed us a large rock that turned out to be made from fibreglass.

'Good to hide bombs,' he said gleefully.

'Indeed,' I replied fruitlessly.

'Then boom!' he said, indicating a large explosion.

'Marvellous ...' I didn't really know how to respond.

Ali was off again, leading us through a small entrance that turned into a vast tunnel complex. Within the tunnels were prayer rooms, kitchens and guns ... so many guns. We ended up in a bunker that still had a vast machine gun poking out of the observation window. Ali pointed along the length of the gun to a hill about a mile away.

'That was Zionist command post. Every day we fired at them from here,' continued Ali proudly.

This seemed strange to me because, if the whole point of this massive secret base was to provide a place to hide from the Israelis, then firing an industrial-sized machine gun at them daily from the centre of the base seemed to be a curious logistical decision, but once again I kept my counsel.

Meanwhile Harry had placed himself behind the machine gun in the gunner position. He suddenly started to make incredibly loud machine-gun noises, like a four-year-old in the playground. Ali looked stupefied by his behaviour and I had to admit that I was on his side.

'AKAKAKAKAKKAKAKAKAKAKKAKKAKAKAKK,' screamed Harry.

'Harry ...' I tried to get him to step away from the machine gun.

'AKAKAKAKAKKAKAKAKAKAKKAKKAKAKAKK,' continued Harry, enthusiastically mock firing his new toy.

'Please, sir, this is not correct.' Ali was looking stern.

'AKAKAKAKAKKAKAKAKAKAKKAKKAKAKAKK.'

'HARRY STOP!' I shouted.

Harry stopped and looked annoyed with me. Ali looked annoyed with me. I wasn't sure why I was annoying everyone, so I exited the bunker to find Chris. He was looking at a vast row of ordnance on show. He drew my attention to a particularly unfortunately named Russian missile called the Fagot.

We'd only been outside for two minutes when I heard Harry making more shooting noises. I turned to see that he had now installed himself on an anti-aircraft battery and was rotating it manually while pretending to shoot up into the air. It would be fair to say that Harry was having a whale of a time.

I tried to distract Ali from Harry's behaviour by asking him a question.

'Are you not worried that the Israelis will bomb this place?'

'They have already sent many secret agents here as tourists.' He eyed Chris suspiciously.

'Did they give it a good review on Trip Advisor?' I laughed, trying to get Ali to join in, but his face was thunder.

It was time to say goodbye to Ali. He didn't seem very sad about this. We asked him to send our regards to his cats, but he didn't react. We'd started to make our way towards the exit when I noticed a sign saying, GIFT SHOP. It was dark-tourist heaven. Everything Hezbollah-related that you ever wanted or didn't know that you needed was there. There were Hezbollah key rings, paperweights, pens, banners, posters, books, DVDs, T-shirts, sunglasses ... the choice was extraordinary. The store was packed with other museum visitors, mostly heavily bearded, rather muscular men who, not too long ago, would have been keen to chain me to a radiator. I decided against asking one whether they knew my fellow Old Haileyburian, John McCarthy, and concentrated on the shopping.

I went for a key ring and made a mental note to make sure not to forget about it and have to explain its presence in my bag the next time I visited the USA. As we got into our car another Israeli jet was overhead. I gave this place a maximum of five years before it was bombed to smithereens.

We drove to the Christian town of Jezzine, which, at an altitude of 950 metres, is the summer resort for the south of Lebanon. It is the southern version of Brummana, the main hill resort near where I had grown up. From June to September it, like Brummana, is buzzing with life – restaurants and bars packed with young bucks up from Beirut determined to catch the eye of the plethora of beautiful Lebanese girls playing it cool in the heat of the Lebanese summer.

It is an attractive town that sits overlooking the vast Wadi Jezzine, a steep-sided valley. The main hub of the place is a bunch of restaurants and cafés that overlook the impressive waterfall that pours into the Wadi. The town's most famous son is the gloriously named Carlos Slim, once the richest man in the world, Señor Slim's father having emigrated from Jezzine to Mexico in the late nineteenth century.

We checked into Hotel Iris, a modest but perfectly adequate hotel with a view down to the town. After half an hour of 'freshening up' we went into town. This was probably Chris's first experience of staying in a two-star hotel for some time, and there was a look of profound panic in his eyes as we set off. We wandered down the main street and past a rather fearsome statue of what I presumed was God. He was carrying a very aggressive-looking curved sword and appeared to be taking no prisoners. Clearly the God of Jezzine was a vengeful God. I guessed you had to be to survive in this part of the world.

I found a cashpoint that worked. Lebanese cashpoints offered you US dollars or Lebanese pounds, both of which were accepted anywhere in the country. This would probably be my last opportunity to get some cash for a while, so I took full advantage. We then installed ourselves on an empty terrace above the waterfall and drank arak, the Levantine version of Pernod. It is very much a Marmite drink, and both Chris and Harry loathed it. They ordered Mexican beers, a Lebanese favourite in which beer is poured into a salt-rimmed glass containing copious amounts of fresh lime. It has very little to do with Mexico, but it is delicious and more than several were consumed.

We chatted to Caroll, who told us that we were the first people to ever book a walk across Lebanon with him. It turned out that he was a motorcycle nut and normally organised motorbike tours. He used to do them in Syria until the war there decimated his business.

'That was when I moved to Germany,' he said.

'Germany . . . you live in Germany, not Lebanon?' I asked.

'Yes.'

'So, you flew over from Germany for our trip?' I was gobsmacked.

'Yes.'

'Oh . . .'

I made a note to do a bit more research next time. I'd organised what I thought was a local lady hiker to guide us and now it turned out that we'd got a motorcycle man who lived in Germany instead.

Harry wanted a bit of clarification about Hezbollah and the difference between Shias and Sunnis. I'd once had lunch with an anthropologist who had given me the clearest explanation. When the Prophet Mohammed died, he had two heirs: Ali, who was his son-in-law, and Abu Bakr, his father-in-law. Mohammed had not made his succession crystal clear. He decreed that 'whoever follows me is the closest to me'. As Abu Bakr had been physically the closest to the prophet's deathbed, he became the first Caliph of Islam. His supporters were Sunnis and became the Muslim establishment. Others, however, felt that Ali, as his son-in-law, should be the successor and supported him. They became the Shias and were forced to flee to the countryside, becoming, to some extent, outlaws. You could still see this division in modern-day Lebanon with Sunnis mainly living in the cities and the Shia being in the poorer southern part of the country.

I love that Harry has such an inquisitive brain beneath his devil-may-care exterior. I've known him for ever. We first when we were nine years old. We were competing against each other in an inter-school athletics meet. Not for us the Olympian pursuits of discus, javelin or shot-put. Our chosen speciality was the soon-to-be-an-Olympic-sport of throwing the cricket ball. I think that it had been decided by school authorities that it would be too dangerous to allow us to handle javelins (still true to this day, to be honest) and so we had to throw a cricket ball as far as we could.

I vividly remember going into the final throw-off against this freckly boy with an unruly mop of curly ginger hair. The end result is not important (I won with a mighty throw of 53.27 metres) but I particularly remember someone shouting, 'Well thrown, Joly!' from the sidelines. It was the comedian Dave Allen, who had a son in my year. This might very well have been the moment that I decided that I wanted to be a comedian ... but it wasn't. I just remember Harry coming up to me, annoyed that he had been beaten.

'Joly? That's a stupid name.'

That was it. We were friends for life.

Three years later, Harry and I went to the same public school. Quite why these private schools were called public schools was beyond me. Much like cricket, it was just another layer of complicated code to confuse foreigners. Harry and I became firm friends and we discovered that our fathers had been at the very same school together. It was all very British. My dad had loathed boarding school. Once he had been sent off from Beirut he could only return once a year and was farmed out to dull relatives in Durham. How he must have longed to return to the exotic thrills of Lebanon. I'd loathed boarding school enough, but the thought that I didn't have the sweet release of holidays back at home in Lebanon would have tipped me over the edge. Even his annual return was kyboshed by the advent of the Second World War and he was not to return home for years. No wonder we shared this bond of emotional incontinence.

Harry is always a curious mixture of intense shyness and unbelievably outrageous behaviour when alcohol blunts his natural reserve. He was not to stay at my school for too long. Three years in, he was finally expelled for letting off fireworks, but this was just the straw that broke the camel's back. He moved on to Stowe, another public school, where he managed to last about three terms before once again being expelled. He was not one for rules or education although he has a fabulous brain and the driest sense of humour of anybody I know. I couldn't think of anybody in the world with whom I would prefer to have a conversation. He knows and accepts me for who I am despite having a profound and understandable mistrust for anybody in the media or creative industries. Harry is a practical person. When something goes wrong in our house my wife wouldn't even consider thinking of asking me to do anything about it. She would be instantly on the phone to Harry, who lives in nearby Cheltenham, asking him whether he'd mind helping out as there was no 'man of the house'.

After a time running the family fertiliser business, Harry now builds houses and rents them out. He would invariably turn up in a filthy old Volvo, the inside littered with curious man tools, wearing paint-spattered trousers and a torn, stained old jumper with a roll-up constantly dangling from his mouth.

The real secret is that we really make each other laugh. I laugh harder with Harry than with anyone else in the world. I love him. We had been on many adventures together – inter-railing through Europe, Greek island hopping, Canadian lake holidays – but Harry had never been to the Middle East. I was curious to see what he would make of it, and it of him.

It was getting late in Jezzine and we were setting off early the next morning. I tried to settle the bill, but the waiter was not happy with the banknotes I gave him. I explained that I had literally just got them out of the cashpoint that we could see across the road, but he was having none of it and claimed that they were counterfeit. We had a bit of a standoff until Caroll stepped in and covered it, but it left me with an unsettling feeling that I might have a wallet full of dud notes.

On the way back to the hotel, Caroll suddenly asked us whether we wanted to go cutlery shopping. This seemed like a weird post-drinks thing to do, but it turned out that Jezzine was famous for cutlery and there was a store that Caroll knew. We all groaned inwardly. I really didn't want someone with us the whole time who kept guiding us into tourist traps and shops owned by his 'cousin'.

Lebanon is not a country like Egypt or Morocco where you are almost forced into every shop you walk past. The Lebanese are way too sophisticated for that sort of stuff. I remembered being in Marrakesh in the early 1990s with a girlfriend. We had rejected repeated offers of a guide and were wandering around the main souk when a man came out of nowhere and spat in my girlfriend's face. Before we could even react, a stranger emerged rapidly from the crowd, punched the spitting man in the face and sent him packing with a volley of abuse. He then turned to us.

'I can only apologise on behalf of my city for the behaviour of this animal.' He looked mortified. 'It is my duty to be your guide now and to make sure this does not happen again. He has brought shame on my city. I shall be your guide and insist on no money for this service.' He smiled and beckoned us down a long alley.

There was very little we could do. He had clearly saved us from an unpleasant situation and we were in his debt. Pretty soon we were trapped in a series of tacky stores that were all run by 'my cousin', from which it was almost impossible to extricate ourselves without giving massive offence. We eventually got rid of him about two hours later after we had bought some serious tat. I had insisted on giving him a generous tip. Later that evening as we wandered past the Café de France on the Jemaa el-Fnaa, I spotted our guide smoking and laughing with the spitting man. We had been royally stung but I had a begrudging admiration for the depth of their deviousness.

Back in Jezzine, we entered the shop and dutifully looked at a range of cutlery, but I was far more interested in a photograph on the wall of the shopkeeper kneeling in front of a vast pile of dead wild boar. There must have been fifteen or more of these huge animals displayed before him.

'Did you shoot these boars?' I asked him.

'Yes, in one day,' he replied proudly.

I loathe hunting, but this was quite the feat as these were big, aggressive animals.

'With a shotgun?' I asked.

He looked at me as though I was insane.

'No ... with AK ...'

He produced a Kalashnikov from beneath his counter.

'Oh, bravo ...' I said, thinking that this had somewhat changed the odds in this epic boar versus man battle.

'You want cutlery?' the man continued, still holding the AK-47, a sales technique that was surprisingly effective.

'Umm, no thank you, maybe tomorrow we come back ...'

We backed out of the shop and made it very clear to Caroll that we were not in the business of tourist tat. We were mountain men, men of the mountain. He nodded and then Harry piped up.

'Caroll, is there a shop round here where I can buy some Coco Pops? It's an essential for me.'

This rather destroyed our mountain-men look but we popped into a grocery store where we got some water and a box of something called 'Choco Pops' that appeared to be a local bootleg version of Harry's favourite cereal. That was it. We were ready.

# DAY 2

# JEZZINE TO DEIR AL-QAMAR

I awoke at 7 a.m. and changed into my walking gear. A thin, stay-dry top from Patagonia, my merino pants, a pair of shorts, a sun hat and some thick hiking socks under my walking boots. I filled my CamelBak with water and dropped in a tablet that was supposed to dissolve and replace my electrolytes ... whatever they might be. The CamelBak went into a pouch in my rucksack from which there was a tube that ran down one of my straps to dangle near my mouth for me to suck on when necessary. In the other part of my rucksack I put a charger for my phone, ear pods, a pot of Vaseline, some sun cream, lip balm, a couple of plasters and a fleece in case it got cold. I felt that I was ready, but I had no idea what to expect. It was a little like the crazy lists that my parents were sent to get their kids ready for boarding school, curious things like garters, tuck boxes, S-belts, complicated colour codas of socks and jumpers and ties. They duly got everything, but it was only once school started that you really knew what you needed and what was utterly pointless.

I joined the others at breakfast downstairs. The table was, to Harry's disgust, covered with fresh fruit, tomatoes, Arab bread, labneh, za'atar, olive oil, olives, apricot jam. Harry looked around nervously for milk but could not see any. I asked the old lady who appeared from the kitchen for 'halib' and was chuffed that my kitchen Arabic was coming back to me so fast. Growing up in the Christian part of Lebanon I was bilingual in French, but my Maronite friends would never talk to me in Arabic as they considered themselves Phoenicians as opposed to Arabs, and so I never osmosed the language as easily as I could have done if I'd been brought up in West Beirut. I could understand most of what was going on, however, and it wouldn't take me long to pick it up should I ever live in the Middle East again.

The old lady reappeared with a sachet of Coffee-mate and handed it to Harry, who looked stupefied by the whole thing. Finally, a bowl of boiled eggs was put on the table and Harry decided that this was to be his best bet for food as at least 'eggs are for breakfast, unlike cheese'. Caroll couldn't stop laughing. He gave us each a little Tupperware box, which we filled with stuff from breakfast. This would be our lunch. Harry put five boiled eggs and nothing else into his box. He forlornly put the Choco Pops back into his kit bag, unopened.

We had a local guide for each leg of the walk and we'd assumed that Caroll would put our main luggage into his van and drive to our next destination so that our stuff would be there when we arrived. This was not his plan. It turned out that he was going to walk with us, then get a taxi back to the van and then drive it to meet up with us again. This didn't seem like a great plan, but we had almost zero experience in alternative hiking logistics.

Our local guide turned up. His name was Nabil and it was immediately clear that he was a man of few words. He was wearing a pair of trainers, jeans and a T-shirt. We looked like we were about to make the final assault on the Matterhorn. We knew we looked ridiculous – Chris, it had to be said, in a different way to us. He was sporting his handmade 'walking blazer'. He was also wearing a natty pair of handmade brogues and had a large flower pinned to his buttonhole. I had to admire his panache but feared there might be trouble ahead.

We set off, marching down Charles de Gaulle Avenue, in fact a small road, a reminder of the fact that Lebanon had been under French control before independence. We'd done about 200 metres when Harry demanded that we stop. The valve on his CamelBak was loose and water had poured down his trousers, soaking them and making him look as though he'd had an unfortunate accident.

'If I was wearing pants, this would be a problem. As it is, I'll be dry in no time,' proclaimed Harry smugly.

'You are not wearing pants?' asked Caroll, in obvious astonishment.

'Don't ask ...' I warned Caroll off the subject, but he remained looking very disturbed.

'You will be in much discomfort,' continued Caroll.

'I've already been through this, Caroll. There's no use.'

We moved on in awkward silence with Caroll still occasionally staring at Harry in disbelief.

Spirits were high; it was a gorgeous morning, the sky was a violent blue, the sun was out and birds were chirruping in the plane trees that lined the road. At the edge of the town we stopped by the Jezzine spring, one of the many sources that fed the al-Awali River as it made its leisurely way down the valley to the Mediterranean far below us at Sidon.

Looking back, that was the end of our brief innocence. We

had a photograph taken of the three of us. We looked fresh, excited, blissfully unaware of what was to come.

Moments after leaving the spring, Nabil took a sharp right and started going up some steps. They appeared endless and, after ten minutes or so, Chris and I were suffering. Harry was doing a bit better and was managing to keep up with Nabil while having a roll-up constantly dangling from his lips. I could see Caroll checking us all out and realising that this was going to be trouble. After what seemed like an hour we eventually reached the top and Chris and I collapsed in a heap as I told Caroll that I needed a 'writing break'. We were going to need a lot of these in the coming days. Annoyingly, Harry seemed to be fine and he started to rub it in as he rolled another cigarette.

'I wonder whether this whole thing is a good idea for you two. I'm concerned about heart attacks.' His mocking tone cut us both to the bone.

Chris and I were both relatively lazy but very competitive. We got up and we were soon up a path that led away from a panoramic view of Jezzine, heading towards our destination of the village of Niha. We stopped for another writing break by a deserted house that had a hand-painted sign on the door that read: WELCOME TO KRYSTAL'S 22ND BIRTHDAY. I imagined Krystal getting the approval from her parents. 'I'm going to have it at Elias's place in the mountains above Jezzine. Apparently, it's a lovely spot and the house has been in the family for generations . . .' I pictured her arriving and looking at the dilapidated, burnt-out house with the sign hanging outside and Elias coming to the broken window wearing nothing but a gold medallion, a half-empty bottle of vodka in his hand. 'Surprise baby, happy birthday . . .'

We knew that the first day was marked as a 16-kilometre walk and only classified as *difficult*, and so we'd been hopeful that we would cope fine. Chris asked Caroll, who had a GPS clipped to his rucksack, how far we'd gone.

'We must have done six or seven kilometres?' Chris panted hopefully.

'We have done three kilometres so far, and we have climbed three hundred and fifty metres. We cannot keep stopping like this if we want to keep on schedule,' Caroll said sternly.

I couldn't look at Chris's face as it was so devastated. The flower in his buttonhole had, like his will, started to wilt.

We walked on, down and across a long valley that contained a vast herd of goats, who were all jostling for space under the only two trees in sight. This area, thousands of years ago, like a lot of Lebanon would have been thick with trees, cedar and pines, but centuries of deforestation by one invading army after another had left areas like this denuded. The rock was beautiful however, rising vertically up from the valley in thin lines like a sliced Wall's Viennetta. I tried to get the hang of the walking poles. It wasn't as easy as it looked. If used correctly they could apparently take up to 30 per cent of the effort from your legs when going uphill and could really help take the pressure off your knees when descending. When used incorrectly, however, they could make an already average walker look ridiculous. We had a lot to learn.

However hard we were finding the walk, the scenery and the splendid isolation were already having an effect. I kept looking around and pinching myself. I was somehow being inserted into my forbidden history. Everywhere we looked was a riot of colours from the wild flowers. We floated over thick carpets of poppies, our footsteps as soft as fur.

After about an hour or so we reached a remote plateau, in which were buried about three or four concealed bunkers. We went in and had a look around, but they were damp and long abandoned. Nabil told us that they had been used as ammo dumps in the civil war of 1975–6 and that some nearby villages had used this area for military training. You would never have thought it. A more idyllic spot would have been hard to picture. All around us was silence save for the whisper of a soft breeze in a row of umbrella pine trees that lined the track that led over the next hill.

Chris and I were much happier on flat ground and we were soon in full banter mode and matching Harry stride for stride. Caroll pointed to a large structure on top of a hill in the far distance.

'That is near our final destination, Niha. It is the burial place of the prophet, Job.'

'Nice job,' said Chris.

'Yes, they seem to have done a particularly good job with it,' I riposted weakly.

'Job's a good 'un,' said Chris to Caroll's utter stupefaction.

It would be fair to say that our morale was better as we continued to walk along a fairly flat track with orchards on each side of us. Eventually the track gave way on the left to a steep drop. A Lebanese flag on a long pole fluttered in the breeze. We had a break and sat on the edge gazing into the valley below. Nabil told us that a hiker had died here. It had been a very misty day and they assumed that she had got lost and fallen over the edge. They found her body at the bottom of the cliffs. Chris, who had already told us about his fear of heights, visibly flinched and moved back from the precipitous edge. It didn't go unnoticed by Harry and me but we kept schtum. Weaknesses were ammunition and best kept dry on this trip.

About an hour later, Nabil suddenly veered left off the track and we started to descend steeply through some rather thick undergrowth. Chris finally admitted that brogues were probably not the ideal footwear for this and decided to wear proper walking boots the next day. The buttonhole flower was long gone, and the walking blazer was clearly starting to heat up, as there were damp patches under his arms. I felt that, sartorially, tomorrow would be a new beginning for Chris.

We came out of the undergrowth on to a rocky promontory that gave us an unparalleled view over the Wadi Jezzine. We would happily have stayed there for hours, soaking up the vista, but Chris was unsurprisingly not so keen. We made our way down to a green clearing below, where we lay down in the welcoming shade beneath a fig tree to have lunch. In between cigarettes, Harry slowly munched his way through egg after egg while Chris tried to make his portable Nespresso machine work. Caroll couldn't believe it when Chris produced the equipment from his rucksack. He poured some hot water from a flask into the machine, whacked in a pod and started pumping with his hand. Pretty soon he had two rather gorgeous espressos on the go in matching metal cups. George Clooney, eat your heart out ...

'We are at the entrance to the Citadel of Niha,' said Caroll.

We looked around us bewildered. There didn't appear to be a citadel anywhere to be seen.

Caroll led us to the edge of the cliffs and then pointed at a narrow path that ran along a crack on the cliff before disappearing around the corner. There was a drop of about 600 metres down to the valley floor below.

'Follow the path and all will be revealed,' said Caroll.

'That's not a path, that's a death sentence,' replied Chris.

'Man up, Chris ...' said Harry rather unsympathetically.

'I will wait for you here,' said Caroll, as Chris looked at him with intense jealousy.

We set off along the path with Nabil. Chris was glued to the cliff face and appeared to be in a distinct state of shock. Finally, we inched round until we were on a much wider rock platform. There were holes bored into the floor and caves dug into the cliff face at different levels. Nabil explained that there had been a three-storeyed building here, formed from wood beams attached to the cliff that served as a back wall. The citadel had an incredible view of the main Sidon road to the Beqaa Valley and so whoever was in the fortification could have control over the entire valley and spot attackers from miles away.

'Nobody know who build this in 900 after Jesus,' said Nabil.

'I'm fairly confident that it was probably us,' said Harry.

'Who is us?' Nabil looked utterly confused.

'Us, the British, I'm sure it would have been us.' Harry looked stony-faced at Nabil, who simply didn't know how to respond.

To get off the subject Nabil looked at Chris, who was visibly trembling with discomfort.

'You, why are you afraid of the heights?' he asked Chris in a brusquer manner than was strictly necessary.

'It's just a choice I made,' replied Chris sarcastically and rather brilliantly, considering his personal state of mind.

We all, including Nabil, fell about laughing.

One of Lebanon's most famous sons, Fakhar-al-Din (Fakhreddine), an extremely charismatic Druze nobleman, had supposedly once hidden in the citadel from the Ottomans. In 1607, Fakhreddine had managed to unite the warring Druze and Maronite peoples of Mount Lebanon into what many Lebanese considered to be the first manifestation of Lebanon as a state and it became a self-governed area under the Ottomans. Fakhreddine became the first Emir of Mount Lebanon.

He also made an alliance with the Duchy of Tuscany in 1608 soon after he took power, and this alarmed the Ottomans. They eventually authorised the Governor of Damascus to attack Lebanon in 1613 to try to curb Fakhreddine's ambitions. This was when he supposedly hid out in the Citadel of Niha before going into exile and living with the Medicis in Italy for six years. This afforded him a front-row seat at the Renaissance and when he returned to Lebanon he brought back a plethora of architectural and cultural ideas to the country. The red-roofed, square Lebanese houses that we had been admiring were supposed to have been inspired by Italian architecture.

This precarious eagle's nest, therefore, had massive symbolic importance to the Lebanese in their seemingly permanent fight against invading forces. Fakhreddine was eventually captured and executed by the Ottomans in 1632, along with two of his sons. The empire had tired of this tiresome maverick, but the Lebanese had never forgotten him. At a guess, I'd say almost 50 per cent of Lebanese restaurants around the world are called Fakhreddine after the great man.

Below the fortress was a large flat rock that was currently

bathed in sunlight. Taking advantage of this prestigious sundeck were about thirty furry little creatures soaking in the rays and totally at peace with the world. These were rock hyraxes and they looked like massively fat hamsters, but Caroll insisted that they are closely related to elephants. We were all a little dubious at this information, but subsequent research has revealed that he was entirely correct. Rock hyraxes are supposed to use a sentry system. Two members of a group are nominated to stand guard and alert the rest if an intruder is spotted. As we were high above them we avoided being spotted, so I did have some concerns about their air defence system.

We managed to inch Chris back to safety, where we found Caroll fast asleep under the fig tree. Nabil prodded him with the gnarled old walking stick that he would slump onto whenever he was having to wait for us to catch him up. We climbed back up to the track and continued on towards the Tomb of Job.

By the time we got there, we were into our fourteenth kilometre, a distance that, at home, I could easily cover with the dogs, but the searing heat and the preponderance of mountains had exhausted us. We gave a cursory glance to the building but were frankly more impressed by a wonderful arbutus tree in the oak forest behind the tomb. Nabil told us that the tree was rumoured to have cured a 'skin disease' that Job was supposed to have. We looked at each other knowingly with raised eyebrows but nobody said anything. We were too tired to push the theme and headed on down the steep hill into the half Druze, half Christian village of Niha.

We staggered into Niha and into our first guesthouse. It was the ground-floor flat of a family house just off the main street. It was fine: two bedrooms with bunks for four people per room and a separate kitchen, sitting room and bathroom. We were so knackered that I would have slept in the street but a couple of beers later and we'd all perked up, although we hobbled around the flat like frail pensioners. Our host came down to say hello. He was charming and very chatty although we didn't have a clue as to what he was talking about. We couldn't help noticing that he had no hands. This didn't stop him doing anything, however; he started to lay the table for supper and there was nothing that appeared to be un-pick-up-able. It was almost as if he was showing off as he gradually brought in larger and larger items to place on the table. When he'd finished and disappeared back up to his quarters, I asked Caroll whether he knew how the no-hands thing had come about.

'I think it was a grenade incident.'

'A grenade incident . . . what type of incident?' I had to ask.

'I'm not sure; I think he tried to catch one and throw it back, and it did not go very well,' said Caroll in an understated manner.

'No shit . . .' I said, not really knowing what else to say.

Harry and I sat on small wicker stools outside the house, watching the world go by. Despite it being a small rural village, there was quite a bit of traffic. Almost everybody who drove past weaved unsteadily as they tried to control their vehicle with one hand and watch a movie on their mobile in the other. We were astonished to see a Rolls-Royce drive past and park up two doors down next to a dilapidated tractor. It looked very out of place in this rural hamlet.

Chris and I were sharing a room; he was inside busy unpacking his enormous suitcase. We could hear him pottering around and sighing to himself. This was not his idea of a dream residence. As he passed the door for the ninth time, Harry looked in.

'Are you OK, Chris? Having trouble finding the trouser press?'

We both roared with laughter and Chris raised a single digit to his annoying walking companions.

Half an hour later I went inside to discover that I appeared to be sharing my room with Jacob Rees-Mogg. Blazers and jackets were hung on wooden hangers, his brogues were polished and sporting shoe trees, while a small teddy bear, apparently known as 'Bear', was dressed up to the nines and in prime position on Chris's pillow.

As I was taking in the scene and trying to find a spot to dump my stuff, the handless man came in and informed Caroll that two Greeks had turned up and that Chris and I would have to share our room with them. Chris had what appeared to be a minor nervous breakdown, and I was forced to take Caroll aside and tell him that this was not an option. Chris started stage-whispering that he would pay whatever the cost of two extra people would be just to keep them out. This was definitely not in the spirit of communal hiking, but we didn't care. Caroll went outside with the handless man and much shouting ensued. Eventually it appeared that we had won the battle as nobody turned up and no Greeks were ever mentioned again. I felt bad for the Greeks.

We sat down for supper. It was a feast. We had all hoped to lose some weight on this trip, but Chris and I already knew that we were doomed. Harry, on the other hand, had every chance, seeing as he was so fussy. The food started coming in, all carried precariously by the handless man. He nearly lost control of an enormous bowl of steaming lentil and cumin soup over Caroll but managed to get it back just in time. The dishes kept coming: pumpkin and lamb kíbbe, fattoush and salate al-raheb (monk's salad) that consisted of aubergine, tomato, cucumber and onion. Harry actually ate quite a bit but was then astonished to find that this was just the starter. The main course was ma'loube – a massive mound of chicken, rice, vegetables, raisins and chickpeas.

Caroll started telling us about the hummus wars between Israel and Lebanon. This was when the question of which country invented hummus became a massive issue between the two countries. Caroll got very excited about the subject and proceeded to read long and not always interesting pieces on hummus that he kept discovering on the internet. I finally slipped away to bed when he was reading a piece on how the Lebanese had made the world's largest bowl of hummus. Harry was nodding off over a bowl of Choco Pops and Chris was looking mildly suicidal.

## DAY 3

# NIHA TO MRESTY

I woke up to find that Chris was not in the room. I panicked. Had he been unable to take the hummus chat and topped himself? Had he been kidnapped in the night by Druze militia who suspected him of being an undercover fop? I discovered him lying on the sofa in the sitting room. He had some ludicrous story about me snoring so loudly that he'd been forced to move rooms. Obviously, this was a dirty lie and I determined to try to find out the sordid truth one way or another.

After breakfast we gathered our stuff and set off. The handless man was on his balcony and shouted goodbye to us. We refrained from waving lest it cause a tricky situation. We were already learning the fine art of diplomacy, so necessary when travelling in this kind of environment.

We left the village following our new guide, Marwan. As we were about to leave the little road and take a path up the mountain, we spotted Nabil, our guide from the day before. He was sitting in a truck on his own and looked very surprised to see anyone. We were unsure what he was up to but it all looked a bit shifty.

Marwan was a relaxed-looking man in his mid-sixties who favoured the Harry-style of walking that involved constant smoking. There was a path, but he seemed to think that this was for wimps. Instead, he led us straight up the mountain through thick brush and prickly prickles and a cornucopia of wild flowers. I recognised white orchids, wild lavender and the ever-present poppies. Caroll kept asking Marwan why we were not on the trail, but he just batted away any questions and kept going in a constant cloud of cigarette smoke. Chris and I were suffering from this uphill marathon, but Harry just plodded on like a metronome.

'The name's Bell, Chris Bell. It's not Chris fucking Bonington,' gasped Chris as we climbed higher and higher.

We both longed for a break, but pride was an annoying thing that prevented us from doing what we wanted to do. Occasionally Caroll stopped to point out an orchid or the ever-present yellow genêt d'Espagne (Spanish broom). Normally we would not be that interested but we both hung onto every word, trying to drag out any break. Chris suddenly came up with a brainwave. He whispered it to me and I agreed instantly. The next time we stopped, I pointed at a tree.

'Caroll, isn't that an Israeli tree? I'm surprised to see it here.' I looked inquisitive.

'Israeli? No, this is a Lebanese tree. Many of these grow up here.' He looked confused.

'Yes, I know, but it's known as an Israeli tree in other countries,' I said, looking surreptitiously at Chris.

'Ah yes, the *Arboretum israelius* if I'm not mistaken,' said Chris, looking serious.

'I have never heard this; I think you are mistaken,' said Caroll, looking very worried.

We managed a twenty-minute break as he explained just why this tree was Lebanese in origin and had nothing to do with Israel. Chris and I secretly high-fived each other.

We came over a little crest and briefly joined the official LMT, marked by two horizontal stripes of magenta paint on the occasional rock or tree. After about 500 metres, we turned off the LMT again and started climbing up a smaller, new-looking trail.

This trail, it turned out, had been built by a gang of Syrian refugees under the watchful eye of Marwan himself.

'Where does this go?' I asked.

'Beautiful place,' replied Marwan, marching on upwards.

Halfway up, we came across the Syrian refugee work gang starting to hack another path.

'Where will that path go?' I asked Marwan.

'I do not know yet,' he replied enigmatically.

I'd often been persuaded by guides in the Middle East to visit something that they had a vested interest in, but I'd never had someone actually build their own alternative path before. To be fair, this pirate path did take us through an exceptionally beautiful oak forest, but it became clear as we sat down in a clearing for lunch that there was another plan afoot. We were supposed to be heading to a particular guesthouse, but it seemed that Marwan had his own one in a village called Mresty. This, by coincidence, was where his pirate path ended up.

When we got to Mresty we sat on Marwan's veranda, sipping iced mulberry juice and grape molasses while playing with Shadow, his rather gorgeous husky. Caroll, as part of his curiously organised itinerary, had to find a taxi to go and retrieve his vehicle. This left Marwan with a perfect opportunity to do everything in his power to persuade us to dump our planned guesthouse and stay with him.

We were eventually able to extricate ourselves from a pleasant but awkward situation after an overly long tour of the various bedrooms and a vague promise to recommend them on Trip Advisor. A lot of Middle Easterners are acutely aware that Westerners are often terrified to cause offence and will play on this very effectively to add pressure when in hyper-selling mode to travelling snowflakes. Marwan was doing the same thing. It was the classic 'just come into my shop and have a look, have a cup of tea' never-leave-until-you-buy-something technique so beloved of any Middle Eastern stall owner worth their salt.

Caroll eventually showed up and drove us to our guesthouse, a splendid old house covered in ivy. To Chris's obvious relief there were enough bedrooms for us each to have our own. His rather world-weary look changed as he started to relish a solitary evening of trouser pressing, shoe polishing and whatever else he got up to on his own.

It was only four in the afternoon. We had left Niha very early and so now had a bit of downtime. I asked Caroll to drive us down to Beiteddine, one of the most magnificent buildings in Lebanon. Built between 1788 and 1811 by Emir Bashir II, the first and only Maronite ruler of the Emirate of Mount Lebanon, the building was so magnificent that whoever was controlling Lebanon invariably used it as an administrative base. It was used by the Ottomans and the French when they respectively ruled the country. It was now the official summer residence of the Lebanese President, but parts of the palace were open to the public and it was a must-see on any self-respecting tourist itinerary to Lebanon.

I was looking forward to showing Chris and Harry the beautiful mosaics, the opulent fountains and the rooms decorated with intricately carved cedar wood. Unfortunately, it was Monday and the palace was closed, so we went for a beer instead, which, I have to admit, was more popular than any culture on offer. Caroll suggested we go to the nearby town of Deir al-Qamar, a name that translated to the rather wonderful Monastery of the Moon.

It was clear the moment we drove into town that this was a pretty special place. It had a big central square, spectacular red-roofed buildings in the Lebanese fashion and a number of outdoor cafés and restaurants packed with people enjoying themselves. This was our kind of town. We meandered down little alleys peeking into pre-lapsarian gardens seemingly containing every fruit imaginable. An elderly man halfway up a lemon tree waved down at us and asked whether we were thirsty and wanted some lemonade. We sat in his garden drinking the lemonade of the gods as the old man looked on proudly, awaiting our verdict. All around us songbirds cheeped as the early evening sun turned the limestone a golden honey hue.

'What on earth was there to fight about here?' asked Harry.

'It's difficult to imagine,' agreed Chris as he downed another glass of lemonade.

'Maybe it was just something simple. Some Maronite just wandered into the town square one day and started shouting about how he was sick of these fucking Druze coming over here and stealing our lemons.' My historical conjecture went down well; the garden echoed with laughter.

I was not far off. This town had been the scene of much conflict. In 1860, during the Mount Lebanon civil war, the place had been destroyed when Druze forces attacked the Christian population. It was rebuilt with the help of a contingent of soldiers sent from France by Napoleon III ... which was nice of him.

We said goodbye to the old man and his lemons and continued wandering aimlessly down little alleys until we came to Deir al Oumara, a lovely hotel with a central courtyard that overlooked the valley. We installed ourselves and ordered round after round of Mexican beers until all thoughts of the hardships of walking had disappeared.

Caroll told us about someone who had just completed the whole twenty-seven sections of the LMT in nine days, walking day and night. This seemed to be a bit over-keen in our opinion. It turned out to have been Paul Khawaja, the man who had looked me up and down ten years or so ago and dismissed my chances of doing the trail.

Caroll grumbled that the people who ran the Tourism Ministry were stuck in a time warp and apparently couldn't see the value in something like the LMT. This was crazy for many reasons: firstly, the indisputable beauty of the country; secondly, the idea of the LMT was to provide jobs for people in remote mountain villages, by being guides, running guesthouses, etc. The hope was that if people didn't have to leave their villages for the city to find employment then the villages would be able to thrive. The problem, however, was that nobody was coming. Caroll used to do a lot of tours around Syria until that beautiful country imploded with obvious repercussions for the Lebanese tourism industry because of the proximity of the conflict.

The organisation, Caroll told us, was looking for a new logo as they felt that the current one, a rather basic graphic showing two stick men with rucksacks and walking sticks, didn't really tell the whole story.

'How about a man walking through a minefield with his hands in the air being dive-bombed by an Israeli jet?' I suggested.

'I think this might put people off attempting the walk,' Caroll replied seriously.

'Are we walkers or trekkers?' asked Chris.

'Umm, I'm not certain. Why do you ask?' Caroll was confused.

'Well, I've just looked up the definition of trekking and it says to go on a long arduous journey, typically on foot,' said Chris.

'Aha . . .' said Caroll.

'Soo, I suppose what I'm saying is that we don't necessarily have to do this on foot,' continued Chris, who had clearly been giving the whole walking thing a long think during our long hours of plodding up Lebanese mountains.

'What do you suggest? Do Emirates do a limo service round here?' asked Harry while downing another Mexican.

'I wish . . .' said Chris.

'Why do you decide to walk a mountain trail if you don't like mountains?' asked Caroll.

'We're fine with the downhill bits; it's just the whole uphill part that we find tough,' I said, laughing.

'Yes, we are paid-up members of the Downhill Hiking Club,' said Chris.

'You are the strangest hikers I have ever been with,' replied Caroll, shaking his bald head.

We all went proudly silent and gazed out across the valley, lost in our respective thoughts. Somewhere far below, a pack of jackals started to howl at the crescent moon. Chris visibly shuddered.

We eventually returned to our guesthouse to find a veritable feast laid out for us on a long table in the garden. Harry scanned the table nervously, looking for anything vaguely familiar. There was the usual basket of mountain bread, bowls of olives, labneh, hummus, fattoush and one of my favourite dishes, loubieh bi zeit (green beans braised in olive oil, garlic and tomatoes). Fortunately, for Harry, a large plate of homemade French fries appeared and he relaxed a little, helped in part by a bottle of rather decent local red wine.

## DAY 4

# DEIR AL-QAMAR TO BAROUK

The following morning, I awoke to the sound of screaming. Some long-buried instinct kicked in, and I rushed towards the sound without too much thought or any clothing. Due to the curious layout of the guesthouse, this meant that I ran through the kitchen naked, which did not go down well with the Ethiopian woman who helped with the cooking. She dropped a bowl, but I was now committed so I continued. The screaming had stopped but it had been coming from behind a thin wooden door to the side of the front door. As I got to the door, it opened and there stood a nearly naked Chris, his modesty covered only by a flannel.

'Morning, maestro . . . Off for a run?' said Chris.

'What? No, there was screaming . . .' I panted.

'Oh, sorry about that, the shower was ice cold. I'd skip it if I were you unless you're in a particularly masochistic mood.' He slipped past me and disappeared towards his room.

This would be the last time that I would use my razor-sharp reactions to come to his assistance. I grabbed a towel from the bathroom and returned to my room, apologising profusely to the still traumatised Ethiopian on the way back.

Breakfast was a quick affair, with the Ethiopian keeping a safe distance from me as she gingerly placed stuff on the table. Half an hour later, we set off for the Maasser el Shouf Cedar Reserve in the Shouf Biosphere, the largest nature reserve in Lebanon, consisting of an area of 550 square kilometres of pristine mountain landscape. This is a big place, taking up roughly 5 per cent of the Lebanese land mass and containing several of the remaining cedar forests that used to cover the mountains.

Unfortunately, it was Labour Day in Lebanon. This meant that most of Beirut had poured out of the sticky capital and headed for the cooling hills for picnics. So, when we got to the ranger's hut, there were already quite a lot of day-trippers wandering about. This didn't sit well with us. We were explorers, trekkers, international men of adventure; we didn't want to hang out with this sort. Caroll had a word with one of the rangers, who agreed to take us to the top of the mountain and drop us off above the tree level where there would be nobody. We could then make our way across the ridge and then back down through the cedar forests. The Downhill Hiking Club visibly perked up at this plan of action. First a lift and then some downhill walking? It was perfect.

We hopped into the back of a beaten-up old pick-up truck and roared up the mountain. Now this was my kind of mountaineering. At the top we stopped beside a giant TV aerial. We thanked the ranger for his help before setting off along the ridge. Ten minutes later we had the most spectacular of views. Beneath us, to the west, was the Beqaa Valley, the bread basket of Lebanon. This is the northernmost tip of the Great Rift Valley that runs from the Red Sea and up through Jordan.

The valley is squeezed between Mount Lebanon, the range that we were stood on, and the lower Anti-Lebanon mountain range on the other side of the valley that forms the border with Syria. We could just make out the Orontes, known as the Rebel River as, unlike the Euphrates and the Tigris, which flow south, it flows north from the Beqaa up to Antakya in Turkey. I liked the Orontes. It had a pleasingly non-conformist Lebanese attitude to life.

We turned to our right, to the south, and could see the snow-capped peaks of Mount Hermon and the Israeli border behind the heat-haze. Turning back to look west, behind us, we could see all the way down to the Mediterranean and the Phoenician ports of Sidon and Tyre.

Harry was stunned. It was like an aerial view of Middle Eastern political history and served to explain the Lebanese situation better than a thousand books could do. You immediately realised why persecuted minorities had fled the flat deserts to take refuge in these wild mountains. You could see why the Phoenicians, whose cities were trapped in front of this mountain range, would choose to expand seawards and conquer the Mediterranean by trade. You also realised why Lebanon, an exotic fish surrounded by hungry sharks, had so often been the setting for so much conflict.

Harry couldn't get over how small Lebanon was.

'How big is it, compared to Wales?' said Harry.

'Why does everybody use Wales as a unit of measurement when it comes to countries?' I asked.

'Whales?' said Caroll. 'Why whales?'

'Wales ... the country. Where men are men, and sheep are nervous,' said Harry.

'Like a sperm whale?' Caroll looked utterly confused by the conversation.

'You're getting close.' Harry laughed.

'I'm guessing that they are about the same size,' I ventured.

'As a sperm whale?' chipped in Chris, a bit late to the party.

'Shut up, all of you,' I said.

I looked it up that night. I had found a very useful website that allowed you to superimpose two countries on top of each other. It turned out that I was very wrong. Lebanon is almost exactly half the size of Wales. Lebanon has 10,400 square kilometres to Wales' 20,800. I dug further into the question of why Wales is used as a unit of measurement. It got complicated. Nobody really knows how it started, except that back in the days of empire when people knew little of other places, attempts were made to explain them to a British audience by using local comparisons. The French, however, use Corsica and the Danes use an island called Fyn (also known as Funen). Even worse, because of metrication, Wales is now losing her place to Belgium, which apparently works better for most comparisons. For the record, Belgium is nearly three times the size of Lebanon. You're welcome ...

We marched on and discovered some, now vacant, Israeli tank emplacements. The tanks would have fired over the crest of the little hill directly in front of them and down into the Syrian positions in the Beqaa Valley. There were still bits of expended ordnance, and the occasional ammo tin with Hebrew lettering on it. Chris stuffed one piece of jagged metal into his backpack, becoming yet another person to take up the very Lebanese hobby of war-detritus collecting. As a boy, at school in Beirut, I would take some of my finest pieces (shrapnel, bullet casings and such-like) into school in a little suitcase where I would attempt to make swaps for other items. I would spend hours roaming the pine forests near our home looking for stuff. It all went a bit wrong when I got to my prep school in Oxford (another terrible term – *preparatory school* – these places preparing you for nothing). On the first night I whipped out my collection to show the dorm and was immediately reported to a strange man who taught metalwork and claimed to have once been in the SAS. He confiscated my treasures and slippered me to boot. It was a brutal introduction to a brutal school. *Arduus ad Solem*, my arse . . .

We kept walking along the ridge before taking a track to the left and dropping down below the treeline, where we entered the Barouk Cedar Reserve. On the other side of a small valley we saw regimented rows of cedars that looked very much like they'd had some assistance from humans. They turned out to be the work of Kamal Jumblatt, the Druze warlord, who had planted a vast quantity of cedars in the 1950s in an attempt to reforest the denuded mountains.

To understand the importance of cedars to the Lebanese, one needs to look to history. The cedar tree is on the Lebanese flag and the ancient cedar forests of Lebanon were the oldest documented in history. The *Epic of Gilgamesh*, a poem from Mesopotamia, often regarded as the oldest surviving great work of literature, described the Lebanese cedar forests as being 'one thousand leagues long and one thousand leagues wide'. Now I was not entirely up on the league as a scale of measurement, but it turned out to be the distance that someone could cover by foot in an hour. So that was a thousand hours of walking. That was quite a lot of trees.

The Phoenicians would use the wood to build their ships, which they then used to sell cedar wood all over the world.

Egyptians used the wood for temples and boats. Babylonians used it to build Babylon. King Solomon built the Temple of Solomon with it. Then the Romans came and protected them for their own use. Even as late as the twentieth century, the Ottomans deforested large areas near the Hijaz railway (the Damascus to Haifa branch) so as to provide fuel for their engines.

So, these once massive forests were now gone, tiny shadows of their glorious past, and much of the Lebanese mountainside was now bare. The setting up of the biospheres and several other nature reserves was Lebanon trying desperately to preserve the remnants of their national symbol: the magnificent Cedar of Lebanon.

Only the strongest or the most isolated have survived for this long as the cedar does not like to be planted too close to another as they are forced to compete for water for their extensive roots. It is an apt national symbol as, like many Lebanese sects, the trees survive best when left to their own devices in their remote mountain hideaways.

We entered a grassy plateau where on all sides new cedars had been planted, each with a little plaque at the base. It was a project to encourage Lebanese people to adopt a cedar and to name it after a family member or ancestor, in return for which they paid around two hundred US dollars to help the upkeep of the area. Caroll took us up a steep slope to a cedar that was about fifteen years old; it was dedicated to his father. We stopped by it for a while in silence as Caroll appeared to be in deep thought, obviously remembering his father.

'When did he pass on, Caroll?' I asked quietly.

'Pass on?' Caroll looked up.

'When did he die?'

'He's not dead, he works in Beirut.' Caroll looked at me as though I was an idiot.

We walked on, but I couldn't get the idea of a tree symbolising someone in your past out of my head. How much nicer would it have been to visit a living, growing tree dedicated to my father and planted in the country he so loved? It seemed much more fitting than the lonely grave in the lonely graveyard in Beirut, surrounded by the long forgotten.

A bird stood on the path ahead of us. It stared at us aggressively, in the manner of a cocky gunman manning a roadblock. It refused to move out of the way. We ended up having to inch round it while it stared at us dismissively. I had a flashback. To the garden of our house in Highgate. I had a catapult and, bored of shooting at apples, I'd lazily aimed at a bird in the tree and, to my horror, hit it and killed it. The bird fell to the ground dead. This was three days after my father had announced that he was leaving my mother. I broke down completely. I felt unbelievable guilt. I was so upset, I could barely function for weeks. My mother assumed it was over the divorce. All I could think of was the dead bird lying under the apple tree in the garden.

We crossed over from the Barouk Forest into the Maasser el Shouf Forest to see possibly the most famous cedar tree in Lebanon. It was named after the French poet Alphonse de Lamartine, who travelled to Lebanon in the nineteenth century from his home town of Mâcon in Burgundy. Lamartine apparently liked to sit under this particular cedar to write.

Today, there was no poet underneath the tree. Instead there was a gaggle of Lebanese twenty-somethings all intertwined and not at all inclined to make way for what was an obligatory photo opportunity. One young man in particular had the peculiar confidence of a contestant on *Love Island*; a confidence that only nine hours a day in the gym can give you. He had three gorgeous Lebanese girls draped around him in a modern erotic tableau that could have been a throwback to a scene from the court of Fakhreddine or Bashir II. I said 'could' because it was unlikely that this Muscle Mary had ever read a book, let alone delved into the rich history of his country. I realised that I was getting disproportionately annoyed with this gym bunny and that he might actually be a lovely guy studying metaphysics at the AUB. It was just a knee-jerk reaction to jock arrogance from a former goth who'd borne the brunt of physical bullying from this type one time too many.

We hiked on up the hill, but the paths were now swarming with day-trippers, most in T-shirts and flip-flops, pushing baby strollers, with one man even barefoot. Once again, we looked utterly ludicrous in our full hiking gear and so we affected the look of people who were coming to the end of an incredible journey, and not three twats who'd got a lift up the mountain before a leisurely stroll back down.

We passed by what was reputed to be the oldest cedar in Lebanon, which was over three thousand years old. As we stopped to admire the gnarly old branches, thunder and lightning could be seen and heard far below us in the valley. It took me right back to the bad old days of the civil war. We'd be in the family home above Beirut trying our best to keep calm and carry on as the sounds of battle echoed around us.

I'd been trying to teach Harry some basic Arabic, though it was not something that came naturally to him. I started with two basic words: *shukran* for thank you and *marhaba* for a general greeting as we walked through the country. He occasionally remembered *shukran* but *marhaba* was completely out of his reach. As people passed by, he gave it his best shot.

'Malabar ...' He nodded at a young couple.

'Marsbar ...' He cocked his hat to an elderly lady with shockingly badly dyed hair.

'Marjoram ...' He smiled with his stained teeth at a nervous-looking man in a T-shirt that read SNIFFING GLU WON'T KEEP FAMILY *TOGETHER*!

I took Harry aside and made him repeat *marhaba* over and over until it became a mantra.

Five minutes later and a rather gorgeous Lebanese twenty-something in a very revealing outfit sashayed towards us. I could see Harry suck in his tummy as he let her pass.

'Mybababa ...' he said loudly, while smiling inanely at her.

He sounded vaguely insane and the twenty-something rightly avoided eye contact and stepped up her pace.

By the time we got close to the entrance, the area was packed with people. It seemed that all of Lebanon had decided to spend the day in the Cedars. This was not what we had been after. So, after 13 kilometres, we hopped into Caroll's van to go down and have a look round Sidon. We would continue our walk the following day when everyone else had gone back to Beirut.

As we drove down towards the Mediterranean, we asked Caroll what there was to do in the town.

'There is a very interesting soap museum,' said Caroll enthusiastically.

'A soap museum, in an ex-French colony? I find that very unlikely,' replied Harry caustically.

We could feel the temperature rising. It had been a balmy 25 °C in the mountains, but as we got closer to the coast the mercury was rising fast. I noticed that Caroll didn't quite seem to be himself; in fact, he appeared to be almost nodding off at the wheel. We forced him to stop and plied him with biscuits and coffee in a café before setting off again. The break did him some good; he became perkier and more alert, which was a minimum requirement when driving in Lebanon.

By the time we hit the coast it was 33 °C and incredibly humid. We turned south on the coastal highway and made our way into Sidon, one of the great Phoenician ports. As we drove along packed beaches beside the Corniche, all human life was there. Every hundred metres or so men on horseback pottered around trying to find people willing to pay for a ride along the beach. As we approached the port, the traffic became chaotic and any vague semblance of order was abandoned. Traffic lights were for the weak, signalling was for the insane. Driving in Lebanon is survival of the fittest, or nuttiest. I rather love driving there. It is like a crazy video game, but it's not for everybody.

Harry's face was glued to the window as he marvelled at the chaos. At a roundabout, where technically everybody was supposed to go around in an anti-clockwise fashion, all bets were off. Drivers were not only going around in opposing directions, but one had decided to go straight over – no mean feat considering there was quite the ziggurat on the top of it. To one side, a traffic policeman, rather smartly done up in knee-high black leather boots and sporting a snazzy white helmet, was lying on top of his motorbike smoking a cigarette. He had long given up on any thoughts of controlling his environment and appeared to be the most Zen person in the situation.

We found a bar right next to the old Crusader sea castle that jutted out into the harbour. The castle had been built by English Crusaders in the thirteenth century with stone that they had stolen from Roman temples. The castle was then partially destroyed by the Mamelukes when they booted out the Crusaders. Fakhreddine II rebuilt parts of it in the seventeenth century, only for the Ottomans to damage it severely. It was then nearly destroyed by a British naval bombardment in the eighteenth century and had taken direct hits in the relatively recent civil war. This castle had certainly paid its dues ...

We sat and stared at the goings-on around the castle as we nursed our beers. On the top of the ramparts, we watched Muslim couples coyly courting, while on the sea wall a couple of newlyweds posed for an ambitious photo shoot. In the water, just off the castle, a couple of overly hirsute medallion men roared around on jet skis. There is nothing more obnoxious or irritating than a jet ski, unless you happened to be on one and then, of course, they are excellent fun.

We were in pensive moods. Possibly the abundance of history had made us reflect on our place in it. Chris opined that being fifty was a little like waking up on the second Tuesday of a two-week holiday ... not long to go.

To cheer ourselves up we went for a walk around the town. The castle was interesting but, as I told the boys, once you'd done Krak, you never went back. I was of course referring to

Krak des Chevaliers, possibly the most magnificent castle in the world. It was just over the Syrian border in the north and Harry longed to visit it, but the situation in that country meant that this was not very likely, so we had to make do with Sidon Castle.

The souks were unexpectedly atmospheric. I remembered my favourite story about souks. It was an urban myth, but most likely based in truth. The story was that the first stall you went into in a souk made an assessment as to whether you were a pro, an average or a total mug in the shopping stakes. Based on this assessment the store would give you a different-coloured bag: red for pro, yellow for average and green for total mug. This way the rest of the souk would know when a total mug wandered down their alley.

Having got completely lost in the labyrinth, we eventually came out by the seafront along the walls of a magnificent building. This was the Khan al-Franj, a caravanserai built by Fakhreddine II in the seventeenth century and used by foreign merchants as their base in the city. There they would sleep, house their animals and sell their goods. The centrepiece was a vast courtyard with a fountain surrounded by two storeys of covered galleries.

I adore caravanserai; there is something epically romantic about them. I'd once had a magical night in one in Baku in Azerbaijan. The walls there, as here, were positively steeped in history and I felt a strong affinity with the place; after all, my family had come to this country as merchants, although I think a little too late for caravanserai.

I couldn't help remembering my trip to Baku. I'd been invited out by a dodgy billionaire to attend the opening of a nightclub. He wanted celebrities and journalists to attend and he offered his private jet to sweeten the deal. The jet, normally flying two or three people, was rammed full of travel hacks emptying the bar as fast as they could. The nightclub was an experience: one of the many versions of the Sugababes were miming in the corner and actors were paid to stand outside with non-working cameras to pretend to be paparazzi. It was all very weird, but nothing was as weird as one of the most popular attractions in the city. The Museum of Miniature Books.

'We have over ten thousand miniature books here, most no larger than your thumbnail. We have the entire works of Shakespeare, Tolstoy, Proust ... all in tiny, tiny books,' said the owner proudly.

*BUT WHY? FOR GOD'S SAKE WHY?* was all I wanted to shout. But I bit my tongue and nodded as though interested.

In the stifling heat of the evening, we left Sidon and headed back to the cool welcome of the village of Barouk, which sits at 1,200 metres above sea-level. I knew very little about the village save that it was the birthplace of the man who wrote the Lebanese national anthem.

On the drive back up we spotted a mustering of storks descending on a valley just below the road. I remembered this sight from my youth when storks, migrating from Africa to Europe, would make the mistake of overflying Beirut. Everything from air rifles to tracer bullets would be fired at the poor things in an orgy of violence. You'd have assumed that they would have learned their lesson by now and avoided the country completely.

We stopped the car and got out to watch. It was only a matter of moments before shotguns started going off all around the valley. The Lebanese really could not resist shooting anything that moved and so we hopped back into the van and drove on before they mistook us for potential prey. At the very least we had done the Lebanese travel cliché: we had gone from beach (where we didn't swim) to the ski slopes of Barouk (where there was currently no snow and no skiing).

We arrived in Barouk at about eight in the evening and spent quite some time trying to locate our guesthouse. Eventually, our hostess spotted us and waved us down. We made our way down some steps to the vaulted basement of the three-storey building. We walked into a long room containing a dining table and chairs, a couple of sofas and five beds laid out in a row.

To Chris's horror, a stranger was lying on the furthest bed, reading a book. This was his worst nightmare and he grabbed Bear from his bag and started manically folding clothes, something that I assumed took him to a happy place. Harry and I were fairly relaxed about the whole thing. We'd both survived ten years of boarding school, the last five of which were spent in one long room where you started at one end in 1982 and finished at the other in 1987. Several jokes were made about who was going to kick off the biscuit game at the expense of a clearly nervous Chris, who had not had to endure the ardours of boarding school.

'Mahobo,' said Harry to the stranger, who smiled back, uncertain of what language he was being addressed in.

His name was Daniel, a Lebanese guide whose two Swiss protégés were apparently staying at an uber-luxurious boutique hotel fifteen minutes away. Chris nearly cracked, and I could swear that I saw tears in the corner of both his and Bear's eyes. He disappeared to have a shower and nearly did not reappear.

As in most Lebanese bathrooms, the approach to electricity was relaxed to say the least. This one had a particularly thick electric wire with the ends hanging out and dangling down next to the shower head. Chris came out un-showered, and he and Bear sat down on their bed with desolate thousand-yard stares.

## DAY 5

# BAROUK TO AIN ZHALTA

When we woke the following morning, I was getting a lot less love from Daniel. Despite him being four beds away, my snoring had, according to him, been worse than an air raid. Breakfast was, therefore, a frosty affair and he headed off as soon as he could to meet his Swiss clients.

We took our time getting ready as, for the first time, our itinerary stated *Extremely Difficult* next to the route. We were all racked with fear of the unknown. I felt hiking was a bit like parachuting; probably a lot more enjoyable the second time around, once you knew what was coming. Chris tried to get philosophical and mused that trekking uphill was very much a metaphor for life; rather than enjoying the moment you were always worrying about what was coming around the corner. Harry looked up from his Choco Pops and told us both to stop wittering.

We met our local guide. He was an imposing fellow, about six-foot-two, gym-fresh and sporting the tidy beard of a metrosexual Hezbollah fighter. He was a man of few words and when he did speak, he did not inspire us with confidence, asking us what he should wear for the day. A fleece or a rain jacket? I felt that he was better placed to make that sort of decision, and the fact that he was asking us was not a great sign of his guiding capabilities.

'I am the son of the mayor,' he told us proudly.

'Ah,' I replied.

'One day I will be the mayor,' he continued.

I didn't doubt it as this seemed to be how politics invariably worked in the country. For now, however, we needed to work out whether he needed his fleece or a rain jacket. I looked up to the sky as though drawing on years of experience before telling him to go with a fleece. He appeared pleased with the decision and soon we were marching out of the village.

Once into the forest we got another long lecture on the sex life of the cedar. It was not uninteresting but, as this was our third cedar forest thus far, we were starting to get pretty good on the subject. We also couldn't concentrate, as the words *Extremely Difficult* echoed around our brains. It was the not knowing that was the worst. We constantly feared turning the corner and being faced with some horrific slope. It didn't take long for our worst fears to be confirmed. We started to climb almost vertically on what appeared to be a never-ending ascent. This would have killed us on the body-shock of the first day, but we had already got a bit better. We had also learned some tricks.

The tendency when faced with a steep hill was to try to get up it as quickly as possible. We would almost try to charge the hill to get it over with. We now knew that slow and steady was best. We had to force ourselves into a sort of slow-motion walk that felt abnormal but made a huge difference to our performance. I'd never understood footage of climbers on a mountain, near the summit but making incredibly slow progress and claiming it was another two hours to the top. I now understood it a little better. Our breathing was more controlled and, along with using the poles, the whole ordeal was slightly more bearable.

Even our banter had returned slightly. Up until then the moment we'd started climbing, the 'banter button' would be switched to silence as we huffed and puffed, lost in our own personal hells. Today, however, we all hurled insults at each other with abandon and were much the cheerier for it. There was one problem, however. We all agreed that we loathed the word banter. It was normally a catchall excuse for being a hideous twat, so we discussed what we should call our playful interactions. Chris was all for 'joshing' but I thought this sounded a bit too Victorian. Harry was keen on 'emotional bullying' but we all felt that this might look differently on the page. I suggested 'badinage' and this went down quite well with Chris, but Harry said it sounded 'poncey'. Chris countered with 'ribbing' but Harry and I both felt sure that this was some form of obscure sex act. 'Jesting' was suggested by Harry but not accepted. Then I remembered the word 'persiflage'. The literal translation was 'teasing' but both Harry and Chris, more out of boredom with the subject than any particular love for the term, agreed to using it.

After about three hours of climbing and much persiflage, we finally reached the top and began walking along the ridge. Another view of the Beqaa, very similar to the one from the previous day, lay beneath us. After an hour or so we found a pile of inviting-looking rocks and sat down to eat lunch and savour the view. Chris wandered off to have a look around and found the metal handle of an Israeli grenade, which he added excitedly to his collection. I remembered an energy snack that my wife, Stacey, had bought me just before I left. I took it out of my bag. It was about the size of a tennis ball with the consistency of Play-Doh. I ate it. It was like crack cocaine, Lebanese marching powder ... I had no idea what was in it, but I was up and off within minutes.

Soon I was almost half a mile ahead of Chris and Harry and feeling very smug. I slipped on my headphones and selected *Ghost Alive* by the Boxer Rebellion. I was now striding out over the roof of Lebanon to my own personal soundtrack, ripped to the tits on some hiking rock of crack. This was what it was all about. I wondered whether this was a bit like the endorphin rush that runners were supposed to get, the buzz that kept them hooked. I gazed down at the world beneath my boots. This was truly God's country. The only problem was, which one?

At the end of the long ridge, we started to descend into the Ain Zhalta Cedar Forest, the third and, in my opinion, the most staggering of the three forests in the Shouf Biosphere. It was as though prime cuts of northern California, Switzerland and Narnia had all been compacted into a private garden of Eden for us to wander through.

Halfway down, we found a lovely spot for lunch. Unfortunately, Harry decided to take his shoes and socks off, unleashing a satanic smell that forced Chris and me to beat a strategic retreat. Harry didn't care a jot. He sat alone, eating his way through seven hard-boiled eggs. The Lebanese chicken population had found a keen fan.

Unlike the previous day, when we felt as if we had been part of some form of infernal coach tour, today we had the mountains to ourselves. It seemed unreal in the modern world that you didn't have to share this natural beauty with anybody.

After lunch we made our way slowly down through the enchanted forests, passing the time with our new game. Every time anybody mentioned a wild boar, of which there were traces of many about, we would all shout 'wild boar, wild boar' in the style of Duran Duran's international smash hit, 'Wild Boys'.

The game soon evolved because we were all up for as much ribaldry as possible. Keeping the Duran Duran theme, we agreed that, if anybody said they were hungry, we would all shout 'hungry like the wolf'. If anybody said the word 'Easy' we'd all shout 'you're about as easy as a nuclear war'. For non-fans of early Duran Duran, this might have been very confusing, but it kept us all going for hours and we never tired of it. Caroll particularly enjoyed it. The son of a mayor joined in occasionally but with little enthusiasm and visible consternation.

Finally, we hit a tarmac road. A quick ten-minute walk down brought us to the entrance of the park. It had been a long day. We had walked 22 kilometres, and our legs were screaming. I felt exhausted as the effects of the crack bomb had long worn off, leaving me with a slightly shivery comedown feeling. I honestly had no idea what was in the thing but made a mental note to ask Stacey where she had purchased it from and whether Colombians had run the establishment.

Caroll set off on his daily pilgrimage to retrieve his vehicle while we sat on a bench and started talking to a bored police officer who stood guard there. Harry spotted the man's pistol in his holster. It was like a moth to a flame. Within minutes Harry was trying to persuade him to hand it over for him to look at. The police officer looked very unimpressed but, unbelievably, un-holstered his weapon and, after a little more persuasion, handed it over to a delighted Harry. It was an aged Smith & Wesson and not brilliantly maintained. There were, however, six bullets in it and only four of us standing around him. I knew what was coming before it happened. Harry started waving the thing about, making 'bang' sounds as though he was the good guy in a bad Western.

The police officer immediately realised that he'd made a terrible mistake. Harry turned away from him to point the pistol up at the mountain from where we'd come. The police officer took his opportunity and grabbed Harry's hand, making him drop the pistol, which smashed onto the stone floor beneath us. I held my breath and awaited the report of the gun going off and the sickening thud of the bullet as it entered Chris's buttocks, but it didn't come. The police officer, however, was distinctly unimpressed and started screaming at Harry in Arabic.

'All right, all right, calm down, it was only a bit of persiflage,' said Harry, trying to calm the cop down with his hands.

It was a long and awkward wait for Caroll to arrive back with the van.

On the way to our guesthouse for that evening, we stopped by an abandoned bus at the side of the road just outside the village of Ain Zhalta. The windscreen was riddled with bullet holes, with an incongruous I LOVE LEBANON sticker stuck to the front just beneath the engine. It was an unintentional visual metaphor for the country and too good to ignore.

We climbed on board. The driver's seat was pierced by three bullets and there was what looked like blood on the seat cover. On the dash lay a logbook with the words LEBANESE INTERNATIONAL UNIVERSITY emblazoned on the cover. I looked up the place and found out that it had been established in 2001 and so this incident had presumably happened since then. I tried to make more enquiries but came up blank. Safe to say that this had clearly been a bad day to be a student at LIU.

As we drove on, there was less laughter in the van. Lebanon has a curious way of reminding you that there are two sides to everything, and that no matter how beautiful or wonderful something is, there is always a darker side. Five minutes later, we arrived at the guesthouse in Ain Zhalta, the home of one of the park rangers. It was a cosy place and we were made incredibly welcome. Chris and I shared a room while the 'non-snorers' Caroll and Harry shared another. It was getting a little cold and we were pleased to have ancient oil-burning stoves in the middle of each room.

We strolled down into the village, found a shop and bought a bottle of Lebanese wine from Ksara. Back up at the guesthouse we sat on a little veranda at the front, laughing and drinking away. The wine was very tasty, and our spirits soon rose. From below in the village we heard a voice starting up on a very loud tannoy.

'What are they saying?' asked Chris.

'It's not good news,' I deadpanned. 'The man is telling locals that there are three foreigners in the village and the going ransom rate is a hundred thousand US dollars per person.'

'Bollocks,' said Chris.

'Now he's just repeating some code word … "the cats are in the cradle", "the cats are in the cradle" … over and over again.'

'Ah, top persiflage,' said Harry.

After half an hour the ranger came out looking very concerned. He ran to get Caroll and explained his problem.

It turned out that we were sitting on his neighbour's veranda, whose house was connected to his. They had telephoned him to complain about these strangers drinking and laughing on their property. We quickly moved to the correct veranda, and no harm appeared to have been done.

Supper was magnificent. It was cooked for us by the park ranger, who lived on his own. We had homemade tabbouleh, baba ghanoush and (to Harry's delight) chips.

Permanently on in the background, as in most Lebanese households, was a blaring television. The news was on and talking about the upcoming election. A reporter was interviewing families arriving at Beirut Airport from abroad.

'Have you been paid to come back and vote?' asked the reporter.

'Yes,' they all replied, as though this was the most normal thing in the world.

The local warlords were busy shipping their diaspora back home to vote.

After supper, I posted a photo on Instagram of me posing like a ponce while standing, in what I took to be rather majestic fashion, overlooking the Beqaa Valley. I wrote 'never been happier' underneath it. An hour later I got a WhatsApp message from my wife. She told me that my elderly mother (who lived with us) had seen the post and wandered into the kitchen to inform Stacey that I had never been happier and had no longer any need for a wife.

# DAY 6

# AIN ZHALTA TO SOHA VILLAGE

The following morning saw excessive Vaselining of the testicles. (A sentence I never thought that I'd write.) My bits were in pieces and I needed to take some preventative action. The only positive aspect was that Harry had to be in a far worse situation. I broached the situation at breakfast, already a tense time for him.

'How are the boys, Harry?' I asked.

'What boys?' he muttered, not looking up from his Choco Pops.

'The gentlemen down below. Everything OK?' I smiled.

'What on earth are you talking about, Joly?'

'How are your testicles? Do you have severe chafing in that area? I'm like Vietnam down there.' Code was useless with him.

'No, fine. No problems to report.' Harry continued with his cereal.

I was astonished. Harry was marching commando through Lebanon and suffering zero repercussions. Maybe his method was better? Either that or he had balls of steel.

After breakfast we were all outside soaking up the morning sun when our new guide turned up. She was a very bubbly young woman called Jacky.

'Are you surprised that she is a woman?' asked Caroll.

'No, we have women in the UK, but we were all surprised that you were a man.' I ground my teeth audibly as I always do when I go a touch too far.

Everyone laughed, maybe a little too hard.

'You are brave to come to Lebanon and hike for so long,' said Jacky.

'We have never hiked anywhere before,' I replied.

'Ah, so you are not brave, you are just stupid.' Jacky laughed.

We were going to get along famously.

We were no longer walking in the Shouf Biosphere. We knew this because we'd started following the LMT blazing again – two stripes of purple and white daubed on the occasional tree or rock. Weirdly, the Biosphere did not allow the LMT blazing in their area, which made it very difficult for hikers to find their way. This seemed to be a crazy decision and Jacky told me that I should mention it in my book so that this policy might be changed. We quickly learned that you didn't argue with Jacky.

After a couple of hours' walk through a relatively uninteresting section of the trail, we neared the Beirut–Damascus highway. The mountains around us were peppered with quarries, mostly owned and operated by crooked politicians or their associates. The quarries were like hideous scars on a beautiful body and are becoming more and more of an issue in Lebanon. There are an estimated 1,300 illegal quarries in this tiny country, most digging up sand and sandstone for construction.

We crossed an Ottoman stone bridge and saw an old railway line. It was state-owned and closed years ago, but the employees of the Lebanese Railway still got their salaries. There was a lot that didn't make sense in Lebanon. In the old days, under Ottoman rule, you could take this train from Beirut to Baalbek and Aleppo to join up with the Baghdad to Istanbul line.

Just before we crossed the literal 'Road to Damascus', we found a boy sitting in a container, running a makeshift shop. Pride of place was given to a vast, shiny coffee machine. Unfortunately, the boy had no coffee. We bought a beer and a Marathon bar and cracked on.

We got some very curious looks from drivers as we stopped the traffic and crossed the highway. Lebanese Army soldiers at a nearby military checkpoint looked at us suspiciously but did nothing to intervene. Once over the road we walked up a track peppered with abandoned shoes. There was no explanation for this except the slightly paranoid thought that we might be wandering through a minefield and that the shoes were the only remains of previous hikers. About half a mile above the highway we stopped by a lonely tree.

'Take off your packs and leave them here,' barked Jacky.

'Why?' I asked.

'Because this is where you get taken hostage,' she said unsmilingly.

Jacky had a very Lebanese sense of humour.

She took us up a little incline just off the track to the waist-high mouth of a tunnel. It was an old French military hospital from the Second World War and went into the mountain, opening up into enormous spaces, some of which had been closed off. It would have been used in the fighting between French Vichy forces and the invading English and Free French troops. It was an exceedingly creepy place – damp, cold, and the wind was making eerie sounds in one of the walled-up tunnels. It was quite the feat of engineering. Being injured in battle must have been bad enough, but to have then been dragged down these long, cold tunnels and deposited in underground caverns must have been quite the experience. We didn't hang around and were soon back out in the reassuring sunlight. Harry was not impressed.

'Very typical of the French to be skulking around underground during a battle.' Harry was not what you might call a Francophile, despite being married to a Belgian.

As we walked on, it became clear that the whole plateau was something of a military museum. This made sense as anybody controlling it could also hold the strategic pass through the mountains from the Beqaa Valley to Beirut. Anybody wishing to invade Lebanon from the east would have to go through this pass before they could advance on Beirut. We walked over remnants of recent invaders; Syrian tank emplacements and trenches dug along a ridge. We nearly fell into a couple of well-hidden dugouts. The ground was carpeted with historical military detritus, bullet casings, shrapnel … so much shrapnel of every shape and size.

As we reached the other side of the plateau, we spotted the current military inhabitants, an artillery battery manned by the Lebanese Army and pointing towards Syria and the Beqaa Valley. As we checked it out surreptitiously through binoculars, a fox made a sudden break from cover and bolted across the field in front of us. Oblivious of the military history beneath its feet, it was only concerned with the current threat, which was us, and it bounded up and over a wall and was gone.

We lunched under cedars, sitting on the soft grass in the shadow of the artillery. Jacky gave us some janarek to try. These are sour plums but taste far better than this sounds. They are like lemony apples, about the size of a cherry. I munched content-edly on a handful while Harry and Chris wandered off to inspect the nearby artillery, all the while pretending to be picking wild flowers. I was sure that there would be a shout from the army and that they would be detained immediately but no sounds came from the base and they were able to have a good look at the battery.

Once back from their tour of inspection Harry sat down to roll himself yet another cigarette, while Chris and I discussed our exciting new business idea. It was a range of hiking equip-ment called 'The Lazy Hiker' and aimed at people like us. Our range of products included a walking stick that turned into a three-legged chair and a remote-controlled, wheeled rucksack that would follow you automatically. Chris was adamant that we could take the market, but we often had ideas like this that never really went anywhere. I remembered our grand ideas for enormous hipster Lego tables and the ludicrous notion of open-ing a chain of avocado restaurants.

We walked on, creeping past a dugout that contained a sleep-ing sentry. We didn't want to wake him lest he take us for yet another in the long list of shameless invaders of his homeland.

If you drove north along the coast road from Beirut towards the town of Jounieh, you could see physical proof of this list. A massive rock formation that stretches right into the sea forms a formidable barrier to anybody trying to cross between the northern coastal towns and the southern ones. The rock towers over the Nahr al-Kelb, the wonderfully named Dog River, another tricky element to this natural defence fortification. Today there is a tunnel that takes the driver through the middle of the rock. In the past, however, this was a mighty obstacle to an invading army and many were so chuffed at getting past it they chose to mark the occasion with a boastful plaque on the cliff face. There were seventeen of these plaques. The first was put up by the Egyptian Pharaoh Rameses II in the thirteenth century BC. He had sent an army to fight the Hittites for possession of Mount Lebanon. There followed further boastful memorials from the Assyrians, Babylonians, Phoenicians and the Romans among others. Alexander the Great came through but didn't bother with a plaque (when your surname is Great, you clearly don't need to show off). There was nothing to mark the Crusaders nor the Ottomans, but the tradition was restarted by Napoleon III, who left one after he'd sent an army to stop the Muslim massacre of Druze and Christians in 1860. There were also plaques from English and Free French troops celebrating their defeat of the occupying Vichy forces in 1941, followed by a final one from the Lebanese celebrating the departure of the last French soldier in 1946. There was no sign, however, of modern-day invaders (Palestinians, Israelis, Syrians and Iranians, Americans); it was actually a wonder that there was any room left on the cliff face.

After half an hour we summited a tiny hill that we realised marked the end of this 'war' plateau. Below us was a sheer drop of hundreds of metres and a spectacular view down across red-roofed villages to the distant Mediterranean.

'Now what?' said Chris, peering nervously into the abyss.

'We take the path.' Jacky grinned.

'What path?' Chris looked about frantically.

'That one ...' Jacky pointed to a barely discernible line a little down from the clifftop. It was technically a path, although many a mountain goat would have shaken their heads and announced to their fellow goats that they were moving to the city.

Chris was not happy, but we had little choice, so we eventually set off with Jacky leading and Chris keeping his eyes firmly on Jacky's feet ... or so he claimed. We inched our way across. Every so often, Chris would release a barely discernible whimper, a subtle hint of the unfettered turmoil raging within. After ten minutes or so we had traversed the drop and entered the Valley of Lamartine, another beautiful place named after the French poet who had visited Lebanon in 1832–3 and supposedly sat on a rock in this valley to write as well as under the cedar we had seen a couple of days before. Lamartine seemed to do a lot of outdoor writing. Chris was showing signs of post-traumatic stress disorder, so I tried to console him with some gentle words from Lamartine's epic poem, *La Chute d'un Ange*:

> Tell us on what day, of all our days, were our roots born,
> Rocks that provide both shelter and food
> From our floating dome-peaked mountains,
> that lived through innumerable
> suns extinguished by the firmament.
> Stars of the night, scattered by God,
> Speak, when is the right moment?

'Oh, Dom ... please shut up.' Chris was not yet in a receptive mood and my translation was almost certainly not doing the original French any justice ...

The modern-day Lebanese had honoured the special nature of this spot with some extreme fly tipping, something that rather soured the moment.

The Lebanese might live in one of the most beautiful countries on earth, but the majority have not yet learned to appreciate it. Rubbish is everywhere and is a distinct problem. In 2015 there had been mass demonstrations in the capital organised by a group called *You Stink!* after rubbish started piling up in the streets when the waste collections stopped after the main refuse site was declared full. The ever-increasing mountains of rotting rubbish became a potent symbol for the corruption and dysfunction of the Lebanese state. We tried to ignore this affront to our sensitive literary senses and started uphill again.

'Just five minutes more,' said Jacky, striding out ahead of us.

This was not to be the last time that we would come across the Lebanese 'five minutes'. There appeared to have been some sort of terrible mix-up in the dictionary as these five minutes could often become an hour, as long as it was reiterated every ten minutes. There was logic there somewhere, but we were unable to crack it.

Up above us, in the middle of a small cedar forest, flew an enormous Lebanese flag, two red stripes with a cedar tree on a white background in the middle. I tried to check what the design of the flag stood for. The red stripes were thought to represent Mount Lebanon and the Anti-Lebanon mountain ranges, with the white being the Beqaa and the cedar being ... the cedar. This sounded pretty tenuous to me, the sort of thing somebody comes up with after the event to give what was admittedly a pretty cool flag a touch more depth.

As an amateur vexillologist, I was rather into flags, and I tried to teach my kids as many of them as possible when they were growing up, along with the capitals of the world.

Fave capital? Got to be Tegucigalpa, capital of Honduras.

Fave flag? I rather love the Nepalese one as it is the world's only non-quadrilateral flag.

I admire the fact that the Nepalese thought, *Why should we have a flag that is rectangular? Let's go crazy, sod everybody else.*

We entered the forest and climbed another steep, rocky path until we came to the Lebanese flag, the first to be flown after independence in 1943. Dotted around the forest was an assortment of abandoned artillery that pleased Harry no end. We took a much-needed break as he placed himself in the gunnery position on every cannon and mimed firing off a salvo of shells down onto the coast. Jacky stared at him in disbelief. I felt sure that she would tell her small children off for this sort of behaviour but here was a fifty-year-old man in full flow and she didn't really know what to do but giggle nervously and hope that he would stop soon.

After another twenty or so 'five-minute' periods, we arrived at our destination, Soha Village. This was a charming little mountain hotel with tiny cottages dotted around the main compound. The place was set up for Beirutis who wanted to get away from the hot, humid coast and relax in the mountain air. The occasional hikers such as ourselves popping in for the night would not be something on which to base a business plan but we were very chuffed at staying somewhere almost posh.

We were tired, hot and sweaty and longing for a shower but, obviously, our bags were in Caroll's van back where we'd started and so he had to try to get a lift there to bring them back. He'd phoned a local taxi driver who was clearly quoting too much for the trip as Caroll got quite heated. I understood most of the conversation and particularly enjoyed Caroll telling the guy that he expected a Rolls-Royce for that price. Eventually a price was agreed, and the guy turned up twenty or so minutes later in the usual beaten-up old Mercedes that constituted most taxis in Lebanon.

We had no choice but to wait for Caroll's return before we could wash, so we chatted with the owner, Tarik, and admired the stunning view from the terrace. He and his wife had lived in California for fifteen years before returning to set up this idyll. As we chatted over cold beers and even colder strips of carrot dipped in lemon juice, Tarik told me that his kids went to Brummana High School, my old school. I hesitated as to whether to bring up my favourite fact about the place: that I had spent a year there in 1975 at the same time as Osama bin Laden. Brummana was a sleepy Maronite mountain town not far from the family house. I was sent there after a stint at the Lycée Français in Beirut, before I was despatched to boarding school in England.

Obviously, I didn't remember bin Laden. For a start he was sixteen and I was six and, from a photograph taken of the bin Laden family around that time, he resembled an extra from *The Partridge Family* as opposed to the global bogeyman he later became. When I told this story in my book *The Dark Tourist*, the school denied that he had been a pupil there, despite my having uncovered the fact from a member of staff. I supposed that I could understand their reticence. Brummana High School was a Quaker school, established in 1873. The Quaker philosophy is renowned for strong pacifist views and having produced a pupil such as bin Laden might not be the best advertisement for a school.

'You might know some of our more illustrious former pupils ... Osama bin Laden, Dom Joly? Don't go, please, we haven't finished the tour of the school yet.'

I decided to keep my Old Boy news to myself. I normally did the joke about looking him up on Friends Reunited but I let it go.

Jacky told us that her family ran a vineyard. She just got better and better. Her father-in-law was a master winemaker and they had quite the business set up in her home village of Mtein, for where we were bound tomorrow. Things were definitely looking up and, after a couple of beers, we forgot all about our aching limbs and smelly clothes. This was fortunate because, half an hour later, a sheepish Caroll returned in the taxi. He had forgotten to take his van keys with him. He retrieved them and set off again as we settled down to watch the sunset and desperately try to keep downwind of our hosts.

# DAY 7

# SOHA VILLAGE TO MTEIN

I awoke to a vicious attack. One of the guesthouse's dogs had snuck into my room, having rather cleverly opened the door, and was now on my bed demanding attention by rolling around on me and licking my face furiously. He was utterly gorgeous, and I missed my own dogs, Truman and Fitzgerald, who must have wondered where I'd disappeared to. Soon they would doubtless have a conflab and decide that Stacey had finally kicked me out. They would be confused as to what to do, and would go and speak to the pigs, Stanley and Sir Francis Bacon, who always knew what to do.

'Morning pigs,' said Fitz.

'Morning dogs,' said Stanley, who was a nice pig.

'What do you want, mutts?' said Sir Francis, who was a slightly less nice pig.

'Have you noticed that Dom has gone?' asked Truman.

'Of course we've noticed. What do you think we are, dogs?' Sir Francis said sharply.

'No need to be rude, we just wondered if you knew where he'd gone,' said Fitz.

'I'm afraid we can't tell you that, privileged information and all that . . .' said Sir Francis.

'Francis—' Stanley was cut off.

'He is off on a trip looking at other dogs. Apparently, you two are not quite cutting the mustard.' Sir Francis smiled a thin, cruel smile.

'What? No, he can't be,' Truman whimpered.

'Are you telling the truth, pig?' asked Fitz.

'I'm afraid so. I think it's the great kennel in the sky for you two. I hear they're after a pair of spaniels.' Sir Francis grinned.

'Oh dear . . .' whimpered Truman.

'Bugger,' said Fitz.

'It looks like it's going be a nice sunny day,' said Stanley, trying to change the topic. Stanley was a nice pig.


I vowed to try to talk to my dogs on Skype. My new canine companion and I walked down to breakfast. I felt guilty, like I was having breakfast with a mistress. Harry and Chris were already there. We went through our usual routine of moaning about our tired, aching limbs and asked our usual question.

'How much uphill is there today?'

Jacky laughed.

'It's OK, it's a big day but just some uphill.'

We immediately knew that we were in for a terrible day. We did not like uphill. In fact, even Caroll had started calling us the Downhill Hiking Club as we got so excited whenever the terrain pointed downwards. Caroll claimed that going downhill was much worse and far more damaging to the knees. I accepted his point about steep descents and knee strain, but I was never going to be happier going uphill than down. Jacky confirmed that the best approach was not to attack hills too hard, and instead use little steps in a slowing-down-your-pace technique.

'Slowly, slowly catches monkey,' she said.

I had no interest in catching any monkey. I just wanted to constantly walk downhill, become the hiking equivalent of those people who are helicoptered up to the top of mountains and then ski down. What would be the problem in that? Jacky and Caroll smiled benignly at me as though dealing with a simple child.

Speaking of simple children, Harry was still having problems coming to terms with a Lebanese breakfast. The table groaned with bowls of loveliness. It was all too much for Harry. Caroll offered him some cheese and he exploded.

'Cheese, Caroll, is for the evening. There is a natural order to things that must not be disturbed, and this meal is all wrong.' Caroll looked confused as Harry poured himself a generous bowl of Choco Pops and then looked around vainly for milk.

'Caroll, is there any milk in this entire country?' Harry looked as though he was in pain.

Caroll disappeared into the kitchen and returned with a small jug of hot milk. Harry put his head in his hands. Abroad was not for him. It was a frightening place. Meanwhile, I was in clover as a basket of fresh manakish was brought to the table. This is a Levantine breakfast special, a kind of thin pizza dough with za'atar and olive oil on top and baked in the oven. Za'atar is the ground zero for Lebanese cuisine. It consists of dried hyssop leaves mixed with sesame seeds, dried sumac, salt and other spices. The recipe varies across the Middle East, but the Lebanese version is by far the best, although I might be a touch preju-diced in the matter as I grew up on the stuff. The smell was orgasmic and everything about the experience, from the oil soaking into the paper it was wrapped in, to the first bite, to the deciding whether to eat it folded over or stretch the experience out by having it flat, delineated my childhood happiness.

At school, at morning break, a boy would roll his manakish cart into the playground, laden with things, but I would never be given money when I went to school. Every day I'd have to deal with the heavenly smell and the sight of my schoolmates buying and consuming their manakish. One day I snapped. In the general scrum of hands and bodies grabbing manakish and proffering money I slipped my hand in and grabbed one. I'd started to walk away when I heard a shout and then felt a hand on my shoulder. I was caught. I was mortified and ashamed. I was handed over to a teacher, who gave me an unbelievable bollocking, but for some reason never told my parents. The humiliation and the shame of the whole thing still washes over me with a shudder.

As usual, I fought between filling up with energy for the walk ahead and not stuffing myself too much so that the walk would be too much effort. After breakfast, we raided the breakfast table to fill our plastic lunchboxes. When we'd started the trip, we'd packed our boxes full of stuff. As the days passed, however, Chris and I noticed that we were putting less and less stuff into our boxes: we were getting used to a light lunch on the road but Harry was now on about nine boiled eggs a day.

Chris tried to get more information out of Jacky.

'Jacky, when you say a big day, what do you mean exactly? Are we talking length of walk or steepness of trail?' Chris was in slightly terse CEO mode.

'It is long walk today. Much walk uphill and also much walk downhill . . . then uphill again.' Jacky smiled sweetly.

'So, is this a very difficult day?' Chris persisted.

'No, I have done many times.' Jacky hoisted her pack onto her back.

'Sorry to keep asking this, Jacky, but as a percentage, where do we stand with uphill versus downhill?' Chris was now getting testy.

'One hundred per cent fun. Now we go there.' Jacky set off straight uphill, pointing towards a distant peak.

Chris groaned and fumed inwardly. It was funny to watch but I felt exactly the same way. Our guides appeared to have been trained to say whatever was necessary to get you over the next hill. This might work with some people but both Chris and I are the type that need to know everything, good or bad. We found it hard to deal with the 'just five minutes' policy but couldn't get this across. Harry didn't seem to care and just plodded on regardless. We hated Harry.

We climbed for an hour or so until we reached our destination, a small gap in the mountain top that allowed us to have a look at the next valley. Below us were about ten perfectly round irrigation pools, all with a subtly different colour of water and home to what sounded like a million frogs. The valley itself was stunning and we soaked it all in until Jacky pointed out a red-roofed village on a little promontory on the far distant side of the valley.

'That is my village, Mtein,' she proclaimed proudly.

'In how many days will we get there?' asked Chris.

'Tonight, we get there tonight.'

'Tonight! That's about four days' walk!' Chris was starting to lose it and Jacky didn't seem to realise. A combination of terrible clothing choices – Chris was drenched in sweat – and a touch of black dog had temporarily broken him. But we were a team and, as team leader, I remembered the wise words that Bear Grylls had once given me before he threw me off a boat, two hours from the Pacific coast of Panama, to spend two miserable weeks surviving on a desert island with a bunch of people who even I hadn't ever seen on telly.

'Be nice ... it's the most important thing in survival,' said Bear, as he contemplated what he might have for breakfast once he'd dropped us off.

'For God's sake, Chris, let's just crack on and stop grumbling.' It made me feel better to tell him off as I could pretend that I didn't feel exactly the same way myself.

Harry sparked up another roll-up and looked at us both with quiet amusement. Chris's glasses had misted up with condensation, so I couldn't quite make out the expression on his face, but I could take an educated guess.

We started down the mountain, weaving our way through the pools. The sun was beating down on us and I longed to dive into the water, but the slopes were sheer and slippery, and I didn't want to end my life as frog food. We stopped at a pile of stones that turned out to be a spring and drank long and deep from the ice-cold water. Chris splashed the water on his face and it appeared to revive him somewhat. We marched on with new determination, mainly because, for now, it was downhill.

We descended into the treeline and started to make our way through a large pine forest. These were the magnificent umbrella pines, the type that produce the snobar (the pine nut so loved by foodies around the world).

Reaping the pine nut was very intensive. I remembered the guy who used to come and do our pine trees at home. He was an old man with big baggy black trousers that seemed very impractical for the job ahead. He would carry a long stick with a metal hook on the end. He would shimmy up the trees and use the hook to dislodge the pinecones. Once he had cleared the trees of cones, a massive job, he would gather them all and lay them out in the sun on top of the gatehouse to dry and open so that the valuable pine nuts could be extracted.

For a kid, the pinecone made a perfect mock grenade. I would sneak up to the gatehouse, stuff firecrackers into the openings of some pinecones, light the fuses and hurl them at arriving cars. This didn't go down very well in Lebanon. Firstly, the pine nuts were an expensive crop and people objected to them being blown to smithereens. Secondly, Lebanon was very much not the place to pretend to be throwing grenades at people, as I learned when one gentleman got out of his car carrying a handgun and let off a couple of shots in my direction as I scrambled for both cover and a cover story should he manage to somehow get into the property. Thankfully, he got back into his car, turned around and drove back and away from the house.

I am now more versed in grenade etiquette, having recently attended a HEAT (Hostile Environment Awareness Training) course as part of my role as an ambassador for Save the Children. The course took place in a large Scout camp on the outskirts of Kettering. For grenade training, we all had to stand in a circle around a man who lit a massive bird bomb, a glorified fire-cracker. The moment the fuse was lit we all had to turn, take one step and hurl ourselves to the ground while shouting 'GRENADE'.

There was a good reason for shouting as it emptied your lungs and made them less liable to damage from the percussion, but I couldn't help wondering what the workers at the massive Argos warehouse that neighboured the Scout camp thought when hearing a group of Scouts constantly shouting 'GRENADE' followed by mystery explosions.

'Blimey, Scouts have changed since my day, Brian ...'

The sun was now high in the sky and beating down with intense heat, so we were thankful for the shade of the forest.

Jacky, however, started asking questions. 'Dom, what do you do for a job?'

'I'm a writer, but my main job is as a comedian.'

'A comedian? So, you are supposed to be funny?' She looked at me with an expression that indicated that this had not been the case so far.

'I'm not a stand-up comedian. I don't tell jokes.'

'So, you are a not funny comedian?' Jacky smiled.

'Many would agree with you there,' interjected Chris, who had perked up somewhat.

'He's incredibly unfunny,' agreed Harry.

'I do a different sort of comedy ...' I continued, ignoring them.

'Like what?' said Jacky.

'It's difficult to explain. Take here for an example. I would love to get a squirrel costume and an over-sized nargileh, and set myself up in a little spot next to the path and wait for a hiker to come by.' I loathed explaining my comedy as it always sounded so odd.

'You'd be shot immediately.' Jacky laughed.

'Again, they'd not be the first to want to do that,' said Harry.

'So, you make children's television?' continued Jacky.

Chris and Harry fell about laughing. I fell silent and marched on through the pines bemoaning the lack of respect my particular brand of comedy garnered from ignoramuses.

For the first time, I could feel blisters forming on my feet. Between us we had brought enough plasters to seal the Hoover Dam, but we had not had any problems so far. I stopped and removed my boots to put some preventative strips over the sore areas. Things were tricky enough without open sores developing on my tootsies.

We kept seeing single shoes lying by the side of the path.

'Must be more landmines,' said Harry.

Chris looked nervously at Jacky's face to see if he was close to the truth. There were so many single shoes that I thought of a genius business plan.

'We should open a shoe shop for amputees. This is the perfect country to start it up in. A place specialising in single shoes.' Nobody thought this was a good idea, so I left it there.

I did start to think about landmines a lot, however. I remembered my friend Georges warning me about how they littered the mountains. If I did step on a landmine, then it would be incredibly annoying. It would actually be doubly annoying because, two years later after much rehabilitation, I'd have to do the whole walk again on an artificial leg to raise money for victims of landmines. Then, what if, on that walk I stumbled onto another one and lost a second leg? I'd probably have to embark on a third walk on crutches ... I decided that it would not be a good idea to step on a landmine.

Two hours into the walk, Jacky seemed to go a little off-piste. This was her official section of the LMT and Jacky had personally blazed the trail replete with two cans of paint, but we now had a problem. Somebody had suddenly built a new tarmac road over the old trail. Jacky decided that we should try to find a new way through a thick oak forest that clung to a vertiginous slope. Chris was not amused.

'So, this will be the first time you've tried to go this way?' he said.

'Yes,' replied Jacky.

'And what happens if we don't find a way through?' Chris's voice was rising slightly.

'Then we walk back up and try another way.'

Chris remained silent, but a small black cloud appeared above his head.

We started to walk down through the forest. At first, there was a semblance of a path and spirits were high. We came across a little glade that seemed to have an unnaturally vocal set of songbirds. We stopped to listen. It was rather lovely until the avian chorus was interrupted by a shotgun blast from very close by. We rounded a corner and there was a man sitting on a rock reloading his shotgun. Next to him was a small amplifier that was blasting out songbird tunes to attract the poor creatures. Caroll was livid.

'You are not allowed to hunt here. What you are doing is illegal,' said Caroll angrily.

'Go fuck yourself.' The hunter snapped his shotgun shut.

'There are laws against this for a reason,' continued Caroll as we all edged away from the confrontation lest it go live.

'Your laws mean nothing here, this is my area. Go fuck yourself, you bald bastard.' The man turned up the birdsong.

Caroll thought about it for a moment and then moved on muttering to himself. You did not argue with armed men in Lebanon.

Ten minutes later the path disappeared and there was just a steep slope of loose scree. Jacky started scrambling down and we followed tentatively while a herd of goats and an enormous dog looked at us as though we were insane.

'Would you look at these idiots,' said Goat One.

'I wager one hundred infidel dollars that the loud-mouthed one breaks a leg,' said Goat Two.

'Bloody tourists ...'

'The country's gone to the dogs.'

'What's wrong with dogs?' asked Dog.

'Shut up, dog,' said Goat One.

'Nobody likes you,' said Goat Two.

'How dare you speak to a dog like that, my people have been on this mountain a lot longer than you goats.' Dog was furious.

'We goats were made by God for this mountain, that's why we are able to hop from rock to rock with the grace that you can only dream of, dog.' Goat Two was off on one.

'Goats are stupid,' said Dog.

'Brothers, did you hear what this hairy man-friend just said? Are we to let him speak to us in this manner?' Goat One was now on a rock speaking to the rest of the herd.

Above us we heard the dog yelping and many goats bleating in unison as we desperately tried to keep our footing on the descent. Occasionally we could grab on to a little tree or branch, but most were spiky and impossible to use. The brush was so thick that it was very difficult to take a particular direction even if we knew it to be the right one. Finally, we came to a break in the brush along a ridge. We followed it along for about 600 metres and were soon out of the undergrowth and into a pine forest with a soft path of pine needles along which to pad. Jacky was delighted that she had found a new way and said that she would return soon to paint the new trail markings.

We had lunch under an ancient oak tree littered with large rocks once hewn by Romans for a nearby spring. Locals had dragged the rocks under the tree to use as seats for picnics such as ours.

We discussed retirement plans. Harry and Chris appeared to be well set up. I had no plans and got a bit depressed. I'd never been good with money. When I had some, I spent it and then constantly panicked when I started to run out. It was one of the good and bad things about the entertainment industry – the uncertainty. One day I could be about to sell the house and then I'd get a phone call with some offer of work that would sort us out for six months. It was both thrilling and draining, and I really needed to try to work out how to get some financial stability. Actually, I didn't need to work anything out. I just needed to spend less and save more but I lived my life on a you-might-be-run-over-by-a-bus-tomorrow philosophy. *Alea iacta est*, etc. The problem was that when things got tight I'd be more likely to throw myself in front of a bus as I worried about things so much.

That was why this expedition was so wonderful, why I loved travelling so much. Once you were under way, everything could be put in limbo. All you worried about was the road ahead. Life, when walking, was reduced to its simplest form.

How long you had to walk until you reached your destination, ate and fell asleep. That was my life for these three weeks and it was heaven.

After an hour or so we carried on. We still had a long way to go and even Jacky was not hiding the fact. We were now at the top of a ridiculously steep valley, on the other side of which we could see our goal, Mtein.

'And there is definitely no zip-line of any type that could whisk us to your village and a couple of cold beers in three minutes?' enquired Chris.

'It's just that we wish to spend as much time as possible in what everybody says is the most beautiful village in the Orient.' I said.

'I think you are joking with me.' Jacky smiled.

'Possibly about the village, but definitely not about the zip-line ... or the beers,' muttered Chris.

We were tired today and the level of joking between us was set firmly at low. We all retreated into our personal headspaces as we tried to zone out the effort and move on autopilot. I put on some headphones and selected *Skeleton Tree* by Nick Cave: a magnificent album recorded by Cave while trying to deal with the tragic death of one of his twin boys. It was perhaps not the wisest choice with which to drive myself on ...

'*Oh, the urge to kill somebody was basically overwhelming, I had such hard blues down there in the supermarket queues ...*' Cave hammered at the piano as I tried to keep my shattered left knee from crumbling on the almost vertical descent.

This was the first time that the Downhill Hiking Club realised just how bad a proper descent could be. It was almost impossible to stop; you just had to ride the momentum, using your poles to try to alleviate the pressure on the knees while constantly scanning the ground for potential footholds and trip hazards.

By the time we reached the very bottom of the valley we were spent. The sun burned the valley floor mercilessly and only a tiny trickle of what was occasionally a proper river ran past us. We crossed an old stone bridge and began the ascent to Mtein. I had nothing left in the tank and started to lag behind the others.

'*You're a young man waking, covered in blood that is not yours . . .*' Cave was not letting up and certainly not helping much.

I hit the machine to change the tempo. I went for an old favourite: the Australian band, Icehouse. I chose 'Uniform', a pumping pop classic that got my tired legs moving slightly better.

'*Everybody wears the badge, Uniform, uniform . . .*' OK, so Icehouse weren't Nick Cave level when it came to lyrics, but the beat was working.

There was much complaint from the group about me singing aloud. It was clearly not as beautiful as I imagined it to be from within the buffer zone of my headphones.

Our water had now run out. The CamelBaks we carried within a sleeve in our rucksacks were sucked dry and our throats were parched and dry as sawdust. We all concentrated on the pair of feet in front of us, took one step after another and prayed that there had been some terrible mistake in the ETA.

After another two gruelling hours, we finally reached the outskirts of Mtein. We stopped for a rest by the ruins of a Roman grape press. It never failed to astonish us how this country was littered with historical remains that were just part of the rural furniture. The thrill of sitting on rocks that Romans had used to stamp on mounds of grapes destined for Bacchanalian celebrations was strangely restorative, as was the feeling that we were now just half an hour from Jacky's own vineyard. The thought of a comfortable chair, free wine and the removal of walking boots was too much, and I felt the first sting of tears in my tired eyes.

Jacky had one last surprise: the 300-step staircase that finally brought us up into the village. It nearly broke us. There was much wailing and gnashing of teeth, and our newly acquired wisdom of slowly, slowly was hurled aside as we just wanted to get to the top.

We made it. We passed by the ruins of an old water mill and a beautiful old silk factory. These were reminders of the days when sericulture was the backbone of the Mount Lebanon economy. There were originally seven silk factories in Mtein. Raw silk was processed in looms and much-in-demand Lebanese silk products were shipped off to European markets. But there was a darker element to these ruins as well. They had fallen dormant during the First World War when the Allies had blocked international trade routes to prevent Ottoman forces getting supplies. The Ottomans then introduced their own blockade on vital foodstuffs coming in from Syria. Finally, an almost biblical swarm of locusts laid waste to Mount Lebanon in 1915 and the combination of these factors caused a terrible famine in which 200,000 of the estimated 400,000-strong population of Mount Lebanon died. There were bodies piled high in the streets, with people eating cats and dogs and even resorting to cannibalism. The silk economy never recovered. These beautiful ruins were the epitaph of yet another foreign-inspired Lebanese tragedy.

We entered the magnificent town square of Mtein, a step back in time to what Lebanese villages would have looked like three hundred years before. The square consists of five palaces built by the Al Lamaayiin emirs in the sixteenth century. It also contains one of my favourite restaurants in Lebanon, Khairallah. This also happened to be Jacky's surname, although she said it was no relation.

We were staying in one of the palaces off the square, accessed through a splendidly grand gatehouse that led us into a court-yard where we sat and took our boots off. Jacky said that she would come and pick us up later to take us to her vineyard, so we bravely trekked the hundred or so metres to the Khairallah restaurant for some restorative beers.

It was about six-thirty in the evening and the restaurant was empty save for a table of six people who appeared to have been lunching for six or seven hours; the table was invisible beneath food. What Harry would call a big unit was gulping greedily on a nargileh in between massive mouthfuls.

We sat on the edge of the terrace and ordered beer and arak. I love arak. We stared out at the view: far, far on the other side of the valley was the gap in the mountain that we had walked through that morning. It all seemed like such a long time ago. My life of walking, drinking, sleeping, walking, drinking, sleep-ing was the norm now. I could barely remember anything else. My life had shrunk.

We were picked up an hour or so later by Jacky, who had spruced herself up and looked very different from her moun-tain-guide persona. The winery was quite the place – a bottling plant, massive cellars and a beautiful garden with views that equalled the restaurant. Jacky's husband Christian was there to greet us. It was his father who started the business and had been a master blender for many years. We sat round a table in the cellar as we sampled the reds, whites and house arak. The wine was good, the arak superb. They had a slight branding issue with many differing names and logos for their 'château'. Chris immediately offered his services as an advertising guru. He promised to put his design team to work on coming up with a clear, unified logo for them. They appeared delighted and much more wine was drunk. I hoped that Chris would remember his promises in the cold light of morning.

Eventually we staggered back to our palace through the empty streets of Mtein. Our hosts had a comforting meal await-ing us: broad bean stew with rice, homemade fries, a tomato salad and endless hummus. Harry was too drunk to complain.

# DAY 8

# BEIRUT

I awoke in my vaulted basement to hear Chris singing 'La Vie en Rose' while polishing his brogues. I immediately knew that something was afoot. Chris was never cheerful in the morning. He was normally on the phone to Dubai mixing business-stress with concerns about the walk ahead. Today, he seemed not to have a care in the world, and he was back in his non-walking foppish attire. I asked him why he was so happy.

'Harry's knee has swollen up. It looks like we won't be able to walk today.' This was said without a modicum of concern for Harry.

I was totally with him; we whooped, hollered and high-fived each other, before putting on serious faces and going to see how Harry was. He was sitting under the arches with his foot up on a chair and feeling very sorry for himself. Caroll tried twice to check the knee only for Harry to grimace and scream in agony. He was definitely injured. There was only one thing for it . . . a day off and a day trip to Beirut.

The Eritrean cook offered Chris some coffee. He declined and, much to her consternation, produced his portable Nespresso machine. She peered at him suspiciously from the kitchen as he stood pumping away at the machine. Eventually two decent espressos were produced but, to be honest, it all seemed like too much work, especially when the cook plonked a fresh batch of Lebanese coffee on the table. The smell of cardamom wafted across us and the cook looked at Chris in a manner intended to convey her disdain for his coffee-making cheating.

After breakfast we left our palace, piled into Caroll's van and headed off towards Beirut. It was a treat to be tourists again rather than the rugged mountain men we had become during our endless six days of walking. A new 'Metn Highway' had been built since I'd last been in the country and this meant that, rather than weave your way through endless villages down to the coast, you could now roar down to Beirut from your mountain home in no time. Unfortunately, whoever had built this highway appeared to have little previous experience in road building, as they had got the camber of the road reversed so that speeding motorists (basically, all Lebanese motorists) were coming off at corners in their droves. At the bottom of the highway, as we approached Beirut, I spotted that rarest of things in Lebanon – a speed camera. It was pointless, however, as the reverse camber dealt with speeding motorists in a far more efficient manner.

Caroll fought his way through the Beirut traffic and we parked up in what used to be the hub of Beirut, Martyrs' Square. Once a beautiful French-style square with gardens in the middle and surrounded by cinemas and restaurants, it was completely destroyed in the civil war of 1975–6 when it became the Green Line, the demarcation line between Christian East Beirut and the Muslim West. Now, it was a bit of an urban mess. A couple of original buildings remained on one side but most of the area had been cleared and it was a massive car park.

In the centre was the last statue to be placed in the square before the war started. It was by an Italian sculptor, Marino Mazzacurati, in 1960 and commemorated the hanging of a group of Lebanese patriots (of all faiths) who had spoken out against Turkish rule in 1916. The statue was pockmarked with bullet holes and shrapnel wounds and had been kept as a reminder of the bloody civil war that I'd watched rage around us from the terrace of the family house above Beirut.

As we wandered up to the statue, we were brushed aside by a procession of women holding large photographs of, I presumed, the people hanged by the Turks. Others carried the Lebanese flag; they were accompanied by a man who had that international look of a politician on a photo opportunity. They trooped up to the statue, posed for some press photos with the politician, sang the Lebanese national anthem for the television cameras, and then they were gone. The women left, and the politician got into a smart tinted Mercedes and sped off. It was all a bit peculiar and was over before it started.

We started to walk around the newly rebuilt centre of the capital. It was all tastefully done but it felt like a new Cotswolds house; it needed a couple of hundred years to wear in. We walked past a memorial to Samir Kassir, a journalist for the *Al-Nahar* newspaper who had been killed by a car bomb in 2005. Nobody knew who did it but Kassir was famous for his anti-Syrian articles. There had been a period when the Syrians had targeted Lebanese MPs with car bombs. An acquaintance told me that they would hear the explosion and wait to be told which MP had been eliminated that day.

We passed under the shadow of the ruined Holiday Inn. It had just opened when the civil war started and was bitterly fought over as a good sniper position, the victors hurling the vanquished off the roof. Just past it, on the shoreline, was the St Georges Hotel, a place where the great and the good used to hang out and water-ski. It was also where Rafik Hariri, the former Prime Minister of Lebanon and the man behind the reconstruction of the city, was assassinated by a staggeringly large bomb (more than a thousand kilos of TNT) as his motorcade passed by the hotel on 14 February 2005.

I remembered being on the terrace at home on 14 September 1982 when I saw the mushroom cloud following a similar explosion down in Achrafieh. It was the newly elected President, Bashir Gemayel, being assassinated. He was the son of the Maronite godfather, Pierre Gemayel, and his election, backed by the Israelis, was a serious power-play quickly quashed by his assassination, which was widely blamed on the Syrians. His brother Amine was elected President a month later but the anger at the assassination led to the massacres of Palestinians in the camps of Sabra and Chatila. Every explosion had a thousand echoes in Lebanon.

I thought of Sarajevo as we walked. It was the only city that I'd visited that was even remotely similar to Beirut. It was also a place where Christians and Muslims had lived together, until centuries of resentments and ancient wrongs rose to the surface. Sarajevo's equivalent to Beirut's car bombs were the craters caused by mortars lobbed into the city by the besieging Serb forces. Locals had painted red petals around the craters, turning them into Sarajevo roses. I felt curiously at home in Sarajevo. I'd gone there to visit the site of the assassination of Archduke Franz Ferdinand, the shot that was heard around the world, the spark that set off the First World War. I hadn't realised just how badly the attempt had gone wrong and how it so nearly never happened.

Franz Ferdinand, the louche heir to the Austro-Hungarian Empire that occupied Bosnia, was on his last day in Sarajevo, on an official visit with his wife. There were six assassins waiting to have a go at him as he drove down the Appel Quay that ran along the River Miljacka. The first one chickened out, the second hurled a bomb at the car. It bounced off and exploded underneath it, allowing the Archduke and his wife to keep going. They took refuge in the town hall until their security decided that they should head to the railway station and get out of town. All the other assassins had been put off, except for one – Gavrilo Princip. He knew that the Archduke was supposed to do a tour of the Old Town and waited on the corner of the street where the car was due to turn off the Appel Quay. The Archduke's security had wisely decided against the Old Town visit, but nobody had told the driver. So, he turned off the quay and then, having been shouted at by the security guy, stopped to reverse back right next to an astonished Gavrilo Princip, who could not believe his luck. He shot both the Archduke and his wife dead.

What did I learn from my Sarajevo trip? Possibly my favourite *Dark Tourist* fact ever. The number plate on the car that the Archduke was riding in (which is now in a museum in Vienna) was 11-11-18. The last day of the war that the assassination started. Spooky, huh?

Back in Beirut, we wandered through what used to be the old souks but was now a fairly generic but pleasant outdoor mall. Posh Beirutis passed us hauling large bags of designer detritus. A young woman attempted to take her cat for a walk on a lead but, as is the way with cats, it was the cat deciding where to go and her following rather awkwardly. It reminded me of Jack Dee's comments on the matter: 'A dog will just follow you everywhere around the house, whatever you're doing it will look at you adoringly and say I looooovve youuu. Whereas a cat will just watch you out of the corner of its eye and if you try something like putting up a shelf, will say scornfully, you don't do it like that, you idiot.'

We visited a church near the centre where icons of Jesus on the wall were riddled with bullet holes. Stepping out of the church, we were immediately in the shadow of a mosque. Religions stood shoulder to shoulder here. I tried to find the little Anglican church in which I was christened and where we buried my father. It used to be on the point of the bay opposite the St Georges Hotel, but the developers of new Beirut had shoved all the ruins of old Beirut into the sea and created a whole new land mass, so the church was now inland, which was most confusing. I used to loathe having to go to this church on Christmas Day and Easter Sunday when I was a kid. I would have massive fights in a futile attempt to resist wearing a tie. Every family photo from those days showed a grumpy little me, with arms crossed, looking very sulky about the tie situation. I knew very early that suits and ties were never going to be for me. My father, however, although not really religious, felt a strong responsibility for the church; he even removed all the stained-glass windows during the civil war and kept them safe in a well-protected bunker in the garden of the family home.

We met my sister and her husband for lunch in an Armenian restaurant called Loris. It was located in Gemmayze, an area around which Beirut's nightlife scene revolves. Everyone in the restaurant smoked like chimneys while tucking into heavily spiced sausages and aromatic yoghurt dishes that ruled out any chance of intimate contact for the next couple of days.

My Arabic had improved slightly in the last week and I wanted to get some new vocab off my sister, who had read Arabic at St Andrews and really knew her stuff. She gave me some crackers. My favourite was *zoubab*, which meant a huge, deaf rat. Quite how anybody would know that a rat was deaf was not the point. I just loved the fact that there was a specific word for the occasion. She gave me some others to try out.

*sana'a*: to insert a finger into a chicken to ascertain whether it's going to lay an egg.
*istaghraqa*; to pretend to be drowning.
*aqsara*: old Arab word for 'to run like a dwarf'.

I asked my sister if there was a word for 'unfit Europeans who only like to walk downhill'? There wasn't.

Caroll was incredibly keen for us to visit the National Museum. About ten minutes into lunch he realised that this was never going to happen. Beer, wine, arak flowed like it was going out of fashion and, before we knew it, evening was encroaching and Caroll was making frantic signs that we needed to go as we had a big drive ahead to get back up into the mountains. I also think that he was worried that we might not be in a fit state to walk the following day, but he was too polite to say so.

We said our goodbyes and headed out of Beirut. On the way, we drove past my first school, the Lycée Français. I had vivid memories of the place – chiefly, being sent out of classrooms to stand by the door waiting for the school sadist, Monsieur Gaston, to find you. He would walk the corridors and deal with any pupil sent out of his class by violently beating you on the hands with a metal ruler until you bled. I spotted the play-ground through the fence. Every time an Israeli jet would fly over, about a thousand little schoolkids would point their fingers at the sky in the shape of anti-aircraft guns and make 'akk akk akk' noises. Harry would have loved it.

The narrow road that passed by the school was heavily guarded, as next door to the school were the headquarters of the ISF, the Internal Security Forces. They looked like a nasty bunch, swaggering around in tight black T-shirts and combat trousers, stopping cars at gunpoint to let their own guys drive in and out. I wanted to get out and have a quick look round my old school but was forced back into the van at gunpoint and told to 'bugger off' in the Arabic equivalent. These weren't people you argued with and so bugger off we did.

Jacky had sensed our dislike of uphill walking and had suggested that we do the next leg of the LMT in reverse. She felt that we should do Baskinta back to Mtein as this would avoid a long and tortuous 5-kilometre climb out of Mtein. This also meant that we could have another big night at the Khairallah restaurant when we finished, so it was a double whammy. We loved Jacky.

We drove north out of Beirut along the coastal highway before turning up and heading into the mountains again, head-ing to our bed for the night – the convent of Mar Sassine in the village of Baskinta, about 70 kilometres from the capital. There

142

were many army checkpoints on the way as the following day was the general election and if anything sparked off trouble in this country, it was an election. As we drove through villages we encountered massive rallies from various factions making last-minute appeals for their candidates.

We reached cloud level and were suddenly enveloped by a thick white mist that made it almost impossible to see the road ahead. It didn't last long, however, as we burst out above the clouds into the evening sun and the majestic sight of Mount Sannine, one of the country's tallest mountains at 2,628 metres, bathed in the gorgeous red light of magic hour.

The convent of Mar Sassine, where we were staying, was built in 1729 and dominated the village. An enormous, gaudy metal cross, about 10 metres high, stood to the side of it, a present from a former inhabitant of Baskinta who had emigrated to Brazil. He had originally wanted it to be placed on the summit of Mount Sannine but this had turned out not to be possible, so he gave it to the convent instead. We were shown to our rooms by Sister Claire, who had been a nun there for thirty years. In the hall, a television was on and a group of about thirty people were lounging about watching it. They were election officials who were going to oversee the ballot the following day. They were in good spirits and beer, doughnuts and cigarettes appeared to be the order of the day.

We went down to a little dining room under thick stone arches where yet another table laden with food awaited us. Sister Claire fussed around us like a mother at her toddler's tea party. She produced some very fine homemade arak and an incredibly sweet homemade wine that was almost sherry.

After supper, Sister Claire guided us towards the convent shop. It was packed with jams and syrups and good things. I remembered that nothing quenched your thirst on a hot day more than a cold glass of toot – mulberry syrup, mixed with water and ice. I bought three bottles from the delighted nun. As I headed back to my room, I happened to pass Harry's room and the door was ajar. He was busy necking a bottle of red wine from the bottle. We each had our own methods of training for the walk ahead.

As I lay in my spartan room, with just a wooden cross on the wall for company, I was kept awake by two cats who sat right opposite each other on a low roof right below my window. They spent all night miaowing and hurling abuse at each other.

Cat One: You're a twat.

Cat Two: No, you're a twat.

Cat One: Forgive me, but you're a twat.

Cat Two: Rarely have I encountered as big a twat as yourself.

Cat One: I'm told that you are scared of mice.

Cat Two: Well, I'm told that you are a twat.

Cat One: Only a twat would say that.

Cat Two: Said a twat ...

This went on and on. As it was the election the following day, possibly the cats were just getting into the spirit of things, but I knew that my dogs would never behave in this fashion. They were better than that. How they would have loved to come on this walk with me. Sadly, they were too badly behaved. I once took them up to Hadrian's Wall as I was walking along it for a TV show. They behaved unbelievably badly. They chased sheep, peed on a man dressed as a Roman centurion, harassed ramblers and generally made a nuisance of themselves. They had a brilliant time, but I couldn't trust them in Lebanon.

# DAY 9

# BASKINTA TO MTEIN

I awoke to no singing from Chris. This could only mean one thing. Harry's knee was better, and we would be walking today. There was singing at breakfast as it was Caroll's birthday, but this soon turned to concern when there was no sign of Chris. Harry told us a story about a friend on a cycling holiday who was found dead in his room, and Caroll panicked and sprinted up to knock on Chris's door. He was alive but, I think, rather hoping we'd forget him and walk on. He eventually appeared at the front door of the convent looking a little more dishevelled than his usual, immaculate self. This was not going to be a good day for Chris.

Jacky arrived in a beaten-up old taxi from Mtein. She was in a great mood and spirits were high as we set off through the village. We passed traditional Lebanese houses, squat and square with red-tiled roofs and vine leaves growing up the walls. Presently we got to a school where the vote was being held. There was a long queue outside and a heavy military presence. Lebanese army soldiers lined the road and waved us through in a bemused fashion. I asked Jacky whether she wanted to vote. She stuck up her thumb and it was stained in a purple dye. She had already voted in her village before setting off. It was her only choice as you had to vote in your own village, which was why so many people were flying back from abroad to return home.

We soon left Baskinta and started down a steep descent into what Jacky told us was 'the valley of the skulls'. Once at the bottom we crossed a crystal-clear river and started to climb up the other side using our new, slow-but-steady technique. As we climbed, I asked Jacky about Druze reincarnation.

'Can you come back as anything?' I asked.

'Yes.'

'If you're bad, do you come back as a slug ... or Dom Joly?' asked Chris, who had perked up at a chance to slag me off.

'If you're really bad, of course, you come back as an advertising executive.' I grinned at Chris, who accepted defeat.

Jacky looked confused but was happy that we weren't grumbling for once.

'Jacky, why is it called the valley of the skulls?' Chris asked.

'I think because many people over the years have fallen off the paths and died at the bottom of the valley.' Jacky didn't appear to be joking.

Chris fell very silent.

We reached a little plateau and passed by the house of Sleiman Kettaneh, a famous Lebanese writer who had lived there in isolation until 2004. I could see why. It was an idyllic setting and perfect for the writer who wanted to be left alone to think in the serene ...

Clang, clang ... A cacophony of sound bounced off the valley walls. Harry had discovered the rope to a large bell that sat on top of a small chapel near the house. It made a hell of a noise, so we all decided to move on quickly as a large group of locals with pitchforks and shotguns were presumably on their way towards us as we spoke, prepared to repel invaders.

We left the nursery slopes and started the real climb. Chris immediately knew that he was in trouble. Jacky pointed to a long and vertiginous cliff face.

'We have to walk along this all the way until we can climb up and above,' Jacky said.

'Nobody told me it was going to be like this. I'm not happy.' Chris was not happy.

'Follow me. I will walk in front of you and you will be OK,' said Jacky.

'I'd be OK if somebody had told me it was going to be like this before we set off this morning.' Chris was not in a good way.

Eventually he agreed to follow in Jacky's footsteps. He kept his eyes firmly on the back of her boots and didn't look up once. He refused any attempt at conversation. He just wanted to get this part over with. We walked like this for about an hour. It was steep, and the path was narrow but, apart from the occasional rock coming loose and plummeting down to the valley floor far below, it was not too bad.

An hour later, things were ratcheted up a notch. We came over a little incline and were now directly beneath the massive cliff face. Halfway down was a thick water pipe that ran along the edge.

'No ...' said Chris, knowing what was coming.

'Yes,' replied Jacky.

'Jesus Christ!' Chris's face had gone white as a sheet.

Even we baulked a little at the 'path ahead'. Walking along a steel pipe would be considered fun most of the time but the name of the valley now started to make sense. Harry and I cracked on while Chris shuffled very slowly forward with the ever-attentive Jacky coaxing him on. About half an hour later, Harry and I waited at a spot where we could sit to see how Chris was getting on. He got to us about ten minutes later.

'How are things, Chris?' I said jovially.

'Can't talk,' he mumbled as he continued on, his eyes locked on to Jacky's feet.

'What on earth is that smell, Chris? Have you soiled yourself?' Harry dissolved into chuckles as Chris moved on, too focused to riposte. The problem with having been sent to a boarding school is that, however hard you tried, base, toilet humour was always the go-to option.

The scenery was the best yet. Across the valley, we could see Baskinta and the convent. It felt as though we could almost reach out and touch it. The peaks of the mountains behind were flecked with streaks of snow that had fallen the night before. Lebanon seemed to unravel itself like a beautiful onion, every layer being more beautiful than the last.

Eventually the pipe came to an end, and we were back on solid ground ... what little there was of it. We had to flatten ourselves against the cliff wall and shuffle along with a precipice falling away below us. I could swear that I could hear Chris weeping but kept this to myself lest Harry go for the jugular. Then Chris started talking.

'What the fuck am I doing here? Why am I doing this? Seriously, why am I doing this? This is not fun.' It was almost to himself rather than to us, so Harry and I bit our respective lips and inched on along the precipice.

After four hours of sheer unhappiness from Chris we reached solid, but not flat, ground. We started climbing again, which, compared to dropping fast onto hard rocks below, was a welcome relief for Chris. After ten minutes or so, we came across what looked like a small meteorite strike, a blackened area, about 6 metres across, where all the rock was molten and exceptionally heavy. It was totally unlike anything else around. We picked up bits of fused stone that looked like components of a shattered spacecraft. It was all very odd. We would have taken samples with us but nobody needed anything heavier in their pack and so we left the site for others to discover.

We summited and found two beautiful Roman sarcophagi. The Roman dead needed a good vista, a tomb with a view if you will. It was rather sweet to think that these dead Romans had enjoyed this view together for the last two thousand years. The Romans really had got it together and put later civilisations to shame. In a little valley below the sarcophagi lay a ruined Roman temple that was currently being overwhelmed by a large herd of hirsute goats. We sat under a walnut tree and ate our lunch. At least we tried. Within ten minutes we were invaded by the curious goats, who wanted to try everything we were eating and were not going to take no for an answer. Harry, who had fallen asleep in the grass, disappeared under a mound of goats who seemed particularly enamoured with him.

Eventually a goat dog appeared on the scene. He seemed very embarrassed that he had lost control of his herd.

Goat Dog: What on earth are you morons doing? I turn my
    back for one second and you're hassling tourists.
Goat 1: They're not tourists. You don't really get tourists
    here.

Goat 2: They're bloody hikers. Imagine choosing to do this sort of thing? I smell a midlife crisis.

Goat Dog: It doesn't matter what they're bloody doing, Ahmed. You're making me look bad. They'll think that I can't control you hairy bastards.

Goat 2: Well, to be fair, you can't. Remember when we blocked that motorway? Hardly our fault was it? No, a certain someone had decided that rolling around in a field of clover with some tramp like some lovesick puppy was the order of the day.

Goat Dog: You take that back. I will not have you talk about Farida like that.

All Goats: Oooohhhh! He's in love with Farida, he's in love with Farida . . .

We got up, made a path through the gloating goats and continued on towards Mtein.

As we walked we started to sing the Proclaimers song 'I'm Gonna Be (500 Miles)' to keep our spirits up. Jacky's spirits visibly dampened.

We could now see Mtein far below us and this gave us new energy. At least we were approaching downhill this time and didn't have the legendary steps of Mtein to finish us off. I wondered what had happened during the day. The voting would have now finished, and the counting begun. Who knew what lay ahead for Lebanon in another chapter of its turbulent history? When we finally entered the town, eight and a half hours after we had left Baskinta, the populace looked a little tense as they awaited the results to see which village they'd drawn to fight next.

We headed straight for the Khairallah restaurant and ordered beer and food in gargantuan portions. There was a big family celebration going on along a large table in the corner, but the rest of the place was empty. The people that had been there two days ago had obviously finally finished their meal sometime that afternoon as the remains were still visible. We sat on the edge of the terrace and tried to cheer up Chris, who appeared to be suffering from more PTSD.

After a couple of beers and several araks, a twenty-something Lebanese guy detached himself from the family table and came over to us. His name was Raf and he lived in London half the year round and was very surprised to see foreigners. He was tall and thin, wore a leather jacket and had a touch of madness in his deep brown eyes. Raf plonked a portable speaker down on the table and demanded that we choose the music. He reminded me of Richard E. Grant in the tearoom scene in *Withnail and I*: '*we'll buy this place and we'll install a fucking jukebox in here and liven all you stiffs up a bit ...*'

Glancing over to the family table you could already sense that Raf was a little bit of a disappointment to the family. I felt that this scene had been played out before and that it was never pretty. The grandmother looked over nervously while the rest of their table tried to ignore the whole situation by engaging in heightened, slightly false conversation.

'Play your music,' demanded Raf.

So, I chose the Boxer Rebellion's new album *Ghost Alive* again and whacked it on. Raf stopped in his tracks when he heard the delicate refrain of 'Here I Am'. His eyes locked into a thousand-yard stare and he was suddenly no longer with us. He was back in the thick of whatever recent tragedy had befallen him, and we all sat quietly as he swayed from side to side to the music.

'This is very sad music.' He looked me in the eyes. 'You must be very sad man, but there is much beauty in sadness.'

Raf started to sway again, his eyes now closed, in a world of his own.

We all sat in silence again, not looking at each other, not knowing where this was going. The song came to an end and I pressed pause. Raf stayed swaying with his eyes closed for another thirty seconds as whatever personal movie he was screening reached its concluding scene. He opened his eyes and took in his surroundings, as though for the first time.

'NOW WE DRINK!' he screamed, making us all jump and his grandmother's head plummet into her hands in despair. 'I have a special thing that we will do together. We shall drink like men.' He walked off, past his family table, and disappeared into another room.

We all looked at each other in slight panic.

'Where's he gone?' I asked.

'To get a gun,' said Harry.

'I think he's going to do a Columbine in here,' chipped in Chris nervously.

'Shall we run?' I asked.

'Too late,' said Harry.

Raf re-entered the dining room, stopped at his family table for a brief argument and then headed towards us carrying a box of stuff.

'We shall see who is a man,' he proclaimed, plonking the box on the table as we all fixed him with rictus smiles.

Out of the box came a champagne bucket, some ice, many

beers, a bag of salt and sprigs of mint. Things suddenly looked a little less frightening.

'We do brain freeze,' shouted Raf.

One of the older men on his table made as though to intervene but was held down by another. He started to pour the beer into the bucket along with all the ice. He then tipped a lot of salt in and all the mint. Once the bucket was full and foaming he shouted at the waiter, a Syrian refugee, to get some straws.

Once these had been provided, we were ordered to all stand around the bucket.

'OK, when I say GO we all suck on straw and try to empty the bucket before your brain freezes up. Last person to suck wins and is man. Is clear?' Raf looked around at us, daring anybody to disagree. We all nodded vigorously.

'So, let's drink, motherfuckers!'

We all bent over the bucket and sucked at the liquid as hard as we could. It was actually rather good, and we did serious damage to the level before Harry came up for air. I followed, leaving Chris and Raf to duke it out for the championship. Chris had a look of steely determination in his eyes, and I knew he wasn't going to lose. This was good news for Chris, who'd had a very bad day, and it would help to restore his morale and confidence. It was not great for us as we had no idea how Raf would react to being beaten. I took a quick look over at his family's table and could have sworn that a couple of them were praying.

Finally, Raf's head snapped back like Gary Oldman in *Léon*. He let go of the straw. Chris kept going, as though to rub in his dominance in the event. I wasn't so sure that this was a good idea.

'BRAIN FREEZE ... BRAIN FREEZE,' shouted Raf as he stumbled about the room. He appeared to be happy with his brain freeze. This boded well.

Chris finished the bucket and stood straight, a little precariously, but strong in victory. All memories of the hideous day had been erased. In fact, looking at him, it appeared that all memories of anything had been erased, but he was triumphant and raised his hand in the air before shouting, 'I am the winner. I claim this win in the name of Her Majesty Queen Elizabeth II and all who sail in her!'

He then crashed back down into a chair and stared out at the mountains in a contented stupor.

Raf approached the table, a little worse for wear.

'You have defeated me. We must go again so I have chance of revenge.' He shouted at the waiter to bring him more supplies, but a senior member of the family quickly closed down that option and the waiter scurried away into another room.

'We must go out together in Beirut. We will burn the whole city down!' Raf was on fire himself.

'I ride a Harley-Davidson. It is here now. Let me take you, the sad man, for a ride.' He pointed at me unsteadily and I mumbled excuses about having to go somewhere else very soon.

'We will do it with no helmets ... like men.' Raf was off again but a female relative had had enough and got up and escorted him back to his table, where he was firmly sat down.

Fortunately for us, Caroll appeared in the doorway. He had retrieved the van from Baskinta and was now ready to take us to the Beqaa Valley for a couple of days off. We were going to Baalbek, the jewel in Lebanon's traditional tourist crown.

We all breathed a sigh of relief, threw some money on the table and headed off past Raf's table. He stared at us with unblinking eyes. Then, just as we'd made our escape from the building, Jacky appeared, having ditched her hiking guide outfit for some serious make-up and glad-rags.

'Hello, guys. Having fun?' she said.

'Yes thanks, Jacky, having a great time, got to go now,' I said, looking for the van.

'I thought maybe we have some drinks?' Jacky looked surprised.

'Maybe next time, something's come up.' We all said good-bye too fast.

I spotted the van and we made a beeline towards it. We jumped in.

'Good time?' asked Caroll.

'Drive, drive!' we shouted as a confused Jacky waved at us from the pavement.

It was time to leave Mtein.

The road to Baalbek over the top of the mountains and then down into the Beqaa Valley was a beautiful one but we could see nothing in the black night and besides – truth be told – we were all a little tipsy. None more so than Chris, who had not just found a second wind but was now riding it like a bull-rider on crack. He was on fire.

'I reckon there was nobody in that whole village who could have beaten me at that.' Chris gave us a toothy grin.

'Oh, for God's sake, we're never going to hear the end of this are we?' Harry was not amused at having pulled out first.

'You're an Irish Catholic, Harry. You should have enormous experience in pulling out.' Chris was certainly not going to let this one go.

'I'm a Protestant,' protested Harry.

'What goes tick tock, tick tock?' I asked in a broad Belfast accent. 'This fookin' van . . .' I continued before anybody could answer.

'What cries like a girl and wets themselves on a small hillock?' asked Harry.

'Chris Bell,' Harry and I shouted.

It was indeed a long drive to Baalbek. We pulled into the town at about ten-thirty in the evening. We were going to stay at the Palmyra Hotel, one of the grand old hotels of the Levant that had now fallen on pretty desperate times. Jean Cocteau, Atatürk and de Gaulle had stayed there, among many other luminaries, but there had been little passing trade since Hezbollah had made the town their main headquarters in Lebanon. As you drove up the main road there were posters of martyrs and fiery diatribes against their enemies played out over loudspeakers. Just before we pulled up at the Palmyra, we passed the massive Shia shrine that sat rather at odds with the magnificent ruins behind, dedicated to Baal and Bacchanalian pursuits.

We were the only people staying in the hotel, so Caroll suggested that we eat at a little hostel down a side street. We parked the van and then walked down streets deserted save for the fleeting glimpse of a woman in full niqab darting in and out of a building. Then, from where I know not, I heard something extraordinary: the sound of a piano, then the unmistakeable voice of Mike Scott. One of my favourite songs of all time was drifting over the thousand-year-old cobbled streets. It was the Waterboys' 'Old England'. Who on earth could be playing this at eleven in the evening in the middle of Baalbek? I never found out, but the lyrics stopped me dead in my tracks.

*You're asking what makes me sigh now?*
*What it is, makes me shudder so?*
*Well I just freeze in the wind*
*And I'm numb from the pummelling of the snow ...*

God, what a song. I loved the idea that some Hezbollah fighter was kicking back to this tale of death of empire and disillusionment. If they were, I hoped that they got the message: everything fucks up in the end (although Scott put it a lot better).

We entered an old whitewashed building in which about thirty people were huddled around a TV that was broadcasting the first results from the election. Hezbollah were expected to do well, and their supporters were watching expectantly while sucking on nargilehs and consuming tiny cup after tiny cup of strong coffee. Someone would clean up if they ever introduced the concept of the mug to the Middle East.

As we entered, the whole place stopped talking and turned to stare at us. It was like that scene from *An American Werewolf in London* when the American hikers stumble into the Slaughtered Lamb (if you exchanged dour English countryside types for bearded youths and veiled women).

'Shall I challenge them to a drinking competition?' whispered Chris, still a little the worse for wear.

'No,' said Harry and I at the same time.

We nodded at the crowd and were then ushered into a small side room, where we were brought an assortment of dishes that we wolfed down while I gave Harry and Chris a little background on where we were. Baalbek, formerly Heliopolis, was at the northern end of the Beqaa Valley and was in a perfect spot for a stopover on the way down to Jerusalem from Syria or from Syria on the way to the Phoenician coastal cities.

Because of the magnificent ruins (the largest Roman temple in the world) it had become Lebanon's most famous tourist attraction, although footfall had been limited recently. In the 1980s, the Shia town had become the headquarters for Hezbollah and many of the English and American hostages taken then had ended up in the town. For me, Baalbek had always been the stop-off point on expeditions into the Syrian Desert. The town was not far from the northern border and we would always stay at the Palmyra Hotel before heading off into Syria, often with the desert oasis that the hotel was named after as our final destination.

God, how I love Palmyra, an extraordinary city in the middle of the Syrian Desert that was also at a crossroads of various civilisations. It had been in the news recently when it had been overrun by ISIS, who had started dynamiting some of the beautiful old buildings and taking sledgehammers to delicate old sculptures. I was more than aware of the wholesale slaughter that had taken place in the Syrian war, costing hundreds of thousands of human lives. And yet, it was images of the destruction of Palmyra that really affected me, brought me to tears. I supposed that it was simply impossible to take in that level of death. The old Stalin quote came to mind: 'One death is a tragedy, a million is a statistic.'

Seeing the destruction of the past in Palmyra crystallised the madness of human conflict. The irony was that when Lebanon was going through its own internecine conflict we would escape to Syria. Now the roles were reversed, and millions of Syrians poured into tiny Lebanon to escape their own conflict. Their desperate, tented encampments lined many of the roads in the Beqaa.

We finished our meal and wandered through the still empty streets back to the even emptier Palmyra Hotel. After we'd knocked on the door for quite a while an elderly man who I recognised from years previous opened the door suspiciously.

'What do you want?' he asked in a quiet, cracked voice.

'We want to stay the night,' said Caroll, in a slightly irritated tone.

'Oh?' replied the old man as though he'd forgotten the original purpose of the hotel. 'Tonight?' He had clearly not been expecting visitors.

'That's the idea,' said Caroll, a little sharply in my opinion.

'Are you fully booked?' asked Harry.

Everyone laughed at this, even the old man, for whom the idea of a full hotel was as ridiculous as these idiots knocking on his door at this time of night.

'Please, come in.' The old man apologetically opened the front doors guarded on each side by ancient stone heads 'borrowed' from the ruins.

It was a shock to enter. I remembered it so well. There was the hotel manager's office on the left, where I'd once been regaled with tales of the Rolling Stones, who had come to play the famous Baalbek Festival in the sixties. The big hall, once full of antiquities and grand old furniture but now almost empty. I peered into what used to be a rather elegant and cosy cocktail bar; the room had clearly not had much use during the Hezbollah years and reeked of faded glamour. I could remember my father, in his 'desert gear' of a beaten-up brown suede jacket, tough trousers, his reading glasses on his head, sitting in there having a well-deserved drink or two after the drive over the mountains. These expeditions had been when he was at his happiest. He was away from the office and the strains and stresses of Lebanese business life. He was on the road, with dogs, children and assorted family, carefree and ready to explore yet another area of the Syrian Desert or return to some of our favourite haunts.

We lugged our luggage up the stairs; musty old images of Lebanon's heyday lined the walls. Posters advertising Baalbek Festivals, skiing in Lebanon, the train service from Aleppo. It was almost too much – *A Wreck of Paradise* – actually, the name of a novel that my dad wrote. I tried to read it once, but there was a queasy sex scene early on and I gave up. Nobody needs that. The one thing I learned from him in the tiny part of the book that I read before the queasy sex scene was that he also hated it when muzak was played in planes as passengers disembarked.

The old man took us down the long corridors, swinging the heavy brass keys that I remembered so well. He put us in three neighbouring rooms, all with balconies that looked out over the spotlit ruins. To say that the rooms were tired would be too kind, they were exhausted, but I could remember what they were like back in the day and was blissfully happy. Chris, less so. He was now sobering up and, I think, probably felt that he had been kidnapped while drunk and was now being held hostage in a three-star hovel.

'Where on earth are we?' asked Chris, still trailing his massive suitcase. He hadn't unpacked and was clearly hanging on to the forlorn hope that there would be another option.

'We are in what was formerly one of the great hotels of the Levant.' My defence of the hotel was interrupted by an ear-splittingly loud volley of heavy machine-gun fire from somewhere just below my window.

Chris hit the ground hard and, at first, I thought he had been shot; a thought that was both exciting in terms of the narrative thread of this book and upsetting in that I was rather fond of Chris. Another massive volley of machine-gun fire echoed around the room and I saw tracer light up the sky through the window. Chris made a strange noise that I was confident came more from a feeling of general concern than from being wounded.

'Ooooooaaaahrghghgh,' proclaimed Chris.

'Are you OK?' I asked as I shuffled along the wall to peer out of the window.

'Ish . . .' replied Chris, still prostrate on the floor.

I peeked out of the corner of the French window. Down below, on the empty street, lit by a flickering yellow streetlight, was a dilapidated military jeep. Two bearded men sat in the front while a third, also bearded – barbers didn't make much money here – hung off the back of a rather large-looking machine gun that had been attached to the rear of the jeep. I recognised it, but only knew it as was what we would have called a *douchka* back in the days of the Lebanese civil war. Back then, long-haired militiamen with bandanas would 'water-ski' through the burned-out streets of the capital holding onto the swinging machine gun in a curious combination of machismo and incompetence.

The man hanging off the back of the jeep pulled the trigger again and the barrel spat fire and lit up the starless sky. I watched the tracer soar into the air, looking in vain for a target. Then I understood what was happening. Hezbollah had obviously got the first results in and they had been positive. This was a *feu de joie* where the Lebanese fired whatever ordnance they had into the air to celebrate a wedding, a birthday, an assassination, a survival, an election result. Harry came out on to his balcony as Chris and I opened our French window.

'More ... shoot more,' shouted Harry enthusiastically down to the street.

The gentleman on the gun turned at the noise and looked up to see three middle-aged men staring at him. One of them, the ginger, was jumping up and down and making encouraging noises. Harry really liked guns. The gunman looked confused. Then the engine turned over and the jeep moved on down the road to celebrate somewhere else.

'Well, that was bloody brilliant,' said Harry enthusiastically.

'Once one became aware that we were not the target,' replied Chris, who really had had quite the day.

'As Raf might say, bedtime, motherfuckers! Tomorrow is culture time!'

I retired to my room and tried to get comfortable on a pillow that had not been changed since the days of Atatürk; it must surely have stiffened his resolve to modernise Turkey.

## DAY 10

# BAALBEK

There was machine-gun fire all night. More and more cars drove through the streets with people hanging out of them firing machine guns into the air. This was a far more effective way of keeping up-to-date with the election results than watching Jeremy Vine ponce around on some Swingometer.

Hezbollah had clearly done very well, and this meant that it was probably politics as usual in Lebanon. People had voted along clan and religious lines, and the hopes of young people for the new secular party of Sabaa had been dashed. Sabaa was an exciting new idea for young Lebanese; something that they could vote for that was not stuck in the trenches of fiefdoms, religion or family loyalty. Sabaa, meaning seven, unfortunately meant zero to the traditional Lebanese voter.

I got up early and looked out over the ruins. It was raining, and I thanked whichever god was in charge that we weren't walking in this. I wandered down the tattered corridors of the Palmyra towards breakfast while dragging my heavy kit bag behind me. I descended the stairs. Unfortunately, so did most of the old carpet. It was attached by old brass stair rods that gave way under the pressure of the bag. I landed in a heap at the bottom with a mass of dirty Persian carpet on top of me. It was not, I imagined, the way de Gaulle would have announced that he was ready for *le petit dèjeuner*.

I got up with as much dignity as I could muster, turned left and opened the glass doors into the dining room. It was even worse. The first room was empty, no furniture whatsoever except for the old mock-up model of the ruins under a glass case. In the far corner sat a Bedouin woman kneading dough before flattening it on a hot metal dome that cooked the thing in seconds. She was making mountain bread and manakish, my favourite food of all time. The freshly baked smell erased my sadness at the state of the place and took me straight back to happier times, when we would all meet in this room for breakfast before setting off for the border and the Syrian adventure beyond.

I sat down and presently from the kitchen appeared the old man who had let us in the night before. He, like the manager of a salad bar in Coventry, kept up pretences beautifully.

'Hello, sir, how many will you be for breakfast?' he asked in French.

'There are four of us. May I sit anywhere?' I replied.

'As of now we have room for you to sit anywhere.'

His white jacket was stained and crumpled, but he still had beautiful manners and a twinkle in his eyes. How he must have longed for the good old days when the great and the good flocked to this place and the walls echoed with laughter and bonhomie. We started chatting in French.

'How long have you worked here?'

'Many, many years, sir.'

'My family and I used to come here every year, on our way to Syria.' I smiled at him.

'Welcome back, sir, although I hope you are not planning a trip to Syria today. Things are not good there right now.' He looked at me as though I might have missed a news broadcast.

'Inshallah they will get better as they have here,' I said just as a massive volley of machine-gun fire from a passing celebrant echoed through the room. The old man raised his eyes in a manner that seemed to convey that things had not really got that much better.

Chris and Harry appeared. Chris seemed to be missing the comforts of his usual level of hotel whereas Harry, who looked even more dishevelled than usual, looked as if he might be doing some building work in the establishment.

After breakfast we set off to explore the ruins. We retraced our steps from the night before and ended up at the entrance. To get there we had to beat our way past several gentlemen trying to sell us Hezbollah merchandise. I explained that we already had most of the current range, having visited the gift shop at the Museum for Resistance Tourism, but these guys clearly felt that one could never have too much Hezbollah paraphernalia.

'Maybe for wife?' One man proffered a cheap yellow baseball cap with the Hezbollah motif of an AK-47 on it.

I briefly imagined Mrs Joly turning up at a Cheltenham Ladies' College hockey match sporting the headgear. The hawker spotted my momentary indecision and pressed on.

'Maybe T-shirt, keyring, flag? Please, sir, everything must go.' He smiled a toothless smile and was clearly proud of his use of this phrase that I imagined he must have seen on some foreign TV advert.

At the ticket booth we were greeted by a rather oleaginous gentleman.

'Hello, my friends, so you are ready for the tour?' He asked, grinning.

'We are OK, thank you. I've been here many times and have no need for a guide.' I replied politely but firmly. I hated having guides. I'd rather learn nothing than admit to being a tourist. It was a hangover from my gilded youth. I could still remember my mother saying: 'We're not tourists, darling, we're travellers.' It was a mantra embedded deep within me.

'Mr Caroll has organised for me to be with you. I have come from my village to be with you today.' Again, the smile was cavernous and tooth-free but had a hint of steeliness about it.

I had not asked Caroll for a guide. In fact, I had not asked Caroll to accompany us on our walk but, somehow, he was there. It would be difficult to shift this new guy, so I relented. He got our tickets and we entered the vast compound of ruins that made up Baalbek. I knew that he was going to annoy the hell out of me, but there was nothing I could do. I wandered off ahead but our guide, who, with a frayed pinstripe suit jacket and a constant cigarette in his lips, had a slight look of Nigel Farage about him, had other ideas. I decided to call him Toad.

'Please do not stray from me, I have much to say.' I looked at Chris, who had even bigger authority issues than myself, and raised an eyebrow.

Harry, surprisingly, was all over it. He loved nothing more than a bit of history and seemed thrilled that Toad was with us.

'Please, sir, come here and we will talk about entrance before entering.' This was not going to be good.

'This temple here, formerly known as Heliopolis, is the largest Roman temple complex in the world, but it is not just Roman. Every civilisation that has travelled through these lands has added to or taken from this place. For example, the original mosaic floor was taken by the Byzantines to build Hagia Sophia in Istanbul, formerly Constantinople—'

'How did they get the stone from here to Istanbul?' said Harry.

'Please sir, I am talking, do not interrupt.' Now he had lost his only ally in Harry and we were that rare thing in Lebanon, a united front against him.

Toad had a set patter from which he did not like to deviate and that he had given so many times that the words had lost their meaning. Nevertheless, he was going to deliver them as fast as he could and get his money whether we liked it or not.

'Stone from here was also used to build the Temple of the Rock in Jerusalem . . .'

I zoned out and took in the never-disappointing atmosphere of this wonderful place. I loved putting my hands on the thick, stone walls and osmosing their glorious past. Oh, what these stones must have seen. We climbed up the steep steps that led us into the first part of the complex and a line of vast stone pillars.

'The constructors of this place built sloping earth constructions along which they dragged the pillars before rotating them into place,' Toad droned on but managed to catch Harry's interest again as he tried to work out how long the gently rising earth ramps must have been to get the pillars to the required tilt height.

Harry, who built things for a living, reckoned that they must have been at least 2 kilometres long. It was great to have somebody such as him along at these moments. He looked at things that I'd seen hundreds of times through different eyes, the eyes of someone who actually knew what they were talking about. He would point out engineering feats and compare ancient construction techniques to modern-day stuff.

We moved on through the various parts of the complex. Sadly, the classic Lebanese photo op in front of the six 20-metre columns of highly polished red Egyptian granite was denied us as they were under scaffolding. I was glad that somebody was looking after them; there used to be 128 of them. What a sight that must have been.

We had the place to ourselves apart from a group of three French twenty-somethings. One of them managed to get into every frame of every photo that I took. It was bloody annoying, but I was being greedy. Anywhere else in the world, a place like this would be heaving with coachloads of tourists swarming over the stones like ants. I should have been happy that there were only three other people visiting but, somehow, I resented their presence even more. I was like Mariah Carey on a shopping excursion to Harrods; I wanted the entire place to myself.

It was also a double-edged sword. For us it was wonderful that there was nobody around and that we had such a place almost to ourselves. But to the Lebanese, it was catastrophic. It meant that the conflict in nearby Syria and the correlation between Lebanon and 'trouble' were keeping the outside world out and this had a direct effect on local merchants, guides such as Toad and a whole network of linked micro-economies. I almost felt sorry for Toad ... almost.

'Please, do not walk around willy-nilly. Stay with me, please,' shouted Toad at Chris, who was near boiling point.

I was rather impressed with his use of the term willy-nilly. It reminded me of the stallholders in the souks of Marrakesh.

They would assess you as you walked towards them and then use what they thought were phrases that would put you at ease. The first time I went, I was disappointed at being instantly spotted as a Brit.

'Tally-ho, jolly good, time for tea,' shouted an elderly man in front of his carpet stall.

'Pip-Pip, bally-hoo,' screamed another, only his face peering out of a hole in a massive pile of nuts. I was back there very recently, and it seemed that they had updated their patter, but it was still equally obscure.

'Reading, Maidenhead, Basingstoke?' shouted a man from his food stall in the Jemaa el-Fnaa, the massive square that is the centre of all life in the Red City. He was affecting a cockney accent that made Dick Van Dyke sound flawless.

'Beirut,' I shouted back at him, smiling. The guy didn't miss a beat.

'The Corniche, Achrafieh, Hamra Street.'

I had to admit he was geographically correct, but it wasn't going to make me eat at his stall. Did this sort of patter ever work? To me, the moment somebody approached me outside a restaurant or asked whether I needed some help in a shop, our relationship was over. I liked the restaurant abroad that was confident in its quality or reputation and did not need to drag in indecisive tourists. I was, after all, a traveller not a tourist.

'Earthquakes have harmed this site more than the wars of man ... the great earthquake of 1759 did much damage ...' Toad was still rambling on. 'In 1516, Baalbek was conquered by the Ottomans' Sultan, Selim the Grim.'

'Selim the Grim? Was that his real name?' asked Harry.

'Please, sir, do not interrupt, I have much to say.' And indeed, he did, almost none of it of much interest.

We wandered through the Forecourt, around the Great Court and then headed towards the imposing Temple of Bacchus, reading the graffiti left by centuries of visitors. Old graffiti was at least done with some style. Names were carved gracefully into the old stone along with the date of their visit and had, in their own way, become part of the history of this place.

I asked Harry and Chris to stand on a particular column for a photo. Toad had other ideas.

'Please, sir, this is not the best vista. If you could stand on this column ...' He pointed to a nearby fallen column.

'... and I will take the photograph.'

Wearily I handed over my camera to Toad and we all three clambered onto the column and stood, side-by-side, ready for our close-ups.

'OK, my friends, please put your arms around each other for photo.' Toad was gesticulating wildly and getting into his role of photographer.

'No, thank you, we are fine as we are,' said Chris.

'No, sir, you do not understand. Please put arms around each other, you are friends, you are in Baalbek.' Toad spoke as though to a dim teenager.

'No, we are fine like this. Take the photo please.' Chris was low-voiced and measured. This meant trouble.

'Sir, please, you do not understand. I have taken many photographs here. Please trust me and put your arms around your friends.' Toad was shaking his head slightly as though in disbelief at the calibre of tourist he was now having to deal with.

Chris now blew. 'I understand the situation completely. I'm afraid that it is you that have failed to grasp the situation. We are British, and British men do not act like Italians at a beach bar. We will not be putting our arms around each other. We will stand as we see fit and I would ask you to please take the photograph and let's move on.' He folded his arms and waited.

Toad looked utterly confused but took the photo and we got down from the pillar.

'Here is photograph. It is decent but much better with arms around each other like brothers. I do not understand . . .' Toad looked crestfallen and, for the second time that day, I almost felt sorry for him.

'It is our custom and I ask you to respect it as we respect yours,' said Chris.

Chris wandered off and I followed him, leaving Harry with Toad.

'Please explain this to me. You are friends, yes?' Toad asked Harry.

'Yes, we are friends,' replied Harry.

'So, if you are friends, like brothers, why you not put arms around each other? Never in twenty-five years of this job have I seen this.' Toad looked to Harry for clarification.

'It's just the English way. This is what distinguishes us from the Continentals. There are certain rules to life, like no cheese at breakfast, that you fellows might be a lot better off following.' Harry lit a roll-up for effect.

Toad looked like his world had been turned upside down.

'You are not happy with me. You are angry.' He was a shell of the man he had been ten minutes before.

'No, not at all. We just have standards,' said Harry kindly.

Toad and Harry moved on and we entered the Temple of Bacchus, but Toad's heart was no longer in it. He rattled through his facts about the temple and his speech just became a sequence of words that had very little meaning.

'This temple finished by Septimius Severus in 19 AD, interior of temple is divided into a thirty-metre nave and an eleven-metre sanctuary, temple is surrounded by forty-two columns each twenty metres in height, some pillars have fallen and lean on temple wall.' Toad eventually came to the end of his spiel.

'I have finished now. Please walk on your own time around and visit maybe the museum. I will go now.' He pretended to walk off but was clearly wanting us to call him back. We all felt guilty and did call him back; we gave him a handsome tip that pleased him greatly.

'The British are a great culture,' he said, shaking our hands before wandering off towards the entrance muttering to himself.

At last we were alone. We mucked about taking photographs of ourselves pretending to be trapped under leaning pillars and sticking our heads into the mouths of vast stone lions. We were happy, free to be idiots again. We made our way down a long tunnel under the Temple of Jupiter that housed quite an impressive collection of relics and a set of fascinating old photographs of Baalbek.

Suddenly Baalbek exploded. The sounds of machine-gun fire mixed with small arms and the occasional explosion that was most likely a grenade echoing menacingly off the walls. It was probably another *feu de joie*, but you could never be entirely sure, so we exited the tunnel and came out into the soft Levantine light.

The sound of gunfire was everywhere around us. I saw a man standing on his roof emptying a clip from his AK-47 before removing it, flipping it round, inserting a second one that he had taped to the first and continuing to fire into the air with an impressive fluidity. This confirmed to me that it was indeed a *feu de joie*. Judging by the scale of the *feu* there was a lot of *joie* and this could mean only one thing: Hezbollah had cleaned up at the elections. Happy that we were in no danger, we started filming the celebrations. A large explosion followed by a cloud of smoke very nearby provided good footage. Harry was delighted with the whole thing and felt that we should try to bring the practice to Cheltenham.

'Sod the Christmas lights, imagine this going on over Imperial Square. It would be awesome.' He grinned, lighting up another roll-up.

Suddenly from our left we heard panicked voices. We turned and spotted the group of three French tourists. They looked petrified and were sprinting towards us and the exit beyond. All three affected a curious sort of running crouch with their arms covering their heads that I could only guess they had learned about in some French military training manual. The thought did briefly cross my mind of letting them know that we were not under attack and that this was just celebratory gunfire ... but that silly notion did not last for long. We affected poses of courage and indifference, and watched the Continentals cower-run past us. I couldn't help myself; I unleashed a loud chicken sound as the last Frenchman passed us by. This, I told myself, was why we did not hug in tourist photos.

We left Baalbek with gunfire going off all around us. On the way out, we made a brief stop to visit the largest stone in the world. It was in a quarry on the outskirts of the town, where the builders of Baalbek had hewn some of the massive foundation stones of the Temple of Jupiter out of the limestone. Technically it was the largest *manmade* stone in the world. It was certainly impressive, weighing in at around 1,650 tons. This was most likely the reason that it had never left the quarry. The stone was on a tilt as though somebody had tried to move it but had given up. I didn't blame them.

Whatever the reason, the stone sat abandoned in this old quarry and was looked after by a lovely old man who also promoted a series of no-littering campaigns. He charged a little fee and had some knick-knacks and souvenirs that he half-heartedly offered to the visitor but with little pressure. Various articles about him and his work were proudly displayed on the wall. He had the kindest of faces. Lebanon needed as many of his type as possible.

We drove south down the Beqaa Valley. On each side of the road were endless makeshift camps of Syrian refugees, exiles within sight of home with no idea of when they might be able to return. What must they have felt, stuck in a land that used to be the byword for chaos, gazing at the foothills of their country, foothills where the ragged remains of ISIS were still struggling with Hezbollah and Lebanese Army fighters in internecine struggles far too complicated for the US government to comprehend.

We drove for about forty-five minutes until we reached the town of Anjar and the utterly deserted ruins of Lebanon's second most popular official tourist site: an eighth-century Omayyad city built, like Baalbek, to take advantage of the crossroads between Homs and Palestine, Beirut and Damascus. Unfortunately for Anjar, however magnificent, everything paled into insignificance in relation to Baalbek. It was normally wise for the visitor to visit here first to avoid later disappointment.

Chris, however, had other concerns. He was troubled by what he saw as the uneven lines of the construction. He suffers from OCD or, as Chris prefers to call it, CDO (because this is alphabetically correct and therefore more pleasing). When Harry and I had visited Chris in his ex-pat palace in a gated community on the outskirts of Dubai, we couldn't help but notice the fastidiousness of the place. At first, we assumed that Samar, his lovely half-Armenian, half-Palestinian wife, was the clean-freak. She soon disabused us of this notion and showed us a brilliant game that we could play. When Chris left the room for a moment, we would change the angle of his speakers or move a glass trinket a couple of inches and then sit back and enjoy the show. Chris would re-enter the room and, like a nervous fox sensing danger, freeze on the spot. Something was wrong in his ordered world, but he could not work out what. We watched as he mentally went through every little detail of the room until he corrected the offence and visibly relaxed, although he would still remain vigilant for the next hour or so as he knew that dark forces were messing with his mental equilibrium.

Anjar is stupidly close to the Syrian border, so we drove to the frontier post to have a look at what was going on. The road to Damascus was open and there was a remarkable amount of traffic queued up to go into Syria as well as much traffic coming over into Lebanon. I longed to cross into Syria and visit Damascus again, one of the great cities of the world, but sadly run by a totalitarian thug. What history tended to show, however, was that the choice for many a Middle Eastern country was strong rule by a dictator propped up by either Washington or Moscow, or choose democracy and suffer utter chaos as young, often artificially constructed countries disintegrated along religious or tribal lines. Assad, for some, was the dictionary definition of 'better the devil you know'.

From the frontier post, we headed across the Beqaa towards Zahlé, a Christian town that sits at the base of the Mount Lebanon range. It is home to a couple of good vineyards, including Ksara, and it seemed rude not to pop in. The irony of having all these vineyards and wineries so near Hezbollah territory is so Lebanese.

We parked up next to the manicured lawns of the Ksara vineyard and we could have been anywhere – California, New Zealand … vineyards have an ecosystem of their own and are mainly interchangeable. We were taken upstairs to watch a very dull video on the history of the winery before going on a tour of the caves that riddle the cliffs behind the building. Romans had made wine in this very spot and you could see why – perfect climate, access … the Romans really did get everything right.

As we walked up and down corridor after corridor gazing at the bottles and barrels behind cages, I started to develop a thirst. The place reminded me of the kilometres of cellars beneath the Pilsner Urquell brewery in Pilsen, Czech Republic. I'd been there once for a TV show in which I did a joke about trying to organise a 'piss-up in a brewery'. I wandered around Pilsen posting flyers that said, 'Piss-up, Brewery, tonight, 7 p.m.' Then my friend Pete and I sat and waited in the cellars, wearing party hats. Nobody showed (which was the joke) but we managed to enjoy ourselves by drinking pure nectar lager straight from the barrel with no preservatives or chemicals. It was incomparable.

Recently I'd made a TV series called *How Beer Changed the World* (tough job, but somebody had to do it) and I returned to the Pilsner cellars. The Czech-born Australian brew master gave us more of this 'straight from the barrel' heaven. He told us about the scene in Pilsen town square when the inventor of lager poured out the first golden glass and handed it to locals who took to it like ducks to water and lager went on to conquer the world.

Back in the caves of Ksara there was no wine to drink straight from the barrel but there was the next best thing, a tasting room. We all sat on high stools round a spittoon and were given samples of reds, whites and rosés. The spittoon remained unused. I was never one for the gurgling and spitting out of wine ... what a waste. By now a little worse for wear, we decided to go into Zahlé and get something to eat. I'd been told about Massaad Barbecue, a place that should not be missed when in town.

Unfortunately, when we arrived it was closed, as was most of Zahlé due to the election and worries about potential trouble as the results came in.

I checked my phone and asked my social media followers if anybody had any bright ideas about where to eat in Zahlé. I got a message back almost immediately from a Lebanese guy called Edmond who had seen my stuff on TV and wondered if we would like to come to lunch at his place.

Twenty minutes later, we were knocking on his door and being received by a rather startled-looking family. We were probably stretching the limits of Lebanese hospitality, but a fabulous meal was whisked up by staff as Edmond made us jugs of arak and ice mixed with toot. It all went down very well, and we were soon sitting on his veranda overlooking the Beqaa and discussing the election. Edmond's uncle had just won a seat in parliament as an MP and so celebrations were in order, although, unlike in Baalbek, there appeared to be a sense of admirable restraint where firearms were concerned.

Harry was very disappointed. 'Are you sure there isn't a machine gun or an RPG lying about that I can fire off into the air? It just seems so rude not to and I'd so hate to offend anyone.' He kept his bone-dry expression going, much to the consternation of the Lebanese.

It turned out that I had been correct regarding Hezbollah's election results although, this being Lebanon, it was not as simple as it could be. Hezbollah had not made any gains. They had just retained the same number of seats in parliament. However, the Sunni party of Saad Hariri, the son of murdered Rafik and, obviously, this being Lebanon, the current President, had lost a third of its seats.

Hezbollah had, therefore, become a much more powerful partner in the governing coalition. This was bad news for Lebanon as it discouraged foreign investment at a time when it was desperately needed, especially with the added pressure of one million Syrian refugees currently in the country. Israel hadn't wasted any time in declaring that they now saw no difference between Hezbollah and the Lebanese state itself. This was also bad news for the Museum for Resistance Tourism, which might be making use of those tunnels again, sooner rather than later.

We seemed to make a habit of travelling during election times. In 2015, when Harry, Chris and I had gone to Sri Lanka to watch some cricket, the general election was in full swing as we arrived. Posters of the impressively moustachioed President,

Mahinda Rajapaksa, were everywhere. I knew very little about Sri Lankan politics, but it looked as though there was nothing that this President couldn't do. He was pictured cuddling children, teaching at a university, driving a tank, flying a plane and even seeming to be repairing public roads on his own. I assumed he would win as he appeared to have total dominance over the publicity machine but, in an unexpected result, he lost and actually handed over power.

It was time to leave the Beqaa. We said our goodbyes to Edmond and drove back towards Baalbek before turning west on the road over the mountains to the coast. As we approached the mountains, I asked Caroll to stop the van. There was something familiar about the fields of green next to the road. I hopped out and approached a field ... there were acres and acres of hashish.

Hezbollah turned a blind eye to farmers growing the stuff, as for many this was their only solid income. It was still unbelievable to see such a massive amount of the stuff growing so openly. I stood in the middle of the field, surrounded by hashish. I remembered a recent visit to Colorado, a state where marijuana had been legalised. I'd visited a grow centre, the sort of place that I was used to seeing being busted by DEA agents in the movies. Now, the whole thing was legal, enormous quantities of hydroponic lights in massive greenhouses, exstoners employed as master growers, discussing their crop like the keenest winemaker.

I'd then gone to a dispensary, where a very stoned man asked me how I'd like to feel. I said that I wanted to feel like Cheech and Chong in those movies, giggly, happy and relaxed. I did not want to be paranoid or go dark. The guy suggested the stuff

I should buy, and I was soon puffing away on a little pipe. I can't remember much of the next seven hours. I dimly remember being in a restaurant that specialised in weird food. There were heads of dead animals everywhere on the walls. I think I had rattlesnake.

Then I was in a microbrewery on a guided tour and was convinced that the guide was speaking in code ... a code that only I knew the real meaning of, so I translated for the others until I was asked to leave. Marijuana is really not for me. Still, it was quite something to be standing in fields of the stuff.

As I took in these fields of uneasy dreams, Caroll screamed at me from the van to get back in. A farmer was approaching us on a tractor and did not look happy. Now, I was used to unhappy farmers. I flew a hot-air balloon and landing maps were full of areas ringed in red with things like 'angry farmer, uses shotgun' on them. I'd somehow expected a marijuana farmer to be more mellow, but farmers are farmers whatever their crop. I took some photographs and jumped back into the van as the angry weed farmer hurled expletives at us from his tractor.

As the sun started setting we started climbing, finally levelling out at 2000 metres to drive across the plateau, a flat, desolate area dotted with oddly shaped rocks and juniper trees. We passed through lonely roadblocks manned by the Lebanese Army. They stared into the car before waving us on, sometimes having to remove a stinger from the road.

As we started down towards the coast from the plateau, a biblical rainstorm hit us. The water started gushing down the sides of the road and was so powerful that it was picking up mopeds and rubbish bins and sweeping them down with it.

Pretty soon we were driving down the middle of a flash flood that would have halted traffic in any other country in the world. Not Lebanon. Everybody just kept on driving, with the occasional lighter car being swept off the road into the ditch. At the bottom of the mountain, we hit the coastal highway along with our accompanying flash flood. We turned right over the torrent and entered our destination for the night. Jbeil (Byblos) is supposedly the oldest still-inhabited city on the planet. (Although, like hummus, there were several claimants to this crown.)

Things were good. We had two nights in the same place before we headed back to our walk. We checked into a modest, seaside hotel that, ten days ago, Chris would have walked straight out of. Now, it was as though he was checking into a Mandarin Oriental.

'There's TV, laundry, a pillow and not one dangling electrical wire in the shower area,' he shouted excitedly from his room to mine.

We met downstairs in the lobby, where we had a couple of pre-dinner drinks. Chris tended to down his first couple of drinks at lightning speed.

'I drink to forget ...' he said as he downed his second drink in one.

'To forget what?' I asked.

'I can't remember.'

We left the hotel refreshed and traipsed happily through the ancient streets until we reached the little harbour that felt like we were in the South of France. I was taking them to a very famous Lebanese establishment. We were going to the Byblos Fishing Club or, as we all knew it, Pépé Abed's.

Pépé Abed was the Lebanese Hugh Hefner. He was an adventurer and entrepreneur who like many of his type loved to wear a captain's hat and very much enjoyed the company of famous people and beautiful women. He opened a series of nightclubs and restaurants in the fifties and sixties, of which the Byblos Fishing Club was probably the jewel in his crown. If you've been to the Mediterranean, then you know the type of place: a relaxed seafood restaurant on the water with fishing nets and other marine detritus dotted around. There would be the odd black-and-white photograph of David Niven or Tony Curtis on the wall from when the place had been a 'scene'. There are restaurants like this all around the Mediterranean, and I think I've probably been to them all.

Pépé used to get every famous customer to have a photograph taken with him and this would go on the wall ... and Pépé had quite the wall. There were photos of Anita Ekberg, Václav Havel, Ginger Rogers, Brigitte Bardot, Shakira, Kim Novak, Max von Sydow, Gloria Estefan and ... among many, many others ... Dom Joly.

The last time I'd been to Pépé's had been in 2004, two years before his death. *Trigger Happy TV*, the UK comedy show that I had sold to eighty countries, had made me quite well known, and news of my fame had even reached this little corner of the Mediterranean. Of course, it always helps when you are followed by a camera crew. I was making *Dom Joly's Excellent Adventure* at the time. By chance my father had been having lunch in the restaurant that day but he would not be filmed, and so I had to go through this curious charade of talking to camera about growing up in Lebanon with my family on the next table pretending that they weren't there.

By then Pépé was very frail, but he was clearly excited that his place still attracted celebrities, whatever the questionable calibre, and so we sat down and had our photo taken together. Now it was on the wall with a little plaque underneath that read DOM JOLY, STAR OF UK COMEDY SHOW, TRIGGER HAPPY TV. I had to admit to being quite chuffed that I had made it to this Lebanese wall of fame that I had stared at all my life.

Typically, there were dissenting voices.

'Wow, you barely made the wall,' said Chris, pointing out the fact that I was in the very top left-hand corner.

'Yup, one more famous visit and you are gone.' Harry laughed in a surprisingly harsh manner.

'The good news is that should a visitor to this restaurant be over seven foot tall he will be at eye level with your photo,' said Chris.

'Well, if there was somebody over seven foot tall, chances are that they would be a famous basketball player and so their photo would take his place anyway.' Harry and Chris howled with laughter and I chuckled along as best I could.

They were very mean friends, and I did not like them any more.

We took a table overlooking the little fishing boats bobbing up and down in the harbour and ordered cuttlefish, octopus, squid, a selection of fried fish and a couple of bottles of white Musar. Life was good. Two hours and several more bottles of Musar later and talk returned to my photograph on the wall.

'All jokes aside, Dom, I think you should be seriously upset at your position on this wall,' said Chris with a serious face on. 'I mean, if you can't get a better position than the Foreign Minister of Gabon then you need to reassess your career choices.

I think we need to have a word with the maître d'.' Chris smiled a cunning smile.

'Sod that,' said Harry. 'I've got a knife and I reckon that I could get it off the wall and then put it in a better place. How about right next to Brigitte Bardot?' Harry held up a rather large knife that I had not seen before.

He got up unsteadily and headed over towards Brigitte Bardot's photograph. His plan was clearly to prise off the photo next to her to make way for mine. The problem was that the photo in question was of Camille Chamoun, an ex-Lebanese President, and I felt that this might be taken the wrong way by locals. Chris grabbed Harry and brought him back to our table.

'We need a subtler plan,' said Chris, who now had his most subtle-plan-thinking expression on his face.

'Like what?' asked Harry, putting his knife away.

'Like I pretend to be Dom's agent and have a word with the maître d' to let him know how upset Dom is with his position on the wall.' Chris smiled at me.

I was too drunk to care and it all sounded quite fine, so I nodded my assent.

'Leave this to me,' said Chris, standing up and smoothing down what was left of his hair. He wandered over to the maître d', while Harry followed him, filming discreetly at a distance. He put his arm around the man and guided him towards my photograph.

'You see this photograph ... Do you know who it is?' Chris pointed to my photo.

The maître d' peered high up at the wall but could clearly not make much out.

'No, sir, sorry. I see nothing.'

'That . . . is Dom Joly, one of Great Britain's finest comedians and a personal favourite of Her Majesty Queen Elizabeth II,' said Chris.

'OK . . . like Mr Bean, yes?'

'Sort of . . . yes . . . anyway, I am his agent and he is sitting in the corner over there and he is very unhappy at his placement on the wall. He feels disrespected.'

'He is here now?' The maître d' turned to look back at me in the far corner. I looked very sad and gave him a mournful wave. He turned back to face Chris. 'So, Mr Joly would like to know whether it might be possible to exchange photographs with a lesser celebrity so that fans might be able to enjoy a better view of his face. I was going to suggest that we exchange him with Gloria Estefan who, I think we both can agree, has peaked showbiz-wise, whereas Mr Joly is still climbing fast. Perhaps you caught his television advert for Wickes, the building suppliers?' Chris raised his eyebrows quizzically.

'No, I did not see this.' The maître d' looked apologetic.

'Well, if you get a chance, Google it, because it really is some of his finest work. Anyhow, what about swapping him for Gloria?' Chris was now in hardball mode; the mode that had taken him to one of Arabian *Forbes*' 'Top Ten Thousand People to Watch in the Advertising World'.

'I think he has good position here. He is number one. We have photographs in back rooms that nobody sees.'

'I think that diners would actually be put off their food by this photograph of Gloria Estefan.'

'OK, I ask grandson of Mr Abed.' The maître d' gave in, and Chris patted him on the back and returned to our table.

The maître d' came over with a free bottle of Musar and welcomed me back and apologised for any disrespect. I was gracious and accepting of his apology and even gave him a hug when we eventually staggered out of the establishment at about one in the morning. He handed Chris and me two badges informing us that we were now members of the Byblos Fishing Club. Harry was not given one. I agreed with this decision. After all, a place has to have standards. I have not yet returned to check on the status of my photograph and that of Ms Estefan, but I feel sure that the decent thing has been done. Sorry, Gloria, but that's showbiz . . .

Back in our hotel I tried to sleep but I clearly had what was intended to be Harry's room as there was a thick plastic sheet on the mattress. I turned on the telly and found myself watching a news report from Beirut. There were street fights breaking out all over downtown between followers of Hezbollah and those of the Future Movement, the party of the Prime Minister, Saad Hariri. The rival gangs were roaming the streets on mopeds looking for each other so an order was given to ban mopeds for seventy-two hours. It felt like a tiny Band-Aid over an ever-expanding wound.

# BYBLOS

This was our big rest day. Nothing planned, nothing on the agenda except for a stroll around town. This was lucky as nobody got out of bed until midday. We had pretty much emptied the Byblos Fishing Club of Musar, and we were now paying the price. I stumbled downstairs to breakfast, but it was too late: they were already serving lunch.

Harry was sitting on the balcony overlooking the blue Mediterranean below us. It was a gorgeous sunny day, zero sign of the downpour of the night before. The beach looked very inviting and so Harry and I wandered down and had a swim. We were alone on the beach that stretched down towards the harbour walls. Offshore, standing on pin-sharp rocks, were a couple of fishermen expertly keeping their balance while waiting for a bite.

We walked back up to the hotel to find Chris nursing a coffee. We all sat and took in the view in silence. It didn't last long. Talk began on one of their usual attack lines as to how much better it would be if Bill Bryson was writing this book.

'If Bryson was doing this there would definitely be a film spin-off,' said Chris.

'Yes, his books sell so well, and he's just naturally funny. He doesn't appear to have to work at it like you do, Dom.' Harry laughed.

'Take *A Walk in the Woods* – it's basically the ultimate travel book about a walk, making anything coming after it defunct,' added Chris.

'And it was made into a film,' said Harry.

'Hardly the ultimate walking travel book,' I protested. 'What about *A Time of Gifts* and *Between the Woods and the Water* by Patrick Leigh Fermor? He walked all the way to Istanbul just before the Second World War. Those are the two greatest travel walking books to my mind.' I was clearly dealing with ignoramuses.

'Yeah but was there a film made of those books? No there wasn't.' Harry laughed.

'So, in your opinion a book is only good if it gets a film spin-off?' I asked. I was trying to sound relaxed, but I was getting a bit pissed off.

'Obviously,' said Harry.

'It's a shame that this won't be made into a film as I quite fancied being played by Robert Downey Jr,' said Chris dreamily.

Our alliances shifted as quickly as a Lebanese coalition, and Harry and I now teamed up.

'Robert Downey Jr? You must be joking. I was thinking Bob Hoskins,' I said, pleased that the fire had been diverted from me.

'Who was that bloke on *Magnum P.I.*, the little English guy in shorts? Higgins. Yes, you should be played by him.' Harry was enjoying this.

'I presume you would accept nobody but Clint Eastwood to play you, Harry?' I laughed, but I knew that this was true.

'Of course, he'd jump at the chance.' Harry smiled, a roll-up suddenly dangling from his lip.

'Dom, presumably you'd like a young Johnny Depp to play you but I'm afraid it would be Robert Smith.' Chris was desperately trying to get back in with Harry.

'All this is pointless anyway because Bryson is not writing this book, so it won't be made into a film, end of.' Harry and Chris laughed.

The coalition was back together. Politics was a fickle mistress.

We set off on a stroll around Byblos. There was a souk area that was mostly bars and restaurants on ancient cobbled stones under natural ceilings of purple bougainvillea. A couple of merchants half-heartedly tried to offload the usual Lebanese tourist tat, but their hearts weren't really in it.

We visited the twelfth-century Crusader castle, built from the local limestone and remains of Roman buildings. The Romans had been so construction-happy in Lebanon that they appeared to have been an almost infinite source of building materials for later arrivals.

Harry and Chris were in love with Byblos. Chris was already Googling house prices and deciding which part of town he wanted as his weekend place. We found a restaurant that served some traditional English food for Harry as he had tired of Lebanese fare. He ordered a spaghetti bolognese and a bottle of wine, and all was right with the world again. One bottle led to another and, by about five o'clock in the afternoon, we were considering returning to Pépé Abed's to have another word about the placement of my photograph. Fortunately, cooler heads prevailed, and we staggered back to the hotel for a well-earned rest. We all decided that we were bored of each other and needed a break. Every breakfast, lunch and supper had been spent together and I think we all just wanted to veg and watch TV. I hopped into the lift and went up to the third floor. I opened my door and flopped on the bed as I turned on the TV. This was bliss. I started to drift off to the dulcet tones of Wolf Blitzer and CNN. Then my phone buzzed.

I checked my WhatsApp: the message was from Caroll, who we hadn't seen since we arrived in Byblos. 'Dinner with LMT people 6 p.m. Meet in bar.' I groaned.

Not only was this our day off but it was a bit weird for him to organise a dinner without asking us. Also, I was quite drunk and so were the other two. I knew what was coming and, sure enough, a minute later I got a WhatsApp from Chris.

'FFS, there is no way I'm going out to supper.' Chris was angry.

'Yeah, me neither, sooooo pissed off,' I typed back.

'Bloody liberty . . .' continued Chris.

Fifteen minutes later, and I started to feel guilty. We couldn't just ignore Caroll. I tried to contact Harry, but he didn't really do WhatsApp and was uncontactable. I was sure he was already asleep, and I knew that I'd have to take one for the team. I WhatsApped Chris again: 'I'll go, have a drink and a quick meal. You stay here. No problems.' I started to get dressed. 'Thanks mate,' replied Chris.

I wandered downstairs to the bar. To my surprise, Harry was there surrounded by quite a few empty beer bottles.

'I messaged you. I thought that you were going to crash.' I said.

'Well, I was, but then I remembered the bar and thought it would be a shame to waste it.' Harry grinned.

'Did you get my message about supper?'

'No, I thought we were doing our own thing.' He necked his beer.

'We were, but then Caroll took it upon himself to invite some people from the LMT to supper with us.' I grimaced.

'LMT ... what's the LMT?'

'The Lebanon Mountain Trail, the thing we are walking across Lebanon on, remember?' Harry was quite drunk.

'Oh ... yes ... of course. What day are we having this supper with them?' Harry indicated that he'd like another beer to the concerned barman.

The lift door opened and out came Chris, dressed up to the nines, the full blazer, brogues and pocket square.

'I thought you were staying,' I said.

'I couldn't let you do this alone.' Chris was a decent man.

'Do what alone?' slurred Harry.

It was going to be a long night.

Fifteen minutes later Caroll entered the bar with a man and a woman both wearing the practical garb of the off-duty hiker. The woman was the head of the LMT and the man was one of the people who had started it up and helped originally blaze the trail. They were both earnest and good people, very concerned with the environment and massively keen walkers. We were drunk, unfit layabouts. This was most likely not going to go well.

Caroll made his introductions, and I very much got the feeling that the head of the LMT had not yet taken on board the fact that we were the people walking her beloved trail. She stared at Harry, surrounded by empty beer bottles and smoking like it was going out of fashion. Then she turned to the athletic frames of Chris and me, hanging off bar stools. She gave us a nervous smile and ordered a water.

'So how are you finding the trail?' she asked.

'I just follow Dom. We just do everything he tells us to ... he is very bossy,' said Harry, downing another beer.

'And, how does it compare with other trails you have done?' She looked quickly away from Harry to me.

'Umm ... we haven't really done any other ones. I did half a day of the Cotswold Way once but that's about it. We're not really hiking people normally.' I smiled at her.

'And you have decided to do the LMT with no experience?' She looked appalled as opposed to surprised.

'Yes, we probably should have done a little more training before starting, but Chris lives in Dubai and there are no hills there, although he did join the Dubai Polo Club and that has a Stairmaster.' I smiled again and felt very tired.

Suddenly, Harry jumped off his bar stool and, as though he had only just spotted the presence of a woman, grabbed her hand and kissed it in a rather exaggerated manner.

'*Enchanté*,' he said, while awkwardly bowing like a rubbish musketeer. 'Margabaala ...' he continued, thinking perhaps that his effortless command of the Arabic language might impress.

She stepped back a couple of paces and, thankfully, Caroll suggested that we head out for supper.

We made our way past the old quarter of town into more modern Byblos. We ended up at a place that was less picturesque than anything we'd frequented but was rammed with locals, which is always a good sign.

'Is this your first time in Lebanon? You must try the food, it is sooo good.' The LMT woman stared at me intently.

I had to admit to feeling a little annoyed that this woman had not done her research on us.

'No, I grew up here. I'm pretty familiar with the food, to be honest,' I replied, possibly a little curtly.

'Madame, do they do spaghetti bolognese here, Madame?' slurred Harry.

'Umm, no, I do not think so.' She looked at Caroll in disbelief before turning to me. 'So, tell me about your book.' She was quite an abrupt woman and the way she phrased this really got my back up. It was as though I was having to pitch the thing to her and I really wasn't in the mood.

'What would you like to know about it?' I replied defensively.

'What is the point of it?'

'That's what we're all wondering,' said Harry as the beers arrived.

'It's a travel book; I'm a travel writer,' I replied quietly.

'So, it's like a guide book?' she continued aggressively.

'No, it's not a guide book. It's a book about doing the walk.' I looked at Chris despairingly.

He jumped in. 'If I may ... Dom is a very well-known comedian and a travel writer of some repute. This adventure we are doing is the subject of his new book.' God, I love Chris. I hate having to explain myself and my job, mainly because it sounds so flimsy when I do so.

I zoned out of the conversation and focused on the food, which, even by Lebanese standards, was exquisite. Towards the end of the meal things relaxed a little. Chris had taken over for me and was asking questions whose answers he was completely uninterested in, but he was good at this sort of polite small talk.

This was his bread and butter in Dubai, the endless business schmooze in which the greatest skill was to fake sincerity. I think this was why he enjoyed being with Harry and me so much. He could say what he thought with no need for any filter.

'Lebanon is like fattoush ... you know what is fattoush?' the woman asked Chris.

'Yes, I know what is fattoush,' Chris replied charmingly.

'Fattoush is a Lebanese salad, a mix of many things thrown into a bowl together.'

'Yes, I know,' repeated Chris patiently. 'What is the meaning of the colours of the LMT emblem?' he asked, pretending to give a shit. He was referring to the white and purple stripes that were daubed on rocks and trees to show us the path.

'White is for the mountain, for the labneh, for the snow, for the flowers; purple is for the famous dye made by the Phoenicians. It represents the rich history of this country.'

Chris nodded at the information and subtly checked his watch. 'And whose idea was it to set up the LMT?' he asked. God he was good.

'Well, originally it came from a British man who was a keen hiker. He came and walked these mountains and was astonished at their beauty and so he suggested that we do a trail like the one in the Appalachians in the US.' She looked to the man for help.

'The one Bill Bryson wrote about in *A Walk in the Woods*,' the man said helpfully.

'Peace be upon him,' howled Harry.

'Blessed be his name.' Chris collapsed in giggles.

I was starting to think that this might all be a set-up. I gave up and hurried the meal along as best I could so that we could go and watch television.

After a couple of hours, we made our excuses.

'Thank you so much for this evening, it was wonderful to learn about the history of the LMT.' Chris was still schmoozing.

'Yes, thank you, I hope you enjoy the book when it comes out.' I smiled a big, false smile.

'Madame, *enssshhhanté* . . .' slurred Harry as, for some reason, he suddenly became a kind of French dandy and went down on one knee again while kissing her hand.

Nobody knew why Harry was speaking in French as the language had never featured in any conversation that evening. Eventually, with a final 'Marbubba' we were off to bed and blessed sleep, because tomorrow, thank God (whichever one happened to be on duty), we were back on the trail as we seemed to just get into trouble when we weren't. The devil made work for idle feet.

## DAY 12

# NAHR BRAHIM

It was not a happy breakfast. Chris appeared and announced that he was feeling nauseous. He was quickly followed by Harry, who looked like death warmed up. He informed us that he'd had violent diarrhoea all night and had not made it to the bathroom on several occasions. Harry was a little bit obsessed with his bowels; it was an almost constant topic of conversation for him and he would keep us regularly up-to-date on his 'movements'.

When not going on about his own movements, he liked nothing better than to talk of those of others. He regaled us with one of his favourite travel stories featuring a rugby-playing friend who had gone to India on holiday. He'd got incredibly ill and was staying in a hostel with communal showers and bath-room (you know where this is going, and I apologise in advance). He'd woken up one morning, staggered into the showers that three other foreign guests were already using, bent over double in pain and projectile excreted all over the showers with extraordinary violence. The guests were covered, the showers were covered, and Harry's friend was chased out of the hostel by a large Indian lady brandishing a stick, shouting, 'You are very bad man, very bad man.'

Praying that Harry wasn't quite this bad, we hopped into the van and set off for the Nahr Brahim, a river valley where I often used to go and swim as a kid. At least one Sunday every month we would drive down to the coast, head north and then, after the town of Jounieh, turn inland again and wind our way up the river valley to a secret spot where we could picnic and jump off rocks into the crystal-clear water.

Today, we were going to be joined by my nephew, Paul. I was looking forward to some new blood on the trip.

Paul was the son of my half-brother Marc-Henri. When my mother had first arrived in Lebanon in the 1950s, she had been working for the Foreign Office. She'd grown up in Somerset, at the base of Exmoor. When she was posted to Lebanon she fell in love with both the place and a man called Lionel Gorra. Lionel was half-Lebanese, half-Swiss, and a powerful early champion of trying to keep Lebanon's heritage intact. He'd promoted ecotourism before it was fashionable and had walked the mountains of Lebanon with many of the people who had gone on to make the Lebanon Mountain Trail an actuality. Lionel and my mum got married and had two children, Anne-Dominique, who now lived in Greece on the island of Evia, and Marc-Henri, who, following Lionel's death, lived in his historic old house in Zouk Mousbeh above Jounieh.

Paul was thirty years old and a photographer. We'd arranged to meet under a bridge just off the coastal highway where he'd been dropped off by a friend. The weather looked ominous; dark clouds hung over the mountains.

We picked up Paul and started to make our way up the Nahr Brahim. I had so many memories from this valley: biting on a corned beef sandwich that was also home to an angry wasp that stung me in my mouth; stumbling across a cache of grenades in a cave when I'd gone for a little walk into the bush ... all part and parcel of the Lebanon picnic experience.

As we drove up the valley, Paul informed me that this was his family valley. There were two big families that lorded it over the place: the Zoueins and the Barakats (Paul's mum, Mouna, was a Zouein). I asked him whether we'd be in trouble if we bumped into some Barakats but he was non-committal and so I didn't push the matter. This area, the Kesrouan, had a long history of being the Lebanese badlands. It was very difficult to access, and certain villages had only just had electricity and roads leading to them. Outsiders were known as '*ghrab*' and there was a saying about them: '*Ghrab minyekol habra*' (Outsiders want to eat our best meat). This was not a traditionally hospitable place and I was glad that we had Paul with us.

The valley had good reason to mistrust outsiders. It had suffered terribly in the Great Famine during the First World War. Paul was developing a horror movie about vampires during the famine and told us that if we stayed on we could be extras. As we drove up and up, I could see (and hear) that Harry was not in a good way. Finally, we got to a little hut where we would start the walk.

We were off to climb the Jabal Moussa (Mountain of Moses), a place where the residents of the valley had erected a huge statue of the Virgin Mary plus a giant cross. On the Day of the Cross (14 September) every year, locals met at the base of the Virgin and all fired their AK-47s into the air because ... well, it's what Jesus would have wanted.

We set off just as the rain came down, and begrudgingly got our unused ponchos out of their tiny little packs. We knew that we would never be able to get them small enough to fit back in again. We trudged up the path through thick brush. Somewhere far below, a machine gun was being fired almost constantly. This was certainly not a Hezbollah area and so the shooter was either celebrating a Maronite candidate's win, berating a Maronite candidate's loss or settling a parking dispute. I half-expected a group of French hikers to sprint past us in panic. Sadly, none came. We were alone on the mountain except, it seemed, for wolves as we found several tracks in the mud.

We clambered all over an abandoned old farm. It was hidden in a little copse of walnut trees. I could easily have lived there and briefly thought about asking if it was for sale, but then remembered that I was neither a Zouein nor a Barakat and I really didn't want to start any more problems in this argumentative valley. After an hour or so we reached the summit. We rested beneath the giant cross and took photos of the Virgin Mary but, if we were honest, it was all pretty underwhelming. There were too many signs along the trail with historical facts and information about flora and fauna. It all felt a bit too manicured and was so different from the rest of our journey. It didn't help matters that it was pouring with rain and that we were all very hungover. We didn't look like a very impressive set of hikers.

We started the descent on the other side of the mountain by clambering over some fairly large boulders. Chris's vertigo kicked in again and we slowed to a snail's pace as we attempted to get him down. Just as we got over the boulder field and reached a steep donkey path, I slipped badly on the wet mud and fell heavily, snapping one of my walking poles in half. Fortunately, I was all right. Having not really walked with poles before, I was now stupidly reliant on them. It did often look as though we might be off skiing, but they really took the strain off our ageing knees. Having said that, none of our guides used them at all, except for one who deigned briefly to use a stick that he picked up along the way.

'Moses came down from the mountain with two tablets of stone and a touch more dignity,' I said, picking myself up.

'Well, I came down from the mountain with six tablets of Imodium and it's still not worked . . .' replied Harry in a slightly threatening manner.

Nobody said anything. We walked on down in silence save for the steady pitter-patter of the rain on our ponchos.

Things got really spooky when we descended through the cloud. It danced and swirled around us, occasionally revealing glimpses of the valley below before snatching them back. Then we came across a simple homemade cross, made of branches and planted right into the middle of the path. It was all a bit *Blair Witch*. Had we upset the Barakats? Should we sacrifice our Zouein to assuage them? Should we tie Paul to the cross to assure our safe arrival at the bottom? The hangover and the spooky weather were really getting to me, and I was glad when we finally arrived at a deserted church that marked the entrance to the village of Chouwen. The village was more a random collection of houses, and Paul said that it had not long had electricity as access was quite difficult. We sat down on a wall overlooking the river below and started to open up our lunch packs. Paul, who had not organised a lunch for himself, had other ideas.

'I will go and see what people can make for us.'

He disappeared and returned five minutes later with a large, middle-aged woman who Paul announced was prepared to cook us some lunch, if we fancied it. Spoilt by our two days off, we relinquished our packed lunches and questioned the woman as to our options. There were no options: it was chicken sandwiches and chips, or nothing. We were thrilled, and all trooped down to her garden and sat round a table under an awning as she disappeared to go make lunch.

My phone rang. It was Rachel Johnson, a British journalist and the sister of Boris Johnson. We were planning to go on the run together for a TV show called *Hunted* in which we would try not to be caught by the organisations of the state for two weeks. (Rachel later pulled out, and I did the show with someone else.)

'Can you talk?' asked Rachel.

'Yes, I'm in Lebanon waiting for some chicken.'

'What on earth are you doing in Lebanon?'

'I'm walking across the country, writing my new book. It's going ...' I didn't finish my sentence. Rachel was not somebody who did much listening to other people and she started on about her worries for the upcoming show.

'I'm not happy about all this handing over of my emails and social media passwords.' The show was very intrusive and demanded that they had the same powers that the state would have if you were on the run.

As she waffled on, I remembered that, back when I wrote *The Dark Tourist*, I had Facebooked the then Foreign Secretary, David Miliband, about my forthcoming ski trip to Iran. He had only just started using Facebook and only had about thirty friends, one of whom happened to be me. He'd warned me to stay away from the area where Iran had her nuclear facility. It was reassuring to have the Foreign Secretary on speed-dial, and

I briefly considered asking Rachel for her brother's mobile number in case the Barakats attacked. In the end, I thought better of it. So, I sat in the Kesrouan garden, half-listening to Rachel finally winding up her list of concerns about our mutual project, surrounded by an ever-increasing army of cats that also seemed to be awaiting the arrival of the chicken and chips.

Conversation in the garden started to get a bit surreal when Harry and Caroll suddenly announced that they both suffered from tinnitus. This was news to me, but Chris was quickly on to it.

'There's a help line for that. I called it, but it just rang and rang.'

There was a long silence after he delivered this joke. Possibly Harry and Caroll didn't hear it because of their affliction, and I just loathe jokes of any form. I hate the pressure they build around how to react appropriately. Would I find it genuinely funny, or would I have to pretend to so that I didn't offend the joke teller? In Chris's case, this is a constant worry. It is one of the problems that I face as a comedian. People hear the word comedian and always assume that I am a stand-up and that I can tell jokes.

'Go on then, say something funny.'

I've never done stand-up. I'm not interested in jokes per se and I always find someone else telling them very painful. It's the same feeling when somebody whips out a guitar or starts singing round a campfire ... it's excruciating and I just long for it to end.

We sat in the garden expectantly for the first hour or so, but no food arrived. Occasionally, a live chicken would wander through the garden as though to taunt us. Two hours in and the cats gave up hope and disappeared. I prayed that they were not being used as a chicken substitute.

'I can see how the famine happened around here,' muttered Harry, whose stomach seemed to have miraculously recovered. 'Did I tell you that story about Richard Harris, the actor, when he had a heart attack in a restaurant?' he continued. 'As he was being carried out on a stretcher he noticed a group of people waiting to be seated. "Don't have the fish ..." he croaked.' We all laughed before reverting to a hungry silence.

Harry told another story. He and a couple of his cousins had been sailing in Ireland and got caught in a rainstorm. They'd anchored in a small bay and got off the boat drenched to the bone. There was a tiny pub on the hill, so they headed there for some shelter. The publican couldn't have been friendlier and told them to take their clothes off and he would dry them while they had a drink. They sat naked but for their sou'westers, drinking for three hours until one of them opened a door to a damp room where their clothes were all just heaped in a soggy pile on the floor.

Paul eventually ventured into the woman's house and came back out confused.

'It's empty. There is nobody there.' He laughed.

We were all confused and there was much discussion as to what could have happened. Was she a Barakat and had decided to refuse a Zouein food? Had she set off to walk to Beirut for supplies? Had she simply been a figment of our fevered imaginations? We left the garden and, feeling rather foolish, set off down and out of the village towards the river. About halfway down, we came across two Lebanese hikers on their way up to the village.

'Don't order the chicken ...' croaked Harry.

We walked through a forest of plane trees, always a sign of nearby water. Thick, lush vegetation everywhere. We joined a track and saw two dead toads, about 20 metres apart, both flattened by some vehicle. It was very curious. The number of vehicles that went down this track a week could be counted on one hand and so how had they got both toads?

'Maybe it was a suicide pact?' suggested Chris.

'Maybe they were just unlucky?' I suggested.

'Maybe they ordered the chicken?' said Harry, who was not going to let this one go.

We passed by a couple of large, ancient circular stones. They were the remains of a carob mill, left in the valley because it would have been too heavy to take away. The carob tree was cultivated for its edible pods that were ground by stones into a powder that was often used to replace cocoa. One of my favourite facts about the carob (in truth, my only fact) is that the carob pod is always the same size and is the origin of the 'carat', the unit of measure for gemstones.

Further down, near the river, was an abandoned water mill next to a building containing a series of little rooms. Back in the day, people would come here, stay the night and mill their wheat for the year. The river roared down past gigantic boulders and right under the steep evergreen cliffs on the other bank. There was a little beach on our side; the place was designed for a picnic and so we had our packed lunches while Paul looked on hungrily. The dodgy weather only served to enhance the magic of the setting.

Thankfully, the water was not blood red. There was a myth that in Phoenician times, Adonis, a keen hunter, was gored by a wild boar in this valley and died in the arms of his lover, Aphrodite. Supposedly, the river ran red with his blood every year. Nobody could tell me if Adonis had been a Barakat or a Zouein.

Lunch finished, we wandered back up to the village, where we hoped to find someone to drive us back to where Caroll had left his van that morning. As we entered the village, the large chicken-and-chips lady was waiting. She was beaming and proffering some chicken sandwiches that positively reeked of garlic and a bowl of sumptuous-looking chips. It was only three and half hours since we'd first ordered them. Time stood still in this valley.

We sat in the garden again, the cats re-joined us, and I was pleased to note that there were none missing. We ate the sandwiches, and Paul pointed out that should we encounter any vampires on the way back we would be more than safe, having consumed half our bodyweight in garlic. Meanwhile, Caroll had negotiated a lift with an old mountain man and we all hopped into the back of his pick-up truck and returned slowly and uncomfortably to the twenty-first century. Paul immediately fell asleep.

Once in Caroll's van we drove for half an hour until we stopped outside a fairly nondescript modern building. It was our home for the night and our hosts were a Greek-Turk and his French wife. They had a large open room at the top where we were all supposed to sleep but I was assigned my own bedroom after everybody made very clear that they did not wish to sleep with me on account of my snoring. Principal in this objection was Chris, who was really laying it on thick in a manner that only perpetrators of the same crime display.

'Honestly, I cannot spend another night in the same room as you. It sounds like the precursor to Krakatoa exploding.' Chris looked to the room for support.

'I can't believe you are saying this. You snore like a gorilla on steroids.' I was not going to take this lying down.

'Dom, with respect, I believe that you should seriously consider putting yourself forward for voluntary medical research. I think you are something of a scientific one-off.' Chris tried to look caring.

'You're just happy that you're not the one being persecuted and you're trying to curry favour with Harry.' I stared at him, letting him know that I knew his type.

'Well, I find the idea of sleeping with either of you repulsive. Please can you both find alternative sleeping quarters.' Harry showed us the door to the stairs.

*As a postscript, when I returned from this trip I bumped into a man at the bar of the Groucho Club who was known by everybody as 'Dr Sleep'. I assumed that he was some specialist drug dealer, but it turned out that he was a big cheese in the world of sleep and had a clinic in Harley Street. I jokingly asked him whether he could cure my snoring. He didn't laugh and told me that it might actually be quite serious, and that I should go and see him.*

*I went to see him a couple of weeks later and he gave me a monitor to wear overnight at home to record my sleep patterns. When I saw him again he had a very serious face on. It turned out that I had sleep apnoea, and very severely at that. The condition meant that I was stopping breathing for periods of up to sixty seconds more than fifty times a night. Not only was this putting strain on my heart and increasing the chances of a stroke but it meant that I was not getting any proper quality of sleep.*

*His diagnosis was tough. I would be in a very bad way health-wise by the time I reached sixty unless I radically changed my lifestyle.*

*The solution? Kick the booze, lose 25 kilos and wear this curious machine on my face every night that forced air into my nose whenever the blockages started.*

*I was in shock at first. Very quickly, however, I realised that I had been given a chance to change. My life has changed completely since that day and I don't think that I've ever felt so present, so alive.*

*In short, snoring is no laughing matter.*

# DAY 13

# AFQA TO AQOURA

In the morning, we were joined by a new local guide called George. He had the look of a rather earnest hippy with a touch of Rasputin to boot. Like many hippies, he appeared to lack that vital organ, a sense of humour. His first impressions of us can't have been good. Harry was sitting outside the house smoking up a storm, while Chris struggled to take his house-sized suitcase down to the steps to the van.

We drove to Afqa, site of the famous grotto and source of the Nahr Brahim. It was one of the great waterfalls of the Middle East (a smallish list, to be fair), situated on a 120-metre bluff that poured into an ice-blue pool of oh-so-swimmable water. The road bridge over the torrent was new, as this was one of five crucial bridges destroyed by Israeli jets in the 2006 Lebanon War. Underneath it, however, were the remains of the ancient Roman bridge. Very nearby were the ruins of the ancient Temple of Aphrodite. There were also traces of the Roman aqueduct that had taken water down to Byblos 1,200 metres below. Hezbollah flags now flew all around the site.

I could have spent all day in a café overlooking the pool, swimming and taking it easy. George, however, was not one for chilling, and we drove a little further up until we reached an army checkpoint. Caroll asked the soldiers whether he could leave the van next to their checkpoint for the day. They must have assumed that he was the world's most polite car bomber. They said no and suggested that we park our explosives in a nearby cherry orchard, well out of blast reach.

After we got out of the van, Harry rolled up a cigarette while I started to plunder the cherry orchard. George had other ideas. He got us in a semi-circle and made us do quite a strenuous stretching session. After we'd looked ridiculous for ten minutes, we set off. Chris was, as ever, keen to find out what lay ahead of us.

'So, George, what is the deal today?' he asked jovially.

'Today? We walk.'

'Yes, well, I gathered that, but what type of walk is it today?'

'Mountain walk. We walk in the mountains.'

'Sorry, George, I don't mean to be rude. I know that we are walking in the mountains but how difficult is the walk today? How long are we walking for?' Chris was just bubbling under.

'Today we walk for maybe nine hours. It is hard, very steep.'

We all slumped into depression. As usual, the truth was never our friend.

We were determined not to let ourselves down in front of George, who clearly thought we were a bunch of idiots, and so we plodded onwards and upwards in the heat of the sun. The view down into the Nahr Brahim valley was astonishing, but we all focused on the boots in front of us in a technique that had had become known as 'Jackying' and marched on.

The path was strewn with loose stones that made our progress even more difficult. After an hour or so, we spotted a tempting ledge that jutted out from the cliff below us. If we could just scramble down onto it then we would have the ultimate

Lebanon shot; a brave hiker surveying the world beneath his feet, the land he had conquered. Harry and I were up for it. Chris wasn't. George didn't think it was a good idea, which made Harry and me even keener.

Clinging onto thin branches, we half slid, half scrambled down through the undergrowth and eventually made it onto the stone ledge. The valley lay below us, a patchwork quilt of villages funnelled into the river valley that disappeared down further steep green cliffs. I wished that everybody could see this view. It would singlehandedly change their entrenched images of Lebanon as this war-torn, tragic place. Harry and I struck a series of majestic poses while Chris took photos from the path.

'This could be the cover shot …' I shouted at Chris. 'Sorry you didn't make it in.'

We clambered back onto the track and continued on up. I put my headphones on and *Script for a Jester's Tear* by Marillion, my musical guilty secret, came on. When Harry and I had been at school, the first three Marillion albums were on constant rotation: *Script*, *Fugazi* and *Misplaced Childhood*. We knew that Marillion weren't cool, but the lyrics and the music were just too good. (I have another guilty secret: *Trigger Happy TV* was named after a Marillion line in 'Jigsaw'.) If you say Marillion to anyone then they normally think of that loathsome song, 'Kayleigh'. Sometimes hit singles kill a band. It's like Stephen Jones, the brains behind Babybird. He is a musical genius plagued by his mega-hit 'You're Gorgeous' but the composer of albums'-worth of dark beauty. The music in Marillion's first three albums, with the exception of 'Kayleigh', is nothing short of spectacular, punctuated by the singer Fish's smart, evocative lyrics. But unfortunately, they looked like a bunch of homeless Yes roadies. This, along with their unrepresentative hit single, meant that they never really got the credit that they were due. If you need a Marillion intro, try 'Incubus' on *Fugazi*. It starts as you'd probably imagine a Marillion song might, a touch pompous and overblown, but hang in there and things start to get rather special from about 1:40 in. The verse that starts at 4:10 is one of my favourite moments in music.

'*You can't brush me under the carpet, you can't hide me under the stairs . . .*'

Anyhow, *Script* came on and gave me a much-needed boost of energy. Soon I was marching past Harry and Chris and then a surprised George, who told me to pace myself.

'We have many distance to go,' he said.

But I could see the summit and had decided that I could make it with the help of Fish and his cohorts. I marched on singing snatches of songs.

'*As you grow up and leave the playground where you kissed your prince and found your frog . . . The rain auditions at my window, its symphonies echo in my womb.*'

I used to know every single lyric to every song. I would wonder why I couldn't learn the words to the poems that I was studying for A levels in the same way. If only Rupert Brooke had joined a prog-rock band. I once quoted a Marillion lyric to my English teacher in an attempt to prove to him that not all rock music was rubbish.

'*Sheathed within the Walkman, wear the halo of distortion, aural contraceptive aborting pregnant conversation . . .*'

OK, looking back it might have been a little forced, but I'll still defend it to my death.

On I walked until, about two hours later, we reached what I took to be the summit. I sat on a rock and took some swigs from my water. We had broken the back of the mountain – I was starting to get this walking business. The others caught up with me.

'Don't rest for too long or it will be difficult to continue,' said George, doing a bit of extra stretching.

'We've done the hard bit, haven't we?'

'No, the hard bit starts now.' He pointed to the left, where a path I had not spotted departed from our track and started to climb steeply up another mountain.

'In two hours we will hit the ridge and then we sit.' George smiled.

I nearly collapsed. Walking was all about being mentally strong and prepared – and I was neither.

The climb was tortuous. My legs ached, my lower back ached, my everything ached. I was still using only one pole as I'd broken the other, and I wasn't sure if it was helping or not. It was surreal how elastic my emotions had become. One moment I was on a high and the world was mine; the next I was dreading every step and physically broken. The only thing that kept me going was taking a look at Chris, who always seemed to look unhappier than me.

We finally summited at 2,000 metres. We came over a grass hillock covered in wild flowers and we were there. Lebanon lay beneath us, the multiple layers of the country exposed, while behind us were the zebra snow strips on Mount Sannine.

We walked along the top of the ridge for a mile or so until we came to a little shrine to the Virgin Mary. There were plastic chairs piled up inside the shrine and we brought them out and sat on the edge to eat our lunch. Chris kept his chair a few metres back from the drop.

George loosened up a little at lunch and was good company. It turned out that he was a teacher by trade, which explained a lot. He told us a joke about Lebanon. When God was making the world, he declared that everywhere would be equal. Once he had finished, however, he was faced with complaints from the angels. Lebanon was clearly way more beautiful than anywhere else, they grumbled. 'Ah, but just wait until you see the people I'm going to put in it,' replied God, smiling.

Caroll said the joke had another ending: 'Just you wait until you meet the neighbours.'

Once we had finished lunch, we headed off again. The walk was easier as the trail went slowly downhill through a series of different landscapes: one moment we were in psychedelically green fields, the next a thin forest of juniper trees and then a plateau peppered with giant rocks. Every corner revealed another more astonishing scene.

I was on my last legs as we entered a little valley full of fruit orchards. We came to a tarmac road and started the final walk down into the village of Aqoura. The hard road hurt my feet but, like a horse that had smelled home, I picked up my pace as I sensed the end of our journey. When we arrived at our guesthouse, we wanted to rush in, throw off our bags and hit the beer, but George had other plans. He made us do a long and elaborate stretching routine that was like some hellish haka. Occasionally, a villager would walk past and try to stifle a laugh at these idiots and their peculiar dance routines.

Finally, George let us go. The guesthouse was delightful, like an Alpine house, all woody and warm with a reassuring smell coming from the kitchen. We sat outside in a garden full of hammocks and daybeds, drank copious amounts of beer and realised that all was well with the world. Even better, my brother-in-law, Michael, had kindly sent up a new pair of walking poles in a taxi from Beirut. I was back in business.

We chatted to our host, who was angry at the way Lebanon was treated on government travel lists. The UK was the only country to have removed Lebanon from the 'Red' list. If you were on this list, then it meant that insurance was nigh impossible and no travel agents would go near the place. This was obviously terrible for the tourism economy. I told him that I hoped that my book might do a little something to counter the situation. George said that it was a shame that our host's mother was travelling, as she was quite the character.

'She knows everything about the area. She knows who shot who, when and why ...'

This was probably the sort of tourist information that was not to everybody's taste, but it was certainly to mine. Supper was a treat. We had an old Lebanese mountain dish, shish barak, that probably originated in Ottoman cuisine as a lot of Turkish food came with a similar yoghurt sauce. It was part of Lebanese Tabeekh, the traditional fare of the mountains, stuff that you would not normally find in restaurants. Shish barak consisted of small meat dumplings cooked in a yoghurt stew. It was perfect – filling, comforting and evocative. I was in a food and beer coma after supper and headed straight for bed. Chris had beaten me to it and was busy ironing his socks.

# DAY 14

# AQOURA TO TANNOURINE

B reakfast was a meal so large that we suspected that it was designed to keep us there for another day. I would have happily done so as the place was so relaxing, like some mountain opium den, sadly minus the opium, which would have helped me get through George's endless stretching routine. Once this was finished, we said our goodbyes. Our destination today was Tannourine, and yet another cedar forest.

As we climbed out of Aqoura, George stopped by a roadside chapel and told us that this was just one of forty in the village. There was a church for each family. People from this village, he said, were pretty entrepreneurial: they used to sell pieces of the 'real cross' to pilgrims. In fact, they sold enough of them to make a forest. They also used to sell land in heaven.

'Those people are now presumably selling bottled water,' chuckled Harry.

We left the village and started climbing out of the valley through orchards, thankful for the shade as the sun was already beating down. We stopped briefly at a spring and dunked our faces into the ice-cold water that came straight out of the mountain. All should have been good. But it wasn't. I hadn't had the sleep of the righteous. I'd had terrible anxiety dreams: about the future, about money, about where my life was heading. I had been in a cocoon, escaping reality since I'd been on this walk, but the real world had suddenly crashed the party and I couldn't keep a lid on it. This was not going to be a good day for me. I'd travelled enough, done enough weird TV shows to know that everybody has a bad day and that the best thing was to try to get through it and to know that tomorrow would be better. Today was going to be a bummer. But I wasn't very good at concealing the fact.

The higher we climbed, the more I got tired; my mental black dog snapped at my heels. It was crazily beautiful, endless wild flowers and great views, but nothing would bring me out of my funk.

As we neared the top of the valley, we suddenly heard a weird sound that we couldn't place. I turned and spotted the source. In the valley below us, flying about 6 metres above the ground, was an army helicopter. The pilot looked left and appeared startled to see us, banking a little too sharply to the right and reducing the gap between his glass cockpit and the ground to about 3 metres. The pilot struggled with the joystick and pulled himself up a little. The chopper lifted and continued up, just making it over a rock that marked the entrance to the pass, and disappeared out of view. It was all rather exciting and briefly got me out of my gloomy mood. But not for long. I was soon way behind the others, trudging up the hill while just longing to just lie down in the soft grass and fall asleep, to wake up on a better day.

I put on my headphones. I thought it best to stay off the Nick Cave. I hit play and 'Bible Belt' by Dry the River came on. I'd come across them when they played this song live on a radio show I was a guest on. It was love at first sound.

*'Darling when the ice caps melt, when the devil's in the bible belt, don't cower in your bed …'*

The power of music to whisk you away from reality, to transform, to heal. I picked up speed and dug in. Far above, the others had stopped and were waiting for me. When I reached them, I could see why they'd stopped, and it hadn't been on my account. We were in a bowl surrounded by mountains. The centre as lush and green as a Cotswold croquet lawn. All around us on the low incline that rose up from the bowl were makeshift targets: cut-outs of people, tyres, sides of cardboard boxes … all riddled with bullets. By our feet lay a carpet of military detritus, remains of RPGs, shrapnel, a couple of mortar bombs, endless cartridges and bullet casings. This was clearly either where locals came to duke it out or an army firing range. Much as I loved the idea of the former, it was indeed a firing range. The sheer amount of ordnance used in this tiny area was phenomenal. It was my idea of a top day out and we started hunting around for military souvenirs, but George was keen to keep us moving as he said that the military didn't like people being there. I popped a couple of large shell casings in my rucksack.

We shuffled out of the bowl and up the track that ran alongside the left of it. It was suddenly very windy, and dust was being blown into our eyes and, for the first time on this trip, I was cold. We reached the top and stopped to look at the view down into the next valley. Once again, the topography changed completely. I was looking down on mist rolling in and out of patches of forest interspersed with the handsome red tiles of traditional Lebanese houses. We started walking down a tarmac road until we could turn on to a track that wound its way past the odd building site. It wasn't the nicest of walks and I could feel black dog scratching hard at the door.

My phone rang; my portal to another life. It was a French girl ringing from the BBC in London. She was interested in doing a story about the recent exposé of French comedy thieves. It had started with French stand-ups translating US routines and doing them word for word in French as though it was their own work. Then a website called CopyComic made a startling film showing a load of my sketches from *Trigger Happy TV* next to almost identical versions of them filmed by the popular YouTuber Rémi Gaillard. People had told me that he'd been stealing my ideas for ages, but I'd just thought that imitation was the best form of flattery. What I hadn't realised, however, was the industrial level and the fact that a whole lot of people thought they were his ideas.

To add insult to injury, Gaillard had recently contacted me out of the blue and suggested that we collaborate. I told him that I would be in Montpellier, where he lived, the following week, so that we could meet up. Then the CopyComic exposé came out and it became clear to me what he was doing. He must have been given a heads-up about it and then contacted me.

I went public and called him out and all hell broke loose. I was assaulted by his fans, claiming I was trying to jump on his bandwagon, and he recorded a series of angry videos claiming that I had stolen all my stuff from Buster Keaton. It was all deeply depressing and, despite being urged to take legal action, I decided to move on. Life was too short.

The French journalist was lovely and said that basic time-frames put Gaillard bang to rights but, like Trump, if you defend a lie strongly enough you dilute the truth.

I gave my version of the story as I walked through the Lebanese countryside; it felt like communicating with another, harsher world. I spent twenty minutes chatting before re-joining the group. They had sensed my mood and, for once, were gentle with me. I appreciated it.

We were now in a field clearly used by hunters. The floor was an inch thick in spent shotgun shells and we crunched our way across this curious Lebanese topsoil.

'Must have been the Cartridge Family,' said Chris to much applause from the group.

We turned down a road and started making our way down into what could well have been the ugliest valley we'd yet walked in. It was not naturally ugly, but somebody had decided to build a concrete dam at the bottom of it despite the rock being porous. The entire surface of the valley was being concreted over to retain the water. It was a clear case of jobs for the boys, and somebody must have got a huge kickback from it. The Lebanese countryside, however, had just received yet another massive kick in the arse. When would they learn?

'Why on earth are we walking here?' I said grumpily.

'It's not the best, George. Are you lost?' added Chris.

'Please wait, you will see,' said George in a patient tone that he presumably always used with recalcitrant brats.

We reached the bottom and found a small stream that we hopped over before climbing back up and then inching along a narrow path under the cliff face that put Chris into a proper mood. Now he and I were moping, and the atmosphere was pretty poisonous except for Harry, who was emotionally tone deaf and very happy just walking along smoking. We finally passed by the construction and descended into a smaller valley where there were no sounds of construction.

'This is why we are here.' George grinned as he approached a set of stairs leading steeply downwards to we knew not what.

'This is Baatara waterfall, a sinkhole, with three natural bridges and a waterfall into a cave.' He looked so pleased with himself that I feared that he might have oversold the attraction.

He hadn't. It was breathtaking. From a viewing platform, we looked down into the sinkhole, covered in thick green moss. A large hole at the top allowed a river to pour water 250 or so metres down through the middle of this natural sculpture. Just to increase the surreal nature of the scene, an opera singer dressed in a massive white wedding dress was standing in the middle of the largest stone bridge and miming to some track for an attendant video crew. The music drifted up and we all stood, speechless, taking in this unexpectedly magnificent scene. It really was a natural wonder of the world.

'How does nobody know about this country?' said Harry, who had already pulled out his binoculars to have a closer look at the singer.

'Unfortunately, the place has been bought by a dentist with very little taste,' a local standing next to us said out of the blue.

'He is adding zip-lines, ugly bars and other unnecessary attractions. This is beautiful on its own. It should stay that way, but it is all about money.' The man sighed and wandered back up the stairs.

We all wondered what grudge he had against the dentist that

made him come down and grumble to every visitor who arrived on the viewing platform.

'She's quite a looker.' Harry was still focused in on the heaving bosom of the opera singer.

'Maybe it's the dentist's wife,' I said as we made our way back towards the steps.

George took us back up to the ugly bar run by the dentist. He had clearly sunk all his money into this venture because his staff had borderline comedy teeth. We tried not to stare as they brought us beer and snacks. George had further news.

'So, I was not going to mention this until now, but there is a very steep crossing ahead. How do you feel about this, Chris?' George smiled.

'How steep?' said Chris, panic filling his eyes.

'Very steep,' replied George.

'Then I feel very badly about it, to be honest, George.' Chris was bubbling under again.

'I'm sorry but I thought you would be upset if I mentioned it earlier,' said George.

'You'd be right there ... although I'm feeling equally upset about it now.' Chris's whistle was about to blow.

'So, what shall we do?' said George.

I knew I had to step in as Chris was about to lose it. I also saw a way for me to end my funk day early.

'I'm not feeling too good myself. George, why don't you and Harry continue down towards the village and we will take the van there with Caroll?' I said.

'What? I smell laziness and cowardice,' said Harry, who wasn't helping matters.

'I'm up for that,' said Chris.

'Good. Well, that's sorted. Harry, you carry on and we'll meet you at the end. It's only another half an hour's walk.' I instantly felt better.

It was the right decision, but we would now have to live with the fact that Harry had walked for half an hour longer than both of us, and he would never let this lie.

'All right, the men will continue on … the ladies will drive to the end.' Harry was often still stuck in the 1970s in terms of political correctness.

Chris and I clambered into Caroll's van and we drove down into the lower part of Tannourine, a beautiful village split into two levels over a series of valleys and ravines. The name Tannourine came from the fact that the village was laid out in a convex shape, similar to an oven called a *tannoor*.

The following day we were going to walk through Lebanon's largest cedar reserve, a forest encompassing some sixty thousand trees. But I couldn't bear to think about more walking. I wanted nothing more than some food and then to curl up in bed with a good book. I was reading *A House of Many Mansions* by Kamal Salibi, an essential book if you want to try to understand the make-up and political intricacies of Lebanon. Salibi undertakes a tough ask: to examine the myths that competing Lebanese factions use to bolster their differing views of Lebanon's future.

We hung around in the centre of the village until Harry and George joined us. Harry was predictably annoying.

'Well, you two just missed the best scenery of the whole trip, a stunning canyon, such a shame that you missed it, but I guess some people just can't hack it.' He grinned and lit up a cigarette.

We ignored him. Caroll drove us all to the top part of the village and parked outside what looked like a building site.

'This looks nice,' I said sarcastically.

'It might be when it's finished,' added Chris.

'Will you two stop grumbling?' said Harry. He had a point.

There was no front door, so we entered through a breeze-block gap and walked up to the first floor, where there had been some attempts to make the place habitable. It was very cold – we were high up, about 2,000 metres – and the weather had turned. It was starting to rain, and dark clouds obscured the world below us. The place had the feel of a budget hotel on a cold winter break in Torremolinos in the late 1970s. There were many buildings dotted around the mountains where only one floor had been developed and the rest sat unfinished. I couldn't work out why until George explained it to me.

'Many parents build the house, get their own floor finished and then hope that their children will come back from the city and build their own flats on the other floors.' It made sense when you looked at it like that, but it was always so ugly.

Our home for the night got even weirder when we discovered some stairs that led down to a basement. It was decked out as a dining room with long tables and chairs plus a small kitchen. The walls were adorned with loads of framed photographs of a blonde woman, possibly slightly too old to be posing in the manner that she was. I recognised her but it took me a while to remember her name. It was Dalida, a French-Italian-Egyptian singer-actress, who found fame in the late 1950s and sold over 140 million records, almost all of them unspeakably awful. She committed suicide in the mid-1980s. Imagine a more exotic Cilla Black. The owner of the guesthouse had been a fan of Dalida and thought that it might be fun to have her as the theme for the establishment. She was dead wrong.

We sat and ate bowls of mujaddarah (a blended mixture of cooked lentils, rice and fried onions, which is better than it sounds) in the empty dining room. It was so cold that we couldn't stay there for much longer and we all soon retreated to our bedrooms and huddled under blankets. Outside, all hell was let loose when a ferocious storm shook the building in quite a magnificent fury.

# CEDARS OF THE LORD

I was first up. The storm clouds had cleared, both outside and inside my head. Black dog would not be joining us today. I felt good. I had a cold shower and dressed. I entered what passed for a sitting room, checking out the view that had been denied us the night before. I could see the cedar forest beneath us and, when I opened the window, I was hit by the sweet smell of damp cedarwood. Mount Lebanon had taken a serious shower and was now cleansed and awaiting our arrival. Chris woke up and joined me. I could see him subtly checking out my mental state.

'Morning, maestro . . . good sleep?' he probed.

'Yes, excellent. I slept right through the storm.' I knew what he was up to and exaggerated my good mood.

'How are you feeling . . . generally?' he parried.

'Generally, very good. Can't wait to get cracking today.' I broke into a big fake smile.

'Right, so . . . no . . . more sad feelings today?' This was his final attempt.

'Nope, raring to go, happy as Larry.' I smiled as his face fell.

It was clear that he did not fancy walking today, especially as George had told us that it was a particularly arduous section. But Chris would have to lead the attempt to bunk off and could not now use me as the excuse. Just then, a terrible howl of pain came from Harry's room. Chris's face lit up again.

'Oh, that sounds bad . . .'

Harry's door flew open and he staggered into the room clutching his knee and grimacing. He fell onto the sofa and started writhing in agony.

'How was your night, Harry?' I asked jovially.

'The worst night of my life. I haven't had a minute's sleep. My knee keeps sending out shooting pain through me. It's utter agony.' Harry tensed up and screamed in pain again.

This was serious. Harry had an extraordinary pain threshold and was normally troubled by very little. Chris was trying to stop looking too happy.

'What do you think it is?' he asked.

'Something in my knee, it's like really painful cramp. It's indescribable,' Harry moaned.

'Do you think you can walk on it today?' Chris asked, knowing this was the big one.

'Not a chance. I can't even move.' Harry screamed again, and Chris turned his head away, but I saw him do a little victory punch to himself.

George came in and asked Harry what was wrong. They had a little discussion and then George said he thought that he could fix it by massage.

'Are you sure that's wise, George? Are you medically qualified?' Chris was a little bit concerned that he might have Rasputin-like powers and manage to cure Harry, allowing us to start the walk.

'No, but I know about these sorts of injuries. I think I can help.' George unleashed a rather creepy smile.

He knelt down next to Harry, who was still lying on the sofa, and grabbed his leg. Harry screamed in pain. George put his hands round the knee and started to dig his thumbs into the sides. Harry's screams were like nothing I'd ever heard, and the lady cooking our breakfast shot upstairs thinking someone was being attacked.

'George, please ... please stop doing that ...' Harry had tears coming down his cheeks. Chris and I were stuck in limbo-land between horror and amusement.

'Don't worry, relax,' whispered George.

'I will, if you stop hurting me,' said Harry with an urgency that I hadn't heard before. This was a man who I'd once pulled from a dock on to a hidden rock with a speedboat as he attempted to mono-ski from land. He was very badly injured but insisted on continuing to ski despite blood pouring out of his side.

'Just be patient ...' whispered George.

'AAAAAAAARRRRRGGGGGGGGGGHHHHHHHHHHHHH,' screamed Harry.

I started to wonder whether George might have had some other career before being a teacher; maybe something in the interrogation field? He appeared to be amazingly relaxed about inflicting great pain on Westerners. After about five minutes of this, George took his hands off Harry's knee. There was almost a 'pop' as his thumbs were extracted from somewhere deep inside the joints.

'Does that feel better?' said George.

'Well, the fact that you have stopped causing me extreme pain feels better, yes,' gasped Harry.

'Do you think you will be able to walk today, Harry?' Chris was ruthless.

'No ... not a chance. I can't even stand up at the moment,' Harry groaned.

'OK ... well, that's a shame but it is what it is. George, I think we clearly will have to cancel the walk today and make other plans.' He was so good I almost believed his apparent disappointment.

But George had other ideas.

'We can do the walk without Harry. Caroll can take him on to tonight's guesthouse. It would be criminal to miss the Tannourine cedars.'

Chris, who had seen quite enough cedars for a lifetime, panicked as he saw his day off being ruined.

'I'm sorry, George, but we are a team and we walk as a team. If Harry doesn't walk, then we don't walk.' Chris was giving it his best Englishman-abroad shtick.

'But yesterday Harry walked alone,' said George.

'Yes but ... that was different ... if Harry doesn't go we don't go.' Chris looked to Harry for support.

'Honestly, Chris, I don't want to stop you guys walking. Go without me and I'll join you tonight.' Harry knew what was up.

I stepped in.

'George, I think it's a real shame that we will miss the Tannourine cedars, but I think it's best we all stay together and do something else today.' I could feel Chris breathe a sigh of relief next to me.

'OK ... but I do not understand,' said George, quite rightly confused at three people who had paid to walk in the mountains and who appeared not to like walking or mountains.

We helped Harry down to the basement for a chilly breakfast. There were French windows out onto a terrace overlooking the forest. All of Harry's socks, pants and walking clothes were hanging on the railing, soaking wet. For some reason he had finally done some laundry and decided that putting them out in a storm to dry would be a good idea. It was the final straw; there would be no walking today.

We had a conflab, and it was decided that there were enough things to visit in the environs. We would have a day as tourists. I'd never seen Chris so happy. For Harry, however, things were going from bad to worse. He'd been seated awkwardly with his leg propped up on another chair. With much pain, he had rotated the chair so that his body now blocked any attempt by George to do any further 'treatment'. All Harry wanted was a bowl of his beloved Choco Pops. With the reverence of a nurse delivering penicillin, the box was brought from his room and placed upon the table by Caroll.

Harry asked for milk. A jar of what we thought was Coffee-mate, unaccountably a Lebanese favourite, was brought to the table. Harry mixed the contents with water and started eating his Choco Pops. He promptly semi-threw up on the table. It turned out that what Caroll had thought was Coffee-mate was actually a jar of yeast. This was not going to be Harry's day.

We left our building site with few regrets. Chris and I helped a distinctly jaded Harry into Caroll's van, and we set off on our unexpected coach trip. We drove through George's home village, Hadath el Jebbeh, which was a Maronite village that overlooked the bottom end of the legendary Qadisha Valley, a place that everyone had kept going on about as being the destination we should be looking forward to the most. I felt bad that I knew so little about what was clearly a very important place for the Maronites among whom I'd grown up.

We stopped at the edge of the village and got our first glimpse of the valley. We'd seen many valleys since we'd started this trip, but nothing had prepared us for this. It was more of a giant gorge than a valley. At the top end, the Qadisha River started its journey down into the Mediterranean in Tripoli, a predominantly Sunni city where the same river was renamed the Abu-Ali. Both sides of the valley were unbelievably steep and deep with a fertile base around the river below. It looked like somebody had delivered a mighty blow to the land with a giant axe, creating a deep and jagged scar through it. In a land that was not short of geographical big hitters, this was the daddy.

The valley was riddled with caves and had been a refuge for the early Maronites when escaping persecution, first from the Mamelukes (a Muslim Sultanate based in Egypt that held power between 1250 and 1517) and then the Ottomans. Almost directly beneath where we were standing was one of the most inaccessible of these: a spot where Maronites from George's village had hidden to escape the Mamelukes who, between 1250 and 1289, had launched a series of assaults against the region as a precursor to trying to conquer the surviving Crusader state of Tripoli, a thorn in the side of the Muslim world. In 1991, Lebanese speleologists and archaeologists including Paul Khawaja, the man who so doubted that I could walk the walk, had climbed down to the cave and discovered eight well-preserved Maronite mummies dating from AD 1283. These mummies were now in the museum in Beirut and, had we not been drunken fainéants, we would have seen them. It was the story of my life.

Many people had come to the Qadisha Valley to make use of the caves for religious retreat. There was a famous hermit living in one of the caves right now, said Caroll. He was called Dario Escobar and was from Colombia.

'Does he receive visitors?' said Harry.

'Yes, for a hermit, he is quite sociable. In fact, he has quite the reputation as a bit of a ladies' man,' Caroll grinned.

'I heard that there was a French hermit in the valley,' said Chris.

'No, I don't think so,' replied Caroll.

'Hermit the frog . . .' Chris awaited his applause. Harry and I were both amused but, thankfully, it went over the heads of our Lebanese friends.

We drove down along the southern ridge of the valley until we reached Dimane, the site of the summer residence of the Maronite Patriarch. It was a huge stone building with the traditional red-tile roof and it sat on the edge of the valley into which Maronites had long descended to hide from persecution. We helped Harry hobble down to a little gazebo perched right above the drop into the valley way below. The view was out of this world. I couldn't wait to get down and explore, although I couldn't help distorting the old adage: 'what goes down must come up'. At some stage we were going to have a hellish climb.

We explored the palace, ending up in the main chapel, which was as sumptuous as the finest in Europe. My eye was caught by a large painting on the right-hand side of the chapel. It was a local interpretation of Rembrandt's *The Stoning of St Stephen*, about a young Christian deacon in Jerusalem who was sentenced to death by stoning on the outskirts of the city. It was pretty graphic: the old women and children all joining in gleefully to smash massive stones onto the prostrate body of poor St Stephen.

'I presume this is a traditional local greeting to hikers?' Harry laughed and turned to Chris for approval.

Chris, however, was not with us. He was standing in front of the steps leading up to the altar and looking very sombre.

'I didn't know Chris was a God-botherer,' whispered Harry to me.

'Me neither.'

We both watched as Chris climbed the stairs slowly, his eyes fixed on the altar ahead of him. He approached it and, after hesitating a second, moved the large candle a touch while muttering something to himself. He retreated from the altar and descended the steps. We wandered over to him.

'Well, now you tell us,' I said.

'Tell you what?'

'That you're a friend of Jesus.'

Chris looked confused for a second and then laughed.

'Oh ... no, it was my CDO. The candle wasn't centred properly, and it was really doing my head in.'

We exited the chapel, Chris's 'CDO' sated and Harry hobbling like a medieval beggar. For once I was almost the normal one.

We drove along the southern ridge until we reached the top of the valley where both sides met at the base of the mountains. We entered the village of Bsharre, a place infamous for its Maronite militancy. It was the birthplace of a well-known Maronite warlord, Samir Geagea, the only Lebanese leader to be imprisoned for war crimes in the civil war until his pardon in 2005. His picture was posted all over the place, as was that of his wife, who was the new member of parliament for the area. The most famous son of this village, however, was Khalil Gibran, the renowned poet and artist, perhaps most well-known for his book *The Prophet*. I was surprised to discover that Gibran was still the third bestselling poet of all time after Shakespeare and Lao-Tze, the founder of Taoism. In Lebanon he was a literary hero, but I was pretty sure that few Westerners knew that he had emigrated to the USA as a young man and that *The Prophet* had been written in English. I certainly hadn't. He lived in Boston and died young, at forty-eight, of cirrhosis of the liver. I was ashamed that I knew very little of his work and was keen to visit his museum.

The museum was housed in a building that used to be the monastery of Mar Sarkis, dating back to the seventh century. It had been bought by Gibran's sister for the express purpose of housing a museum to her brother. The building was similar to the other monasteries in the valley, built right into the cliff, half cave, half building.

It was a warren of little whitewashed rooms and, having paid the entrance fee, we had the place to ourselves. For the most part, it contained his paintings and drawings, which, to my untutored eye, were underwhelming. In fact, lacking a deep love of Gibran as we did, the whole museum left us all a little 'meh'. The most memorable bit was when we descended some steps into a damp cave/room in which we unexpectedly discovered Gibran's actual coffin. We stood in semi-darkness staring at the musty coffin, all lost in thought. Eventually we trooped out of the museum into the sunlight and to an expectant George.

'Did you enjoy?' asked George.

'It was all very nice, but I'd have preferred something like a Meccano museum,' said Harry.

There was a terrible silence. There was nowhere to go from there. George tried to save the situation. 'Gibran hated religion after a priest once told his parents, "Don't educate him, you won't be able to control him." It put him off it for life.'

'That's all very well, George, but I'd still have preferred some Meccano.' Harry lit another roll-up and we helped him into the van.

We drove up and through Bsharre to the base of the high mountain above the village. This was the Cedars ski station, Lebanon's oldest ski resort. People had been skiing here since the 1920s even though the first ski lift was only installed in 1953. Now it had a six-person gondola and three chairlifts to take you to the top of the slope at 2,870 metres, before you skied down into the natural basin. It was pretty decent skiing and, as a kid, I'd learned to ski there as well as at two other resorts, Zaarour and Faraya. If I had a pound for every time I had to convince dumbfounded people that I'd learned to ski in Lebanon, then I'd be a moderately rich man. I have fond memories of buying ham and cornichon sandwiches, wrapped in silver foil, from this sandwich store in Brummana opposite the High School before driving up to one of the ski resorts along with one of my brothers or sisters, getting my first glimpses of independence from my parents. I would tag along with them and listen to their conversations with friends in the slope-side bars, soaking it all in, this strange outside world that I was soon to stumble into.

There had been a snowstorm the night before and the slopes had a very light dusting of snow, although not enough to ski on. The season lasted between November and early April and we were now in May. I could see some proper snow up on the top of the mountain. I really need to do a thing on weird skiing places: Afghanistan, Kashmir, Lebanon, Morocco, Kazakhstan and Iran (where I'd gone to ski in *The Dark Tourist*). But by the time I get around to it, it will be on Netflix ...

We drove up past the resort. An army roadblock checked cars going any further as the road went over the pass and down into the Beqaa Valley. They let us through and we climbed until we reached the pass. The satnav showed that we were at 2,590 metres, and there was a thick bank of snow on each side of the road. The pass was often closed by snow until June and so we were lucky to be able to get access. We hopped out of the van and had a snowball fight. It was insane: an hour and a half from here and we could be sitting on a beach in the sun.

We drove back down to the resort and parked next to the rear entrance to visit the Arz ar-Rabb, the Cedars of the Lord. This was a little area of massive old cedars that had been saved by Queen Victoria. She had heard about the rapid depletion of the cedar forests of Lebanon and paid for a high stone wall to be built to surround the 250-acre site in order to protect them.

Despite this, British soldiers still hacked down cedar trees during the First World War to build railroads. This reminded me of Emperor Hadrian (a man not unfamiliar with walls himself), who, aware of the exploitation of the cedar by the Phoenicians, Egyptians, Assyrians, Babylonians, Persians, Israelites and Turks, issued a decree declaring the forests as an imperial domain and that nobody was to cut the trees down. This was still seen as some form of early conservation ideal but, actually, Hadrian just wanted the exclusive use of the wood for the Roman Empire.

We entered the grove, having given an old man at the gate some money. It was a truly special place; perhaps, compared to the wilder areas we'd walked through, a little manicured and with a touch too many tourists (there were four), but you could not deny the power of these trees to impress. It reminded me of walking through forests of redwoods in northern California. Trees such as these form natural cathedrals infinitely more impressive than anything man could build.

We wandered up and down the well-maintained paths with Harry hobbling along like a grandpa. We stopped by a dead tree, killed by what George rather sweetly called 'thunderlight'. As I stared at it, I started to hallucinate and see images of Jesus on the trunks and branches. I assumed black dog was back. But I wasn't hallucinating. A local artist, Rudy Rahme, who spent five years carving rather beautiful images of Jesus into dead wood, had used the tree as a canvas. I suppose it passes the time.

There was so much cedar fever in Lebanon that we started to feel a little sorry for the other trees in the country. As we left through the main entrance, I almost hoped to see a massive banner on the wall opposite proclaiming, 'CEDARS ARE SHIT – this banner is brought to you courtesy of the Pine Trees of Lebanon.' Sadly, there was no such banner and we sat in the unsurprisingly named Café des Cèdres and ate lunch. The sun burst free of the clouds and lit up the Cedars of the Lord. It was oddly awe-inspiring. The cedars of Lebanon had still got it.

After lunch and some half-hearted shopping for cedar-related tourist knick-knacks we drove back down to a village on the southern side of the Qadisha Valley and checked into a hotel. It was a very basic hotel but definitely a hotel, not a guesthouse, and this cheered Chris up no end. Then he saw his room and reverted to his usual accommodation funk. Harry had taken some painkillers and was falling asleep at reception, so we helped him up to his room and left him to sleep.

That evening Caroll, Chris and I had supper. George had returned to his village, bewildered by his unruly class of Brits. Supper consisted of unbelievably garlicky roast potatoes covered in coriander plus a chicken and spelt-wheat soup. It was simple and delicious.

Halfway through the meal, Caroll received a call on his mobile. He answered and then, after a moment, passed it to me. It was a British guy who was working on some project in the mountains. He had seen online that I was in Lebanon and had spotted the hotel in Byblos in one of my photos. He'd rung the hotel, and they'd given him Caroll's number. He wondered, if I was still in Byblos, whether I fancied going out for a drink? It was all a bit random, but I admired his chutzpah.

I told him that, sadly, we'd left Byblos. I said goodbye and handed back the phone to Caroll. I think he was a little confused as to why strange men were ringing his phone to ask me out for drinks. But, to be fair, I think Caroll was a little confused by pretty much everything about us – our disinterest in walking, our peculiar relationship, Chris's closeness to a small bear, the way we shouted 'WILD BOAR, WILD BOAR' every time the animal was mentioned ...

I longed to be a fly on the wall when Caroll came to tell one of his friends about the trip. I just prayed that he wasn't tempted to write a book about the experience.

# TRIPOLI

M orning came with the sound of Chris knocking on the door. He was in a great mood as Harry's knee was better, but it seemed unlikely that it was good enough to walk on. We all trudged downstairs for breakfast. Harry still looked a little rough.

'You don't look great, Harry,' said Chris cheerfully.

'Yeah, you look like the Six Million Lira Man,' I said, referencing *The Six Million Dollar Man*, a US show I used to watch avidly on Lebanese TV.

'I actually changed my smile when I was a kid so that I smiled like Lee Majors,' said Harry in what immediately went straight in at number one in the 'weirdest things said on walk' charts. We didn't really know where to go with that and so left it hanging. So Harry, so odd.

Lebanese TV had been a very odd thing to watch as a kid. It was mostly American series such as *Charlie's Angels* and *Eight is Enough* along with a plethora of cartoons such as *The Flintstones* and *Scooby Doo*. Most shows were shown in 'VO' (Version Originale), and not dubbed. They would have subtitles, however, in both Arabic and French. Each language would have a totally different interpretation of what was going on, often utterly misguided. People would react to events at different times depending upon which language they were following the show in. The only comedy show I remember was the fairly execrable *Benny Hill Show*. Whoever did the subtitles for this show often just gave up and everybody just watched Mr Hill being pursued by women in underwear in speeded-up time. Some things needed no translation, although an explanation would have been useful.

The group decision was that Harry was still not fit to walk, so we would drive down to the coast and visit Tripoli, Lebanon's second city and, from memory, a bit of a dump. But I was prepared to be wrong. As we set off, Harry brought us up-to-date with his bowel movements, which was a massive relief as both Chris and I hated being kept in the dark about these matters. As we descended towards the flat plain behind the city, we were surrounded by fields of olive trees. I learned something obvious from Caroll that I had never known before. Green and black olives are the same, it's just that the black ones are picked later. Not for the first time, I felt like a complete idiot.

We made a detour to visit yet another abandoned Roman temple, this one at Ain Akrine. It had clearly been an impressive sight when whole. Time, earthquakes and looters had whittled it down to a shadow of its former self, but it was still well worth a visit. It must have made a lovely stopover for travellers between Baalbek and Tripoli who wished to rest and make some form of offering for the trail ahead. Given that we were in a van, we didn't really see any need. We hit the coast at a place called Anfeh, south of Tripoli. Caroll was keen that we stop as he had family there. We agreed. We drove down to the sea and left Caroll having a shouting match with a fully suited-and-booted

Greek Orthodox priest over one of the rare parking spaces. We were unsure if he was family or not.

We scuttled around a graveyard and suddenly found ourselves transported to a whitewashed corner of what could have been a blissful Greek island. A series of huts, each with chairs and access to the sea, was huddled together like some beach-boy refugee camp. We chose one and sat under a parasol as the owner brought us cold beers and a plate of fried octopus mixed with parsley and lemon. It was beyond heaven and talk soon shifted to cancelling the visit to Tripoli and staying here for the day. I was pretty sure that Tripoli was still what Trump would describe as a 'shithole', but then I rather like shitholes.

'Maybe we can come here to celebrate when we finish the walk,' I suggested.

This was a popular suggestion and so we finished our octopus and moved on. On our way back to the van, we went to have a look at the small peninsula upon which had once sat the Crusader fortress of Nephim. It was separated from the mainland by two manmade trenches, filled with seawater, that had served as defensive moats. It had once been a major Crusader site but there was almost nothing left of it as the stone had all been stolen for buildings in the town.

We got back to the van. The priest was still there, standing next to his car, and gave us a death stare as we drove away. We headed the 15 kilometres up the coast to Tripoli, whose name came from the ancient Greek *Tripolis*, meaning 'three cities'.

'We're on a daytripolis to Tripolis,' I said to a silent van.

Ahead of us, the city jutted out into the Mediterranean on a large promontory. It was not what it once was. When Lebanon became independent, it lost out to Beirut as well as losing a lot of trade with Syria to the north. The city of Tripoli is conjoined with the seaside town of El Mina, the site of the ancient Phoenician city, of which nothing remains. We entered the city proper and encountered beautiful, chaotic traffic: cars, vans, buses, taxis came at you from every direction, beeping, honking, revving, screeching, with no quarter given or taken. I weirdly love this kind of chaos, but it's never the sign of a well-functioning city.

We stopped by the Mansouri Great Mosque. It was a Mameluke mosque built in around 1300 among the remains of the Crusader Church of St Mary. Tripoli had more Mameluke architecture than anywhere outside Cairo. The mosque was stunning inside and quite full of worshippers. One man in particular stood out as he was spectacularly lit by a lone beam of sunlight from a small window halfway up one of the old stone walls. It was a timeless scene and could have come from an old painting. Once back outside I realised that I'd played a blinder by having chosen to wear some bright red loafers. I easily reclaimed my shoes from the pile left outside. Harry and Chris took a lot longer and I suspected that Harry might have taken the wrong shoes, but I kept quiet.

We moved on through the city until we got to the Corniche el Mina, a tired-looking seaside road but full of people taking in the sea breezes and watching their kids drive around in a bunch of mini electric cars that you could rent. It was a pleasant enough atmosphere, but aesthetically dull. We drove down the Corniche and then turned back on ourselves and headed for our destination, the legendary Abu Fadi, Malek Samke Harra (the King of Spicy Fish). This was a very well-known eatery, so popular that I knew people who would go on a road trip from Beirut to eat there. We went in and ordered three spicy fish sandwiches. Harry decided to pass.

'Why don't I referee? Last one to keep everything down wins a car.' He chuckled at his own wit, but we were ignoring him, too busy tucking into our sandwiches while sitting on plastic chairs on the pavement outside.

It was seriously spicy stuff, something that I happened to love. You have to be careful when ordering spicy food in Arabic. One of my fave things to order in a Lebanese restaurant is 'batata harra' – potatoes cooked in olive oil, with red peppers, coriander, chilli and garlic. The word '*harra*' means spicy or hot. The word for shit, however, is '*khara*'. Harden the pronunciation of the 'h' to sound like the end of the word 'loch' and you could be in trouble. I had often unwittingly ordered shitty potatoes, much to the amusement of waiters, until somebody had kindly explained the subtle difference. I was fairly sure that we hadn't ordered shitty fish sandwiches and that Abu Fadi himself was not the King of Shitty Fish, but you could never be too careful . . .

I looked out to sea. Just offshore was the site of a major British naval disaster. On 22 June 1893, just two years after my great-grandfather Ernest had arrived in Lebanon, the bulk of the British Mediterranean Fleet was on exercises off the coast of Tripoli. In charge was Vice-Admiral Sir George Tryon, a man known to like to keep his crews battle-ready by testing them with sudden complex fleet manoeuvres managed by a system he had developed called TA, in which elaborate commands could be conveyed by only a few simple signals. Unfortunately, things went very wrong and, during an attempted synchronised manoeuvre, HMS *Victoria* was accidentally rammed and sunk by HMS *Camperdown*, with the loss of 358 lives, including Tryon himself.

'What's for pudding?' asked Harry, interrupting my reverie.

'We are going to Halim 1881,' said Caroll.

I was chuffed with this as Halim 1881 is probably the most famous sweet restaurant in the country and was already in business before the *Victoria* was sunk. I don't have a particularly sweet tooth, but I'd always wanted to visit the place. We got a table and soon it was loaded with plates of sticky baklava and cups of strong Turkish coffee. When we finally waddled out we were in the mood for a siesta, but we struggled on and headed for the old souks. These lay just underneath a large hill, the Alawite area of the city, which had given refuge to many ISIS fighters until the Lebanese Army finally forced them all out.

The souks were bustling, and bursting with counterfeit sportswear, racy underwear and foodstuffs. I particularly enjoyed seeing the beautiful old caravanserai that was now in quite a dilapidated state. Somebody with some imagination could have made a wonderful hotel out of the place and restored it to its original function of welcoming travellers to the town. It was much needed.

We then climbed up to the Crusader fortress, the Citadel of Raymond de Saint-Gilles, the largest in Lebanon. Outside sat four bulky armoured personnel carriers along with a heavily armed bunch of soldiers who looked at us suspiciously.

'What are you doing?' asked a soldier.

'Going to look at the castle,' I replied.

'Why?'

'Because it's there,' I answered a little cheekily.

'You are tourist?'

'God no, we are travellers.'

'Ahlan-wa-sahlan,' he said, waving us through with his M16.

We walked through the gatehouse, whose vast wooden doors were wedged open and currently welcoming to visitors. We were the only people there. We climbed up to the very top and got a magnificent view of the whole of Tripoli for our efforts. I watched as, far below, an old man in a white vest and pyjama trousers repeatedly chased a flight of pigeons off his roof with the use of a broom. The pigeons would swoop about above the neighbourhood until the old man went back inside, at which point they would all immediately settle back down on his roof. Neither the old man nor the pigeons would surrender, and the process played itself out over and over again like some infinite loop. Lebanon was never short of visual metaphors.

Having 'done' the citadel, we walked back through winding streets down to the banks of the Abu Ali River and found Caroll in his van. We drove out of the city and back into the surrounding mountains. We passed through Zghorta, ancient home of the Franjieh family, one of the most prominent Maronite families in the north. Suleiman Franjieh had been the Lebanese President when the civil war broke out in 1975. During the war, his son Tony and Tony's wife and infant daughter were murdered by a Phalangist death squad at their summer home in Ehden. The assassins were led by our old friend Samir Geagea from Bsharre, who was himself injured in the attack. The surviving son of murdered Tony, called Suleiman Franjieh Jr, had just stepped down from being MP for Zghorta so he could try to run for President. The newly elected MP? His son, Tony Franjieh ... Still with me?

The town was packed with well-wishers lining up outside the family compound to congratulate and press the flesh with the new Franjieh scion. I couldn't help but remember how Robert Fisk, the legendary foreign correspondent who lived in Beirut, had described the new MP's great-grandfather, Suleiman Franjieh: 'Christian warlord, mafioso, militia strongman, grief-stricken father, corrupt president, mountain baron and, eventually, a thoughtful, intelligent, rather frightening old man, living out his last years beside the lions of Ehden.'

We crawled through the traffic of well-wishers and briefly toyed with the idea of joining the queue to see what happened. I think we made a good call in not doing so.

We drove on, out of Zghorta and up to our destination for the night, the town of Bsharre from which the assassination squad had set off. Our bed for the night was in a guesthouse called the Tiger House. We soon found out why. It was run by the widow of a well-known Phalangist known as the Tiger. I thought better of asking whether he had been involved in the attack on Franjieh.

It was only late afternoon and so we went for a wander around Bsharre in order to try to find a bar. We found one that sat perched over the Qadisha Valley, where we were finally going as long as Harry was fit the following day. We ordered beers and watched as a village on the other side of the valley started firing machine guns and RPGs into the air.

'Somebody's birthday?' enquired Harry of a local sitting next to us.

'No, maybe election?' answered the guy nonchalantly.

'Happy or angry?'

'Who knows?'

We took in the world-class view along with the 'Lebanese fireworks'. Chris decided to see where we were on the walking front.

'So, Harry, walking tomorrow do we think?' He raised his eyebrows quizzically.

'I should think so, Chris, sorry to disappoint you.'

'Actually, I'm rather looking forward to getting back in my boots,' said Chris.

'Only because it's downhill tomorrow into the valley,' said Harry.

'Fair point.'

Back at the Tiger House we found that Widow Tiger had put more food on the supper table than seemed physically possible. I asked her if we were expecting any other guests. She told me no, and that she expected us to eat it all up. Particularly delicious was a local dish known as *marshousha*, which was made with a plant called dardar (eastern star thistle). The leaves were cooked with onions, bulgur and cumin. It was very simple but so tasty. Widow Tiger was a wonderful hostess, friendly, warm and welcoming. Tiger himself, of whom there were many photos hanging around the house, seemed to be a smiley, avuncular-looking fellow but there was something in his eyes ... a kind of emptiness that I'd seen before in people.

After supper we sat in the communal room heated by a wood-burning stove. As usual in any Lebanese home, the television was constantly blaring away in the corner. Chris seemed a little depressed, as he always did when not in a five-star establishment. He started to browse the internet and I peered over his shoulder to see what he was looking at. It was photos of the first-class lounge in Doha Airport. He just sat and stared longingly at each photo before moving onto the next. He was not a well man.

# BSHARRE TO QADISHA VALLEY

Breakfast was, for Lebanon, a basic affair, made all the worse for Harry when he was informed that, despite this being the Tiger House, there were no Frosties.

'It simply doesn't make sense ...' he kept muttering to himself over and over.

The good news, however, was that his knee was much improved; and that, with a knee support on, he would be able to walk.

Breakfast over, we began our preparations. We filled our CamelBaks with bottled water and some ice-cubes from Widow Tiger and chucked our main bags into Caroll's van. We started the laborious process of smothering ourselves with sunscreen as it looked like it was going to be a scorcher.

As we rubbed the stuff in, Harry's attention was drawn to a jumble of wires that were hanging from a post on the other side of the road. It was as though an electrician had suffered a nervous breakdown and gone rogue. Loose wires, open to the elements, were everywhere. Occasionally one made its way into a central box that appeared to contain individual fuses locked by padlocks.

The national grid, as it is, is very unreliable, often cutting out for more than four hours a day, and so people buy their

electricity from owners of large generators. Harry was astonished at the ramshackle nature of these boxes.

'One downpour and the whole place will short-circuit,' he
said, exploring the set-up gingerly.

'That might account for the power cut during the storm,'
said Chris.

'Oh ... I assumed it was one of your leg-waxing machines
blowing the circuit,' replied Harry, sparking up a cigarette and
looking rather pleased with himself.

Caroll walked over and introduced us to our valley guide, a
local man called Elias who spoke no English. I asked him in
faltering Arabic whether there were any wild animals in the
valley. He said there were wolves, wild boar and even rumours
of a bear. Chris looked a touch nervous at this news. I remembered what we were always told when walking in bear country
in Canada: it was highly recommended that you carry a bell and
ring it vigorously if a bear was spotted. I was walking with a
Christopher Bell, so I told him not to be unnerved if I suddenly
grabbed him and started to shake him. He was not amused.

We started the descent into the Holy Valley by clambering
over a motorway barrier that was there to stop passing cars having
a very bad day. It was almost otherworldly. It felt as if the further
we descended, the further we travelled back into the past. We
inched our way down a vertiginous, centuries-old donkey path.
It was so steep that Chris panicked after the first 300 metres.

'Maestro, this really is not for me. It's far too steep.' He was
dead serious.

'There is another way down, on the other side, where you
can take a car to the bottom,' said Caroll.

'That's the one for me,' replied Chris.

Caroll and Chris disappeared back up the trail, leaving Harry and me to continue down with Elias. About ten minutes later, Elias suddenly came to a stop. In front of him, lying across the path, was a massive black snake sunning itself. If there was anything that Chris hated more than heights, it was snakes. I was glad that he had turned back because the sight of this beast might just have finished him off. Elias tried to move the snake with a stick, to which it took great offence and started hissing menacingly. Eventually, after a bit of posturing, it slithered away into the undergrowth and we continued our descent.

After forty-five minutes, we were nearing the valley floor. We could see Caroll's van winding its way down to meet us.

'Don't tease Chris about this,' I said to Harry.

'Of course not. Not a word,' said Harry, straight-faced.

'I mean it. He'll be very sensitive about it.'

'Yes, we must be very gentle with him.'

A river ran through the valley floor, surrounded by thick foliage. The whole place had the slight feel of *The Land that Time Forgot*. Chris and Caroll crossed the river over a bridge and joined us.

'Hello, Chris, do you need a sit-down? You must be knackered after that, you poor thing.' Harry was ruthless.

'Very funny. Let's crack on,' said Chris as though his entire world was about walking.

'I hope the car seat wasn't too uncomfortable on the way down?'

'It wasn't me who took two days off walking because of my poor little knee.'

'Come on, chaps, let's move on.' I loved being the grown-up.

We followed the trail down the valley for a while and then turned up a track to the right, which took us up to Mar Lichaa, one of the monasteries that were in the valley. It was, like the Gibran museum, built straight into the cliff with the outside wall made of stone and the rear being the cliff face itself. Inside was a series of monastic cells with a communal area. There was also a chapel to the side. I suddenly got a much better idea of what the Citadel of Niha would have looked like and was even more impressed by the people who had built the thing. Above us the valley walls soared upwards like the Wall in *Game of Thrones*. It was easy to see why this valley had attracted people escaping persecution or simply other people.

We re-joined the trail by the river and walked alongside the ever-present plane trees that shadowed the crystal-clear water. Above us waterfalls of all shapes and sizes cascaded down to join the river. Occasionally we would see an abandoned house on the other side of the river. People used to live here until very recently, but almost all had now moved up to the easier life afforded by the villages on top of the cliffs. The walk was easy – flat and beautiful – just what the doctor ordered. We were in fine moods, joshing and laughing. The Downhill Hiking Club were happy to be back on the trail together and not doing too much uphill.

After an hour and a half, we turned off the trail again and climbed up to a still-working convent, Deir Qannoubin. We sat in the soothing shade of a mulberry tree and took in our surroundings while munching on some of Widow Tiger's left-overs and fighting off a multitude of aggressive beggar cats.

The convent was the oldest religious community in the valley and some people dated the building back to the fourth century

AD. There was a musty old chapel that housed a naive fresco of the coronation of the Virgin Mary being witnessed, obviously, by a group of Maronite Patriarchs. This lonely place had been the permanent residence of the Maronite Patriarchs (we could just see the gazebo of the new palace, high above us at the top of the valley) between 1440 and 1790. One of them never left the valley. I wandered into a side room off the chapel to find the preserved body of a dead Patriarch, Joseph Tiyan, lying in a glass case. If I was honest, he didn't look too good. I couldn't help remembering the same look in the preserved body of the philosopher Jeremy Bentham whose body still greeted students entering University College London. Bentham and the patriarch had died only twelve years apart from each other. It must have been the 'in' thing at the time.

As we were about to leave, the convent was suddenly flooded with a school party of bored teens on a field trip from Beirut. It was always astonishing how similar school parties were around the world; the faux insouciance, the annoying outgoing one, the pretty clique, the nerds, etc. They looked at us with deep suspicion. Why on earth would grown men, with all the freedoms that leaving school bestowed on you, choose to come and visit this sort of place? Life moved in slow circles. Once I would have been like them, howling at my parents for bringing me somewhere like this, on one of those long and pointless walks that I would have done anything in my power to get out of at their age. Now I was on one of those walks and keen to know the names of the trees that surrounded us. Time always gets you in the end.

Our next plan was to try to visit Daniel Escobar, the Colombian hermit. I was pretty sure that he was probably on the run from the Medellín cartel and this was some elaborate witness protection programme. However, the fact that he used the surname 'Escobar' put quite a few holes in my theory. It was not often that you met a hermit, for obvious reasons, and I was keen to see what he was like. I had once made a show for BBC1 in which I played a hermit character, all dirty long robes and long grey beard and hair. We filmed him on Exmoor and I would approach people having a picnic and start chatting. The joke, of course, was that he was bored and lonely and really wanted to find out what was happening in *EastEnders*, and what the score was in the test match. People were remarkably un-fased by the sudden appearance of an overly talkative hermit. I wished I'd thought of making him a bit of a ladies' man to boot. 'Sorry to interrupt, ladies, but I was wondering whether you might like to come visit my cave?'

We stopped a wizened old man on a donkey and asked him whether Señor Escobar was in and receiving visitors. It turned out that he wasn't. Apparently, he'd had a spate of visitors recently and wanted to be alone, which, with him being a hermit, was fair enough. I wondered whether he would feel the same if we were three young ladies in tight hiking shorts. But we weren't, and so we would never know. We continued on, hugging the river before the path started to climb a little. We had to stop every five minutes or so just to take in our surroundings. I think the only place I'd been that was more naturally beautiful was Yosemite but that had a hotel where you had to wear a jacket for supper and convoys of RVs puncturing the idyll. Here, you were alone with the hermits. Harry's knee was aching a little but not enough to stop him walking.

'God will heal your knee,' said Elias suddenly.

'Any timetable on that?' asked Harry.

'Maybe we will say a prayer for your knee at the monastery tonight.'

'It's bloody unlucky, Harry,' added Chris.

'Yes,' I replied. 'Imagine having to ask a God you don't believe in to cure you for something you haven't done.'

None of us were religious and, even if we were, Lebanon's fractious history was probably one of the worst advertisements for religion. Not only could I not see the appeal of religion, I never understood the zealous missionary element to it. I would be thrilled for you if you'd found something that worked for you, but why this desperate need to try to make everyone else feel the same way? It's like vegans ... just shut up and get on with it.

Above us the weather was starting to change. Thick, black rainclouds clung to the sides of the cliffs and the valley suddenly became a rather ominous and foreboding place. I felt very small and insignificant as the thunder rumbled and the rain started to hammer down. It felt like we were in a separate ecosystem from everywhere else. You could imagine the sun shining up in Bsharre, but down here in the depths of the Holy Valley, it had all gone a bit Jurassic.

We donned the ridiculous ponchos that we had never been able to put back in their tiny bags. They were awkward to walk with; you couldn't use your poles properly, and after only fourteen days of doing so, I found it difficult to imagine walking without them. Also, we looked like twats. I mean, we already looked amateurish enough walking in our normal gear, but the addition of a poncho was the icing on the Eccles cake.

We trudged on, spirits and clothing much dampened. The path became a lot more treacherous as water started pouring down the slopes and washing away loose stones. We asked Elias how long there was to go. He did the usual Lebanese thing.

'Not long now,' he said.

'How long is not long?' asked Chris from somewhere under his poncho.

'Not long, not long.'

'Yes, but how long?' insisted Chris.

'Maybe three hours,' said Elias.

'That's very long, not "not long" ...' Chris fumed from his plastic wigwam.

'Perhaps four,' Elias said absentmindedly.

I decided to try to harness the holiness of our surroundings. I attempted to empty my mind of thoughts (very easily done) and then started to concentrate on my steps and on my breathing. I slowed down to that peculiar slow-motion gait that felt so unnatural and yet was definitely the most energy-efficient. Step ... step ... step ... step ... step. I broke down the maths. I was doing about 70 steps per minute. Seventy multiplied by 60 was 4,200 steps. If it was worst-case scenario and it really was four hours to go, then it would be 4,200 multiplied by 4, which was 16,800 steps. I started to count them off – 16,800 steps, 16,799 steps, 16,798 steps. This way madness lay.

I started to think about Lebanon. I felt so extraordinarily at home here and yet there was so much that I didn't know. My Arabic was terrible, but I was picking it up so quickly (somewhere in my subconscious lay a massive vocabulary, if only I could access it better).

One of my over-arching memories of the country as a child was fear; fear of my dad being kidnapped, fear of shelling, fear of the gunfire that was constantly in the air, fear of roadblocks, fear of the unseen and constantly shifting enemy – the Druze, the Sunnis, the Shia, the Palestinians, the Syrians, the Israelis – basically whoever happened to be lobbing shells in your direction that particular week. It was a constant fear. It never left you. Sudden noises made you jump. Plans were never cemented. Normality could be stripped away at any time. It was an exciting and adrenalising existence that made everything that we would consider normal pale in comparison. Despite my blocking off and compartmentalising my past, it had always been there somewhere, deep down, my stolen life. It just felt so exhilarating, being in Lebanon on my own terms, making my own memories, on my own expedition that wasn't reliant on tiptoeing around the omnipresent and unspoken disapproval of my father. I'd long ago given up on hoping to change myself to fit whatever projection he had in mind for me that would make him happy. Equally, even if I had decided to try to adapt it was unlikely that he would ever have voiced what it was that he wanted. Indeed, I doubt he actually even knew himself. His death had brought me a certain release. It's a horrible thing to say but it's the truth.

I was dragged out of my reverie by the sight of movement. About a hundred metres ahead of us, just off the path, was a group of four rather scruffy-looking youths in tracksuit bottoms and sweat tops. They were squatting in a little conspiratorial group just above the path, half hidden by a thick bush. I spotted them first and congratulated myself on my razor-sharp defensive reflexes. I had sensed potential danger and was now rapidly analysing the various options available to me. From what I could see they were not armed but there was definitely something not quite right about the situation.

One of the youths stood up and literally pounced from his position to land athletically on the path right in front of us. Was this a robbery? I looked around for a rock to pick up. The youth went for whatever was in his pocket. I tensed. He produced a big bag and proffered it to us. I looked in and it was full of mini-chocolate bars. I couldn't believe it. This pesky path-merchant's business plan was to accost the rare passing tourist hikers and sell them these little chocolates. This sudden insertion of tourist harassment into our holy walk irritated me and I put a firm hand up to indicate that I was not interested and moved past him in such a determined fashion that he very nearly stepped back and over the 200-metre drop below us to his death.

'Just be firm but polite,' I said to Harry and Chris.

They both moved on past the youth. Somebody had to make a stand to show that we were not idiot tourists prepared to buy any old shit after a modicum of pressure. We were travellers and we should never forget this. A couple of hundred metres later, Caroll caught up with us. He was munching on something and had a couple of mini bars in his hand.

'Oh Caroll!' I said. 'You didn't buy stuff off him, did you?' I was a bit disappointed.

'Buy?' Caroll looked confused. 'He was offering us some chocolate, so I took some. They were sheltering from the rain and being nice. They are going to Ehden.'

I felt utterly foolish. I had rudely waved away this youth's generosity and encouraged Harry and Chris to do the same. I had to lose my inbuilt British mistrust of other people's good intentions.

We trudged on, the rain falling even harder and rocks starting to shoot down the steep slopes above and across our path. This was actually getting quite hairy. About half an hour on we came across a pair of fellow hikers huddling under a pine tree. We stopped to chat. They were Belgians and a rather peculiar pair to boot. The man was quite weedy but carrying all their kit whereas the woman was built like a number eight. She was unwisely wearing a long, flimsy summer dress along with what looked like army boots. Her dress was soaking wet; she was shivering and shouting at her boyfriend in Flemish. We asked if we could help. She hurled Flem at her boyfriend again, before he spoke to us in faltering English.

'No ... vank you. Ve are OK,' he said, but his eyes looked odd, as though trying to convey some urgent message.

'Where are you heading to?' asked Caroll.

'I do not know vis. She is the one in control.' He indicated his sodden companion.

She started screaming at him in Flemish again.

'She is unhappy viv ze veather. She iz wery angry.'

He looked defeated.

'Can we help in any way?' said Chris gently.

The man looked quickly at his companion and then back to us, as though ascertaining whether he could get away with asking for a handgun.

'I vink ve vill be OK,' his face saying anything but.

'Enjoy the walk,' I said, smiling sympathetically at the poor guy.

His companion looked at us with unabashed loathing. We walked on as she launched into another verbal assault on him. I started to hum one of my favourite Jacques Brel numbers, 'Ne me quitte pas'.

'Do you miss your Belgian wife, Harry?' I asked, smiling at him.

'More than you could imagine,' said Harry with a poker face.

On the other side of the valley was a deserted old village. I longed to explore it, but the combination of the effort involved along with the ferocity of the rain meant that this was never going to happen. We reached a point at which the valley split. One part (where we were headed) ran north, while the main valley carried on westwards towards the sea. At this split lay a village that we squelched into, trying not to be swept away by a mini-flash flood that raced down the hill alongside us. A couple of cows stared at us dolefully as we trudged past their lovely dry shed.

Cow One: Will you look at these twats?

Cow Two: Wasn't it Noël Coward who said that only mad dogs and Englishmen go hiking in a torrential rainstorm?

Cow One: The actual quote is, 'go out in the midday sun'.

Cow Two: I know that, smart-arse. I was just riffing for effect.

Cow One: Ooh, get you – riffing for effect . . .

Cow Two: Oh do fuck off. Makes a change to hear mad dog rather than mad cow, doesn't it?

Cow One: Too right.

We stopped in the village, hoping that the rain would abate. Anywhere else we would have made for the nearest bar, but this was just a rural hamlet and had nothing like that to hand. So, we made do with standing next to an outdoor fridge that had a loose wire that was arcing furiously in the rain.

'Just to let you know, Chris,' said Harry, 'I hold you entirely responsible for the situation in which I currently find myself. If you hadn't agreed, there's no way I'd have joined Joly on a stupid adventure like this.' He lit a roll-up, which was instantly put out by some water that poured off his hat.

The rain was not going to stop, and after accepting this fact we headed out of the village. To our chagrin we started to climb again. I got quite far ahead so that I could try to capture our unhappiness on my Leica. I got the others to stop and wait until I was ready for them. I shouted 'Go' and they started to climb again. Five seconds after Chris moved an enormous rock smashed down on the exact place that he been standing. I wasn't sure if I had saved his life or put him into a potential death situation by asking him to wait. I decided to go with the saving-his-life scenario, but Chris was past caring. In fact, he hinted that the rock would have been a sweet release.

We climbed for half an hour or so until the path levelled out and we could see down our new valley. At the far end, halfway up on the left, was our destination for the night, the monastery of St Anthony. It was like some kind of Tintin destination. In fact, it reminded me of the monastery that he trekked to in *Tintin in Tibet*. The massive stone building clung to the side of the hill, high above the river, dominating anybody travelling through the valley.

The sight of our bed for the night lifted our spirits and we trudged on with new determination. Chris's mobile rang. It was a cold call from a woman in Liverpool asking whether he'd like to sue someone for the accident that he had apparently recently had. Chris gave the woman shorter shrift than I ever thought possible and the sound of his cursing echoed around the valley to our great amusement.

We finally neared the monastery as evening drew in. The rain had slightly diminished but was still pouring down. We descended to the river and crossed an old bridge before the final climb up to the monastery itself.

As we started up the drive, we passed a large and rather foreboding statue of a monk holding a menacing-looking axe. It was not the friendliest welcome. Fortunately, we were greeted with nothing but smiles in the monastery annexe where we were to stay. A smiling woman produced an unlimited supply of beer and we sat under a little covered terrace watching the rain. We were alone in this vast building. There were no other visitors and no sign of any monks; they were all in the monastery next door and famously anti-social.

Suddenly, there was movement from our right. A very thin, shy little fox appeared from the blackness. We all froze. The fox came closer and stood expectantly in front of me. Harry was munching on a piece of bread. He broke some off and threw it towards the little fox, who snatched it up and started eating it, looking at us in a grateful manner. It was a private moment of communion between wild nature and ourselves. An experience few would ever share . . .

'Boudi!' The smiley lady burst out of the door to greet the little fox. He looked at her guiltily as though he'd been cheating.

She had some food with her that she put down and the fox immediately ignored us and tucked into his supper. There hadn't really been any mysterious bonding going on. We'd just happened to have coincided with supper time for Boudi, the monastery fox. We all sat and watched him eat his supper. His little tail wagged furiously but his eyes never stopped darting about, constantly on the qui vive.

The lady asked us if we wanted to go and see the first printing press in the Middle East, which was in the monastery. Shamefully, nobody could be arsed, but nobody wanted to be the philistine. In the end we just sort of let the idea forget itself in a rather pathetic manner. Harry, Chris, Caroll, Boudi and I sat drinking beer and lost in our thoughts. Suddenly Caroll spoke up.

'So tomorrow I will go back to Germany.'

'Eh?' I said.

'What?' said Chris.

'Is there any more beer?' asked Harry, who never really listened to conversations.

'Yes, I have a group of motorbikers I need to take around Germany.'

'But ... what about us?' said Chris, who was suddenly imagining having to haul his ludicrous suitcase up and down mountains.

'Oh, I have organised for someone else to finish the trip with you.'

We were relieved that we weren't being left in the lurch, but it was still a touch peculiar suddenly to up sticks and bugger off. In fact, the whole set-up with Caroll had been a bit weird from the start. Firstly, we thought that he was a woman living in Beirut, not a bald man living in Germany. Then we assumed that he was just going to organise the itinerary and maybe drive the van. Then he started walking with us, saying he'd do so for a couple of days. Then he did all of it with us. It was either that he thought we were so amateurish he couldn't risk leaving us on our own or that he thought we were such fun that he couldn't not join in ... and now he suddenly announced he was leaving.

I'd actually grown quite fond of him over the trip, but it would also be good to have fresh blood and someone new to grumble to. So, despite the suddenness of the announcement, we raised our beers to him and wished him well. Tomorrow, he said with relish, was a particularly hard day.

'Is that anything to do with having to climb out of the valley?' I asked.

Caroll nodded, and Chris groaned.

It was time for bed and maybe even for a spot of prayer to help us with the following day's climb. It couldn't hurt to try.

# DAY 18

# QADISHA VALLEY TO EHDEN

I awoke to hear the news that Donald Trump had opened the American Embassy in Jerusalem, moving it from Tel Aviv. The Israelis had wasted no time in killing fifty Palestinians, who had demonstrated against the move. Things were heating up fast in our little area of the world.

Harry and I had quite a heated debate about the rights and wrongs of the Israeli–Palestinian situation. This, as anybody who is on social media knows, is a topic that always goes toxic fast and is sadly best avoided. Harry was very anti-Israeli and assumed that I would be too. My stance was something that never went down well either online or in the Middle East – nuance. I was and am anti-extremist on both sides. Just as in the UK, with the Brexit debate, it is the vocal and radical 10 per cent on each side of the debate that are hogging the agenda. The 80 per cent in the middle, who just want to get on with their lives peacefully, have little voice.

If you really want to start to blame people then you could do worse than go back to the post-Ottoman division of the Middle East in 1916 by a couple of pen-pushers – Sykes and Picot – who redrew the entire shape of the Middle East with the stroke of a pen, often totally ignoring existing realities. But the blame-game tends to be a pointless venture. People need to deal with the realities of life on the ground right now and the only way forward is mutual cooperation and communication. Again, just as with Brexit in the UK, both extremes are now so dug into their positions that it is near impossible to find a solution that works for both sides. It has become a question of losing face, pride and, most importantly, memories of past wrongs that are, as in Lebanon, so often the slow-burning fuel of conflict.

Chris joined us after doing some phone business in his room. He looked world-weary. All of us were very aware that this trip was coming to an end, and that we would soon have to leave our bubble and face the real world again. Harry said he didn't want to go home, that we should just keep walking, through Syria, then Turkey and maybe on to Istanbul. We could then do a reverse Paddy Leigh Fermor and walk from Istanbul to London. His seminal travel books, documenting his epic walk from London to Istanbul in 1933–4, are hugely important to me. His beautiful writing about his wandering through a fast-disappearing old Europe is romantic and evocative and, as a teenager in Lebanon, made me long for an adventure of my own. He was the literary equivalent of Tintin in my wanderlust. He was buried not very far from where I live in the village of Dumbleton, in Gloucestershire. I'd gone to visit his grave on a little pilgrimage with my mother. His gravestone had an engraving of a compass on the back of it, which I thought was wonderful.

When we stepped outside, the weather had completely changed; it was a glorious day, transforming our valley from a rather ominous setting to somewhere of staggering beauty. Worryingly, on paper, the walk today was very short, only 9 kilometres. Back in the UK we'd have looked at this and relaxed. Now, as hardened walkers, we knew this meant trouble. This meant 9 kilometres straight uphill.

We put on our packs and were thrilled when Boudi the fox trotted down to say goodbye. How we longed for a dog to accompany us on our travels. I should have borrowed one from my sister Hatty, but it might have upset the delicate political balance of her household.

The trail went directly uphill from the monastery and did not relent for a second. It was more scrambling than hiking and we went onto autopilot.

It was tricky for Chris because we were climbing through dense brush and only occasionally got a clear view of the valley beneath us. So, his vertigo was confused. It knew that we were climbing and that there were big drops beneath us, but the brush offered a false sense of security.

As we climbed I saw signs of wild boar everywhere. They had dug up massive areas under the oak trees to get at every available acorn. I was rather concerned as to what to do if I spotted one. I imagined shouting 'Wild Boar' and getting the call-and-response that we all thought so amusing. I could see them both shouting 'Wild Boar' back at me, blissfully unaware that a muscular porker was bearing down on them. They'd be the victims of the boy who cried boar.

Up and up we scrambled for a couple of hours until we finally came to an idyllic clearing where we ripped off our backpacks and lay down, exhausted. After ten minutes, we were sufficiently recovered to explore the area. A rock gave us an unhindered view down into the valley and we could see the gleaming roof of the monastery. Annoyingly, considering the length of time that we had been climbing, it didn't seem too far away. I moved away from the rock and peed long and hard on a bush while Harry unsuccessfully tried to persuade Chris to get on the rock and have a look down. We sat back down and watched Caroll wander around looking for something.

'What are you looking for, Caroll?' I asked.

'Wild asparagus. It grows in areas like this and it is delicious.'

I watched in a kind of slow-motion horror as he approached the bush that I had just peed on. He squatted down and picked several long, thin green stalks and popped them in his mouth.

'Sooo good,' said Caroll, triumphantly.

I kept quiet – it was too late to say anything – but I politely declined when he came over with some in his hand for me to try. In my defence I felt that, since eating asparagus made your pee smell of it, I was just cutting out the middle man ... or something like that.

As we continued on up, the wild valley gave way to orchards and then finally to a village where possibly the sweetest dog I had ever encountered made a half-hearted attempt to bark at us before rolling over on his back and proffering his tummy for us to tickle. I seriously considered scooping him up and popping him into my rucksack, but just then a little girl ran out and started rolling around with the dog. He was clearly well loved.

Walking through the village, we came to a spring, next to which sat a smiley, gap-toothed old woman who was chopping freshly picked parsley for the tabbouleh. We took some stone steps up and soon we were climbing through a steep meadow absolutely bursting with wild flowers. The valley lay beneath us and the snow-flecked peaks of the mountains soared above us.

It was fitting that we now entered Ehden, traipsing through beautiful streets and marvelling at some of the buildings. We could have been in a hill-town in France or Italy. Ehden immediately became our new favourite place. We eventually came into the town square – cafés and restaurants were dotted around it – and sat in the shade of a couple of giant plane trees. We ordered drinks and took in our surroundings.

'So, this must be the beer garden of Eden,' said Chris to much applause from us. I was livid that I hadn't thought of this myself and consoled myself with several ice-cold beers.

A youth who had been sitting at a café on the other side of the square got up and came over.

'Hello, where are you from?' he asked.

'England,' I replied.

'You are welcome here. Please, you must try the sahlab here – it is very sweet, a local speciality. I think you will like.' And with that he went back to his seat across the square. He wasn't trying to sell anything. He was just being kind to strangers. I loved Ehden.

After an hour we started off again. We were going to stay the night in Ehden but were going to hike to the Horsh Ehden Cedar Reserve, because one could never see too many cedars. We walked up and out of the town and along a tarmac road that eventually turned into a steep track that brought us to the entrance to the reserve.

There was a poster at the gate that explained to the hiker that there was a Maple Trail in the reserve and this had been sponsored by the Bruce Trail Association in Canada. I smiled at this coincidence. The Bruce Trail was Canada's oldest trail, running 890 kilometres from Niagara Falls to Tobermory, at the tip of the Bruce Peninsula. It ran along the Niagara Escarpment, just behind my Canadian in-laws' old house in Ancaster, Ontario. It made me think of home and how much my wife would have loved this place. I vowed to return with her and the kids one day. This country was so much part of who I was and yet they knew nothing of it. I'd been countless times to my wife's country, Canada, and my kids and I adored it. I loved that it gave them roots and a sense of origin. I wanted them to have the same feeling that I had for the Levant. Sadly, I wasn't sure that any of them would ever develop it. Lebanon was a way more complex place to love than Canada. I could only try.

The reserve was, at times, almost Californian with thick moss trailing off oaks that had plunged their roots into large stones that longed to be clambered over. The cedars were spaced out and so had had room to unfurl their impressive branches to their full extent, trapping every ray of sun available. There was a powerful spirituality about these trees. I walked on briskly for fear of becoming a tree-hugger, but the urge was strong. It was a gentle, easy stroll, downhill along well-maintained trails, and nobody was complaining. This was very much a place where day-trippers could come and have a cedar fix and a quick walk in the wild.

Somewhere along the way, we had become walking snobs. Anywhere that had a whiff of too much organisation was anathema to us. This was a silly attitude, and I knew that I should have been much more positive about the Lebanese doing stuff to protect their beautiful country, but I couldn't help it.

We exited the reserve at the bottom entrance where there was a rather enticing-looking place replete with comfortable chairs and good beer. We sat and soaked up the sun while a de-mob happy Caroll got a lift back with a local to get the van. Harry was worrying about something.

'I had two big beers at lunch and I feel wiped. You'd think, if anything, they'd give you energy.' He peered into his glass as though looking for the answer.

'Yes, it is weird. After all, marathon runners always have a couple of pints before they set off,' said Chris sarcastically.

'Do they?' asked Harry incredulously.

'No!' Chris and I replied in unison.

My thighs ached from the climbing we'd done, and I longed to lie down for a while but Caroll was away for a very long time before he finally returned with the van. We didn't bother to ask where he'd been, and we hopped in and were soon back in Ehden. The van pulled up outside a hotel-like building. Chris was immediately excited. It didn't last long.

We entered the massive lobby to find ourselves in a room that looked like it had been decorated by Elton John on Quaaludes. Massive, slightly distorting mirrors, psychedelic colours and gaudy fabrics had all been flung at the place in an attempt to make it 'boutique'. It was the type of interior that you would use should you be shooting a tele-novella on the life of Pablo Escobar. It was so awful that I rather loved it. Chris looked crestfallen.

'There's not going to be a trouser press here, is there?' he whispered.

'You'll be lucky to survive the night without a drug deal going badly wrong and ending up with you being chainsawed to death in your shower,' I whispered back.

'Oh God,' said Chris, a bit too loudly.

The owner of the hotel was delightful and seemed to have been informed that I was someone of a little more consequence than I actually am. I had no complaints and rolled with the fawning, much to Harry's bemusement.

'You know that this is not Bill Bryson? Peace be upon him,' he said to the confused lady.

'Blessed be his name,' muttered Chris.

'Bill who?' asked the lady.

'Exactly, madam,' I said. 'Now please show us to our delightful rooms.'

We were on the top floor and had to wait quite some time as Chris struggled to hump his suitcase up the stairs. The rooms were as I'd expected, not unlike a hooker's boudoir but with the added frisson of no lights in the bathroom so that you had to play Lebanese roulette with the inevitable dangling electrical wire.

We were expected downstairs for a meal with our hostess, but Chris and Harry were having a little rebellion on WhatsApp and demanding that we go out to the nice square and eat in a restaurant. I think for Chris it was a control thing; he'd had enough of not being able to choose what he ate. For Harry it was a lot simpler; he was hoping that they might have spaghetti bolognese on the menu.

It was slightly embarrassing as a meal had been cooked for us, including the local speciality of kibbe Zghortawiye (kibbe from Zghorta), which was a lamb kibbe inflated like a small balloon and filled with fat and meat that cooked inside. I thought it sounded amazing, but this was the final straw for Harry, who insisted on the restaurant plan. So, I negotiated with the hostess and apologised, and I said we'd take the food as lunch the following day.

We headed off to the central square, where we had agreed to meet Caroll and his replacement guide, Gilbert. Caroll would have supper with us and then head for the airport.

We were three araks in when they turned up. Gilbert was a big bear of a man who we all liked instantly. He came from Beit Meri, a village neighbouring the one that I'd grown up in, and we were soon chatting and joking away. It was a relief to us that things would not be awkward with a new guy. Caroll didn't bother with the meal; he had one drink and then announced that he was off. We all said our goodbyes as he got in his van and watched as he drove away.

We ate supper with Gilbert, who turned out to be one of the founding members of the LMT and cared passionately about the future of Lebanon as an ecotourism destination. He was the opposite of Caroll, very macho, and I felt even more emasculated than usual. He promised us that the best was yet to come. I couldn't believe that we could see anything more beautiful than we already had.

We spent the rest of the meal talking about why Lebanon's tourism industry was so bad. Gilbert had his theories. He said that people in the traditional tourist destinations saw ecotourism as a threat rather than something they could work with. It was insane that a country with such long-standing and sharp mercantile instincts was unable to sell itself. Obviously, the other major problem was the political situation, the hangover from the war and the general uneasiness on the part of most Westerners to visit this part of the Middle East.

Supper over, we wandered back through town, stopping off in a late-night store to get Harry a new box of Choco Pops as he was all out. Gilbert started telling Harry that he should try a Lebanese breakfast, but Harry put his hand up to stop him.

'Gilbert, before you start ... please do not waste your breath. You have a wonderful country full of fabulous people, but your local breakfast arrangements are something that require immediate attention. In fact, I think it might just be a major contributing factor to the low tourism footfall here. People simply can't cope with abominations like cheese and olives at breakfast.' Harry's poker face was immaculate.

Gilbert didn't know what to say and simply shook his head in bemusement. I assumed he was starting to realise why Caroll had bailed on us early.

## DAY 19

# EHDEN TO BQAA SOFRINE

We woke at dawn, as Gilbert had told us we had a big day ahead of us. Breakfast was in the vast Salvador Dalí meets Pablo Escobar room. To make matters worse, the local delicacy, sahlab, the thing that the kind youth in the square had recommended, was produced. It was a hangover from the Ottoman era, a flour made from the tubers of the orchid mixed with milk. Our hostess floated around behind us urging us to sample it. It reminded me of the warm yak milk that I'd been forced to drink in the Himalayas. It had the consistency of camel semen and, I imagined, about the same taste. By now, Chris was in a state of catatonic shock; not only was he faced with these culinary horrors but, far worse for him, he was being forced to try them.

Half an hour later we all piled into the back of a pick-up truck that was to drop us off where we had finished the day before at the bottom entrance to the Horsh Ehden Cedar Reserve. We retraced our footsteps of the previous day before turning off onto a trail that took us through a wilder, remote part of the reserve. It was a gloriously sunny day and the sunlight flickered through the ancient trees and warmed our backs as we crossed the forest floor. Occasionally we would come to a break in the trees and we could look down to the coast. For once there was no haze obscuring our view, and all of Tripoli lay beneath us. I could see the little islands off the coast, the Crusader citadel, the stretch of the Corniche, and I had a sudden longing for a shitty fish sandwich.

We exited the forest and were now above the main treeline. The trail became very rocky with just the odd juniper tree for company. In a little valley, we stopped at a spring to refill our CamelBaks. Gilbert had a snazzy new water filter that he had picked up at a trade show in Jordan. It worked a little like one of those cafetières that you slowly pressed down. He filled the thing and started to filter it.

'Is the water not already clean?' I asked him.

'Yes, it is, but I love my gadget, so I want to try it.'

'There are always independent pollutants as well,' Harry added, indicating something with his eyebrows.

I looked up to see that, unbeknownst to Gilbert, Chris was relieving himself about 10 metres above the spring and presumably adding his potency through the porous rock directly into our water supply. Gilbert finished and offered us a drink. Both Harry and I politely declined and watched as Gilbert drank his fill. We had to stop peeing on our guides' foodstuffs.

We started to descend along a rocky trail. On the other side of the small valley was a sizeable herd of goats. The goatherd skipped up the sheer, slippery mountainside as though strolling along a gentle riverbank. He was barefoot and wearing torn jeans and a cut-off T-shirt. He could have been fifty or he could have been seventy, it was difficult to tell. His nimble ascent of the slope, as opposed to our huffing and puffing descent, together with his appearance in comparison with our stay-dry shirts, specialist walking boots and hiking poles, made me think of that passage in E. M. Forster's *A Passage to India* in which Adela Quested notices a physically beautiful 'untouchable' sitting on the floor in the corner of the court. He is pulling on the punkah that fans air into the sticky room. She ruminates on the fact that nature occasionally 'throws out a god, not many, but one here and there, to prove to society how little its categories impress her'.

The trail flattened out and we were knee-deep in a thick carpet of yellow and red wild flowers. The smell was intoxicating, like being gently punched by familiar but elusive memories. We hit a thin track that led us down into an almost perfect meadow, shaped like a bowl. Olive trees and oaks were dotted around, and a large rock in the middle made for the perfect lunch location. Up until that moment, I honestly don't think I'd ever been anywhere more beautiful in my whole life.

'What is this place? Who owns it?' I asked Gilbert.

'I don't know, but I told you my walk was the best.'

'I want to buy this place now and live here for ever.'

'I'm on the phone now doing it.' Chris laughed.

Harry wandered over to a couple of neighbouring oak trees and produced a hammock that he'd bought in Beirut. He rigged it up and lay in the shade, smoking a cigarette in something approaching a state of bliss. Chris, Gilbert and I had our lunch on the rock. I opened my kibbe Zghortawiye, like opening a fresh pitta bread, and, following Gilbert's instructions, used it as a meat pocket to fill with tomatoes, olives and labneh. The result was out of this world.

Having finished lunch, I floated into the middle of the meadow and sank down into a mattress of long grass and flowers. I lay there for twenty minutes, in total silence, save for the buzz-buzz of insects and the swish of the long grass in the gentle breeze. The sun beat down on me. This was it. This was my ground zero. For some weird reason the video for Lenny Kravitz's 'Let Love Rule' came into my head and I started to hum it. I was happy, blissfully happy.

Eventually we had to leave this paradise. I dropped a pin on my iPhone so that I could find it again. Gilbert said it was called Baidar Diyala. I could have spent the rest of my life there.

We entered another valley littered with shattered stone that had a curious blue core. Gradually the valley deepened, and we eventually joined a donkey path that took us right down to the river that ran through it. Two rockpools glistened invitingly, and Harry immediately stripped off and got in. His screams echoed around the valley and he clambered back out. I dipped my foot in; it was colder than ice, a glacial pool.

We walked along the river for a while before starting to ascend on the other side. It was a tricky climb over rocks, fighting through thick undergrowth until we reached a track that ran flat and parallel to the river. We started along it, passing families working in their fields. They all looked mildly surprised to see us, but were very friendly and we stopped to chat with one group.

'Where are you going?' said a wrinkled old man, his eyes squinting in the sunlight.

'Bqaa Sofrine,' we answered.

'Why are you going there?'

'To stay the night,' I replied.

'Why?'

'Because we are walking across Lebanon,' I said.

'Why?'

'Very good question, sir,' Harry replied when the man's question was translated.

We waved goodbye to the old man, who was none the wiser as to what we were doing. Around a corner we came across an unexpected sight. In the middle of the track was a small tortoise, inching his way forward in the same direction as us. I was unsure if he was also doing the LMT across Lebanon but if he was then he'd probably started on the day the trail was opened. I lay on the ground and put my face right up close to get a good look at him.

At first, he withdrew into his shell but soon realised that the idiot prostrated in front of him meant no harm. His little bald head slowly poked back out of the shell and he gave me the once-over with his beady brown eyes. I offered him some za'atar. He took it with good grace and munched laboriously on my offering.

It was greatly reassuring to all of us that there was a slower person than Chris on the trail and we marched on with new determination. It didn't last long, however. Gilbert pointed to a couple of half-finished buildings ahead of us on the crest of a hill.

'There is a big problem coming up. The people in these houses have three dogs that are very aggressive. We had two people attacked and bitten when we did the annual walk.' He was talking about a walk that the LMT organised every year with as many people as possible doing the trail in a group.

'Were they badly hurt?' said Chris.

'One had his buttocks very seriously injured, yes.'

We tried to be adults and not giggle, but it was hard. Gilbert started picking up large stones from the ground and putting them in his pocket. 'I would suggest you do the same as me, get some stones and put them in your pockets. When we approach, we will form a tight group and use your poles as a defence.'

'Whaaat? You're serious about this?' said Chris.

'Very serious, these are big dogs and they are extremely aggressive. I have warned the owners before, but they do not care. If I have to, I will kill one with stones,' Gilbert said matter-of-factly.

I got the feeling that Gilbert was not a dog-lover. There is pretty much nothing that would make me throw a stone at a dog, let alone kill one. It is one of the reasons that I could not live in Lebanon; the way animals are treated is something I'd find very hard to handle. I remembered Gandhi's maxim, 'The greatness of a nation and its moral progress can be judged by the way its animals are treated.'

My sister has the same attitude: that is why she has so many dogs at home. She is a soft touch in a hard country. She hasn't just put up dogs at home but is heavily involved in a dog shelter not far from the house called BETA (Beirut for the Ethical Treatment of Animals). The shelter has over eight hundred dogs and I found visiting the place both harrowing and heart-warming at the same time. Stray or abused dogs are brought into the shelter and looked after, while organisers try to get them adopted, either abroad or by people in Lebanon. Lebanese students volunteer to spend time petting these affection-starved dogs and they flock around you when you enter the place like desperate actors at an open-call audition. I would take every dog if I could. Love of animals is pretty much the only way for my emotionally crippled family to express love. I never ever saw my mum and dad hug or kiss, but my dad would spend nights under the dining-room table nursing a sick dog. I think the technical term is zoophilic but that might have other connotations.

I wondered what it was that had made both sides of my family so emotionally cold when it came to human relations. With my dad, I thought it must be a combination of his era, his schooling and then the psychological firestorm that must have been his war experiences. My mother came from such a different background and yet they had such similar traits. My mother didn't even seem to be very much into animals ...

Back on the Lebanese mountain, Harry started picking up stones.

'What are you doing?' I asked.

'I'm not going to be bitten on the arse by some dog; I'm going to defend myself,' he said.

'I don't think I can.'

'I'm struggling as well,' said Chris, 'although I'm distinctly un-keen to have my buttocks savaged.'

'Not what I've heard ...' said Harry with the comic timing and sad inevitability of an unreformed public schoolboy.

By now, we were all totally adrenalised. Harry and Gilbert clutched the rocks in their pockets while Chris and I advanced on the houses like an approaching Roman phalanx. We moved up the slope in battle formation ready for we knew not what. We got to the dusty yard in front of the first house, where two bearded youths were sitting on a flowery-swingy-sofa thing that would have not looked out of place in a retirement home in Madeira. They looked up in amusement as we crept into the yard.

'What the shit are you doing?' cried one of the youths in Arabic.

'Where are the dogs?' shouted Gilbert.

'They are not here today, relax,' shouted the other youth.

'They bit two people in my party last time we came through.'

'Well, they probably deserved it,' said the first youth.

'You should control them.'

'You should stop walking and use a car like normal people,' shouted the other youth.

'He has a point,' said Chris, when this was translated.

We all relaxed slightly and dropped our poles down to a less offensive position. Harry and Gilbert emptied their pockets of the stones that they had gathered.

'Where are the dogs then?' shouted Gilbert.

'None of your business,' replied the first youth.

Gilbert muttered obscenities to himself and led us on through the yard, down past a cage that looked as if it had been built to restrain the Incredible Hulk.

'Just how big are these dogs?' I asked.

'They are big,' replied Gilbert.

We all subconsciously stepped up our pace and were soon well past the kill-zone and going downhill, so spirits were most definitely on the up. We were still a little jumpier than usual and all secretly hoped that when the tortoise finally made it to that bit, he would be able to sneak past the hounds of hell. We were now de-mob happy and starting to sing Proclaimers songs again, which was never a good sign. Gilbert stopped at an invisible fork in the road.

'So ... Caroll warned me not to tell you until now ...' he said.

Chris groaned audibly.

'Umm, there is a difficult bit before we get into the village we are staying in.' Gilbert looked matter-of-fact.

'When you say difficult, what do you mean?' asked Chris.

'Not difficult at all, just there is a ledge that is very steep ...'

We could tell that Gilbert did not feel this was even worth mentioning, but had been warned by Caroll that Chris was mentally unstable.

'I knew it ... why is it only now, when I am trapped, that I am told about this?' Chris was starting to erupt. I felt like a villager close to the epicentre of an earthquake who should really be frantically packing their belongings and getting ready to flee but didn't want to miss the show.

'It is not very steep to be honest ... I think you will be OK, but I thought I should tell you before we do it,' Gilbert said offhandedly.

'Before what? Not before we actually set off. I'm now stuck without any real choice in the matter.' Chris was going off on one, and we could only stand and watch and pretend that we weren't enjoying the drama.

'I honestly will guarantee you that you will not die,' said Gilbert.

'Honestly, Gilbert, I'd prefer to die than to have no choice over my decisions, a low level of constant mistrust followed by a nightmare terror episode that I am supposed to be grateful for having survived. If I really wanted this sort of thrill, it would be both cheaper and less physically exhausting to allow my wife to hire a hitman to kill me along with a very secure safe word.' Chris had now lost his shit, and Harry and I were trying to look sympathetic while catching each other's eye in order to maximise our enjoyment of the moment.

'Well, if this really is a problem, then we can take the road into the village,' said Gilbert, teasing out a particularly delicate fly.

'REALLY a problem? What, you think, maybe, that I'm making this up for attention?' Chris was now bristling with indignation.

'No ... Chris ... nobody is thinking that at all,' said Harry, in both a very unhelpful and a very insincere tone.

'Well, fuck all of you. I've had enough of people not telling me things, mollycoddling me, not allowing me to take my own decisions.' Chris was now full Krakatoa.

'So ... shall we just take the road?' Even Gilbert looked a little intimidated, like a man who had just taken his first look down into a bubbling molten crater.

'Yes, I think that might be the best option,' I said, trying to slide a heavy cap over the effervescent furnace.

We all climbed in silence for a while until we reached a gravel road that was only used by enormous trucks taking stone away from a nearby quarry. We trudged along the side of it, the village of Bqaa Sofrine below us, with the occasional passing truck coating us in layers of white dust. By the time we arrived in the village we looked like a travelling group of street statues.

The village was Sunni, and it was the eve of Ramadan. As we walked into the forecourt of a four-storey apartment building, we could hear a couple of muezzins doing their stuff. Several kids were playing outside but they legged it screaming the moment they spotted the four white apparitions come down from the mountains.

Their father appeared. A heavily bearded man in stylish T-shirt and jeans. He welcomed us and showed us up to the first floor where a sparse but comfortable apartment awaited us.

Chris had calmed down and we were all longing for a drink. Unfortunately, it being the eve of Ramadan and this being quite a strict Sunni household, beers were not an option.

We sat on the suntrap of a balcony, looking down to the Mediterranean far below. A meal was brought and placed on the table in front of us by a smiley old woman. I was thrilled as we had shish barak again, the yoghurty dumplings with rice. There was also stuffed coussa (squash) and stuffed vine leaves. They had provided enough to feed an army. It was our last night on the move, and we were excited and sad in equal measure. Harry was mainly sad that there were no beers.

The sunset was spectacular – violent red streaks of light made it look like the sky was on fire. As the sun disappeared, the muezzins started to call the faithful to prayer. First one, then two, then three battled it out. Far below, we could see the twinkling lights of the Tripolitan fishing fleet bobbing up and down on the sea. A crescent moon hung in the sky. It was the perfect end.

Harry and Chris went to bed early and I stayed up chatting to Gilbert. He produced his mobile phone and asked me whether I liked music. I told him that I did, and he got a video up on YouTube for me. It started with two men, spotlit on stage, doing the Muslim call to prayer, then a woman appeared and started to sing 'Ave Maria' and the tunes started to twist around each other in a heart-stoppingly beautiful way. I was instantly obsessed with the track and we played it three times in a row as we both sat in silence, lost in thought. The artist was Tania Kassis, a very well-known Lebanese singer. She had given this special performance at Olympia in Paris for an Islamic–Christian concert that was held after the terrorist attacks in the city in 2015.

I thanked Gilbert for introducing me to the music.

'This is what Lebanon could be,' he said sadly.

'It will be,' I said in a determined fashion that I'm afraid I didn't really believe.

I sloped off to bed, leaving Gilbert on the balcony, where he had decided to sleep. It was a hot night; he said he needed a good sleep seeing as tomorrow we would descend into the Valley of Hell. It was going to be a very long day, he said. I expected nothing less.

# DAY 20

# DENNIEH TO QEMMAMINE

I woke up and stared at the ceiling for a while. I was sad. This was the last day and soon we would be back in the real world. I didn't want to go back to the real world; my life had been simplified to a steady routine. It was about getting up, walking with friends, getting to our destination, going to sleep. It was a simple life with simple goals and I started to worry about returning to the world of work, bills and the daily concerns that I had cast aside from the moment that I'd first put on my rucksack.

I packed up for the last time and headed outside to where Harry and Chris were already sitting. It may have been Ramadan, but our hosts had provided us with a slap-up breakfast of manakish, eggs (cooked in lots of oil to show wealth), makdous (preserved aubergine), labneh, tomatoes, cucumber, cheese, apricot jam, shanklish (a type of cheese), olives and freshly baked bread. The full Lebanese. It was heaven ... for most of us.

'Well, I must say I shall miss this the most,' said Harry sarcastically.

'You really do not like?' asked Gilbert, stuffing his manakish with tomatoes and cucumber.

'If you ever visit England, Gilbert, I shall take you to a greasy spoon, where we shall partake of a proper breakfast that will ruin you for life.' Harry smiled.

'I prefer this. I never eat breakfast at home, but this is going to be the new norm,' I said.

'Have you informed your wife?' asked Harry.

'No I haven't, Harry. Mainly because I don't live in the 1970s, so don't expect my wife to cook for me,' I said.

'You mean you have her poorly trained,' said Harry, half-jokingly.

'No, I mean she's my wife, not my cook.'

'Of course, she's Canadian. There's a reason that you don't see Canadian restaurants about the place. No natural cuisine.' Harry chuckled.

'I'll have you know that Canadian breakfasts are amazing – pancakes and blueberries and bacon and maple syrup.' I was annoyed now.

'Well, you'd better get your wife onto it.' Harry could be incredibly irritating.

'I presume your wife does everything for you, Chris?' Harry now turned his fire on Chris.

'Well, she's been known to help ring the takeaway people.' Chris was not for rising.

I had arranged for my brother, Marc-Henri, and my nephew Paul to join us for the last day, and as we finished breakfast we heard the honk of a horn. They arrived in a taxi from Zouk Mousbeh. They were both dressed as though off on a gentle stroll through the park, which made us look even more stupid in our hiking accoutrement.

We all got in a van that Gilbert had organised to take us to Dennieh, the start of our last day's walk. We drove through empty villages as people slept through the day in order to ease the pain of Ramadan. We stopped at Sfireh, possibly the second

most impressive Roman temple in Lebanon and a place that
neither Paul nor Marc-Henri had visited before. One is never a
tourist in one's own home. The temple was almost intact and
had been built by Septimius Severus in the second century AD.
Septimius, a Roman Emperor born in Leptis Magna in modern-
day Libya, died in York after becoming ill while invading
Scotland. It was probably the breakfasts.

We found a hidden staircase within the front wall and all
climbed onto the top of the walls of the roofless temple. The
views were staggering and once again the feeling of history
seeping into my body was as pleasurable as any drug. Clambering
over ruins with my brother took me right back to expeditions
into Syria where we would scramble over every archaeological
site in the country. I didn't want to go back into exile, to what
was now home in England. I belonged here in this magical part
of the world. It was in my blood and I'd blocked it off for too
long. I was finally feeling at home just as I was going to have to
leave.

The van dropped us by a track and we all set off in single file.

'You will see I have left the best until last,' Gilbert smiled.

Paul, being the hyperactive young man he was, started
bounding around us, jumping off rocks and generally arsing
about like a gazelle on speed.

'Please, slow down, be careful where you step. If you injure
yourself, I am the one that will have to get you out of here,'
shouted Gilbert in Arabic.

Paul appeared to have the family trait of not listening to
authority and ignored Gilbert.

'Paul, stop acting the goat,' shouted my brother.

Paul muttered something and slowed down a little.

From the get-go it was clear that today was going to be pretty special. On our first stop, under a juniper tree at the top of a steep climb, we got a clear view into Syria along the coast. We could just make out the port of Tartus, the second largest port in Syria and the site of a major Russian naval facility, something that went a long way to explaining the Russian support for Assad. This was a vital Mediterranean asset for the Russians that allowed their fleet to refuel and undergo repairs without having to head all the way back to Sebastopol. They were not about to lose it.

Just off the coast of the city was the island of Arwad, the only inhabited island in Syria and an ancient centre for boat building. Syria was so close you could touch it, and I longed to visit the country again. So much of my youth had been spent exploring the place. I hoped that there would be peace there soon and that I could return.

We started descending into a lush green valley. Harry and I were ahead of the others and were heading for a spring that we could see on the valley floor. Ahead of us, in the shade of a fig tree, stood two mules. As we approached, a man burst out from behind them, pulling up his trousers as he sprinted away from us at top speed. Harry and I looked at each other and started laughing.

'I guess you have to take it where you can up here.' Harry laughed.

'Do you honestly think that's what was going on?' I asked.

'Well, what else could it be?'

'He could have been having a sneaky dump when he heard us approaching,' I suggested.

'He seems very keen to get away,' said Harry, as we watched the man disappear over a far hill.

We approached the mules, who nuzzled us and appeared to be very grateful for our arrival. They were gorgeous animals and we spent a good five minutes communing with them in a more acceptable manner. We then carried on down to the spring, where the others had already assembled.

The water was ice cold. We took off our shoes and socks and sat on the ancient stone ledge of a long trough that was filled by the spring. We were just discussing who was going to be brave enough to submerge themselves fully in the ice bath when a cry came from high above. It was a goatherd and he was screaming at us and gesturing for us to move. Begrudgingly, we moved and hundreds of his goats poured down the valley, heading for the trough. Within two minutes we were submerged in goats. We sat to the side and tried to keep them out of our rucksacks, but it was too late for Paul's shoes as they were stolen by two goats who had clearly had enough of walking barefoot. It took him a good ten minutes to retrieve them. I could have stayed there for hours. There was something hypnotic about the sound of the little bells the goats wore.

We clambered across quite a loose and difficult path up a side of the valley until we came onto a grassy plateau, surrounded on three sides by high mountain. It had an ancient feel to it, and you could just make out the rough traces of foundations of ancient settlements. It would have been a determined invader who crossed this plateau and still wanted to continue. The urge to settle down and build here was huge, even for someone as practically useless as myself. The scenery reminded me of the Atlas Mountains in Morocco crossed with a touch of Italian–Swiss Alps.

We crossed the plateau in single file, trailing our hands in the long seagrass. At the other end, we joined a track that took us up and away from the plateau. I turned for one last, longing look.

We lunched under an enormous juniper tree that had split down the middle, creating a hole big enough for a man to hide in. A hundred metres away was the edge of a hill from which we could get another unencumbered view into Syria. We were not far from the border and the city of Homs on the Syrian side. I'd recently watched the documentary, *Under the Wire*, about the death of the *Sunday Times* reporter Marie Colvin, who had smuggled herself into Homs from Lebanon in the middle of an awful siege. She must have slipped over the border very near to where we were. Gilbert told us that we had about four hours left to go. Feelings of both relief and sadness blended into one.

We started to follow a trail down into the valley; we just couldn't see how there were four hours to go. We assumed that Gilbert had misunderstood the concept of hours in the same way that Jacky and Caroll had not understood minutes. Gilbert kept assuring Chris that it was downhill from now on. He would say this, in the finest tradition of Lebanese guides, just as he would be starting to climb another massive incline. It was almost like being in an alternate universe, but we didn't care. We had smelled the end and were pretty much on autopilot. As we clambered up one particularly steep bit of scree, Paul's tight trousers split down the buttocks line. Fortunately, he was wearing underpants and able to continue without problems. Chris and I looked at each other and gave a little silent prayer of thanks that it had not happened to commando Harry. Finally, we stopped on the crest of a hill.

'Are you ready to enter the Valley of Hell?' said Gilbert.

'What? I thought we'd been trekking in it all day,' I replied.

'Oh no, that was the aperitif, this is the main course.' Gilbert smiled and walked over the crest as we followed uncertainly.

Below us was the most outrageous valley so far; the drop was vertiginous to the bottom, maybe a kilometre straight down. There was very little in the valley save for a village far, far below.

'That is Qemmamine, our final destination,' said Gilbert.

Harry and I looked down and then both looked at Chris.

'And we are descending this?' asked Chris.

'We are,' replied Gilbert.

'And you didn't think of telling me about it?' insisted Chris.

'I didn't want to worry you until necessary,' said Gilbert.

We all stood back waiting for the explosion. But it never came.

'So be it …' said Chris in a resigned manner. 'Let's get it over with.'

Chris took the lead and started on down the treacherous donkey path. We followed, looking at each other in a surprised manner. The path was ludicrously steep and very soon Chris asked Gilbert to walk ahead of him. I was just thanking the Lord that we had not walked north to south as we would be having to do this uphill, which would have totally finished me off.

The undergrowth around us was so thick that we could not see much except for the occasional break when we could suddenly see all the way down and Chris went a bit wobbly. There were a lot of curious, quasi-psychedelic trees with no bark and a reddish trunk that looked like they had been dropped in from another dimension. At one stage, we crossed over what had clearly been a recent rock fall that had swept away the path.

Even I felt a little dodgy trying to scramble and grip on loose pebbles with a sheer drop to my right. How Chris got across was a miracle and there was a modicum of foul language. After two hours of painfully slow descent, we reached the bottom and started to see the occasional building as we reached the outskirts of Qemmamine. My legs no longer ached; I was free of all the humiliation of that time, years ago in the Himalayas, when, defeated by the climb to Namche Bazaar, I'd had to hire a horse and passed my fellow trekkers in utter shame.

We'd done it. We'd finished.

We entered the village and stopped by a spring. We flung off our rucksacks, shed our poles and doused ourselves in the cold spring water before hugging in a most un-British manner that our guide at Baalbek would have been most impressed with.

We had changed over this walk. Chris had conquered so much more than he thought possible and very much left his comfort zone way behind. I had buried a lot of demons. Harry ... well, to be honest Harry hadn't changed at all, but then maybe he didn't need to. After ten minutes or so, the van that had dropped us off turned up. We were only five minutes or so out of the village when we came across an obstacle. A lorry that had just picked up a load of rock from a quarry was sat right in the middle of the road at a right angle.

'If this is some sort of kidnap attempt, then I'm going to be very annoyed that they left it until we'd finished the whole walk. They could have done it earlier,' said Chris.

We all got out to investigate. There was no sign of the driver and we could only assume that the lorry had broken down mid-turn. Harry suggested letting off the handbrake and rolling the lorry off the road, but this would have meant it plummeting off the steep drop to the side and destroying it. Harry saw no problem in this, as the lorry was delaying our search for beer, but calmer heads prevailed. In the end, we determined that there was just enough room for our van to pass between the lorry and the drop. We were sure it could be done, but not quite sure enough to be in the vehicle when it was attempted.

We all gave directions and hand signals as the driver inched his way past. It took a good few minutes, but he eventually did it and off we went again. But not for long. In the next village, we were stopped by a very old black Mercedes that was parked across the road, the bonnet up, with a man buried deep in the engine. We honked, and he came up for air and started shouting at us to have patience. He had picked the wrong van. We all got out and, despite his protestations, pushed his car to the side of the road. He was keeping mountain men from their beer.

After an hour or so we hit the coastal highway and headed south past Tripoli. We were going to Anfeh to finish off what we'd started several days before. When we arrived, we headed back down towards the huts and our favourite seaside eatery.

The owner greeted us like long-lost friends and we were soon toasting the end of our journey with cold beers and octopus. There was no Ramadan going on down here and we thanked the Lord for it. The sun shone, the beer was good, and we were blissfully happy. Just an hour and a half earlier, we had been descending into the Valley of Hell. Now we were sitting by the sea of heaven toasting our accomplishments. What a country.

A couple of hours later and, having said our goodbyes to Marc-Henri and Paul near Jounieh, we were dropped off at the family home and said goodbye to Gilbert. My sister and her husband greeted us with more booze and Harry was informed that a spaghetti bolognese had been prepared in his honour.

After supper we got a lift down into Beirut. We had agreed to meet Paul in Gemmayze so he could show us a bit of Beirut nightlife. We got gloriously drunk in a tiny dive bar called Torino Express. It was full of arty types in leather jackets and white T-shirts and lit by a seedy red neon light. It was just what we were after and we sat at the tiny bar for hours, scaring away Beirut hipsters with our mountain tales.

At about one in the morning we moved onto a rooftop club called Coop D'Etat where we drank more and watched Harry stagger about trying to dance to some seriously good eighties retro. At about three in the morning, we called it a night and got a taxi back up to the house. I sat in the front chatting to the driver while Chris tried to keep an almost unconscious Harry from drooling onto his shoulder.

# FINAL DAY

On our last day, I was up early and straight onto the balcony to watch Beirut wake up. There was a little activity in the port, on the north side of the city, and I watched a large ship slowly glide into the harbour. I looked south and saw a plane land at the airport, having swung in low over the sea. It was possible that this was our plane landing from London, but I couldn't quite make out the logo. Presently I went downstairs to find Harry and Chris already at breakfast on the main terrace. Harry was in bliss, surrounded by various packs of cereal and with a large jug of cold milk to boot.

'At last, civilisation.' He laughed.

'Soon you'll be back in the land of the fry-up and all will be well for you and not your heart.' I pushed a plate of cheese towards him and he visibly recoiled in horror.

'It can't be soon enough,' said Harry.

Breakfast over, we all headed to the airport. By chance, my sister and her husband were flying to London on the same plane. On my way to passport control, I chucked my rucksack onto the belt taking it into the X-ray machine. I was a little hungover and just wanted to get some hair of the dog down me in the lounge.

My bag came out and I was about to pick it up when a soldier, having been nodded to by an official, approached me and took the bag. He ordered me to follow him to a metal table where he asked me to open it. I did so without thinking and he started to rifle through it. He opened my zipped-up outer pocket and pulled out about seven spent machine-gun bullets, a lump of shrapnel and a large *douchka* cartridge. He placed them all on the table and looked up at me suspiciously.

'Syria?' he barked.

'Sorry?' I replied, not too sure what he was getting at.

'You have been in Syria?' He glared at me.

'Oh, no ... just in Lebanon,' I answered. I'd completely forgotten about my war trophies.

'You have been fighting in Syria?' He looked very suspicious and I suddenly realised that this could be serious trouble.

'Oh, no, not at all. I have been in Lebanon, tourist.' I kicked myself. I was a traveller, not a tourist, but didn't want to complicate matters.

'Why this?' He pointed at the ordnance.

'Oh, I just picked them up in the mountains,' I said nonchalantly.

'In Syria, you fight with Daesh?' The soldier was insistent and had attracted the attention of a colleague and now they were both staring at my booty.

'No ... I was walking across Lebanon. Hiking. I am writing a book,' I said, starting to panic slightly.

'You are journalist?' the first soldier asked, looking at my immigration form. 'It says here comedian.'

'It's complicated. I do a bit of both,' I stammered.

'So why you not say you are journalist?' the solider asked.

'I'm not a journalist really, I'm a travel writer,' I said desperately.

'Have you ever heard of Bill Bryson, peace be upon him?' a soft voice said from behind me. It was Harry and he was enjoying my predicament.

'Blessed be his name,' muttered Chris, who had also now arrived.

'No,' said the soldier.

'Well, he is a very successful travel writer and my friend is a bit like him but without the "very" or the "successful" part.' Harry sniggered.

'So, you are not comedian?' asked the soldier.

'Have you heard of Mr Bean?' said Harry.

'Mr Bean? Yes,' said the soldier.

'Again, my friend is similar but just without the massive international success.' Harry laughed.

'I sold my shows to over eighty countries,' I protested.

'Yes, but that was a very long time ago,' interjected Chris.

'So, you were all travelling together?' asked the soldier.

'Yes, we were all walking across Lebanon,' I said, eager to drag Harry and Chris into my problems.

'Walking across? Why?' asked the soldier.

'That, sir, is a bloody good question,' said Harry.

There was silence for a moment. Then the soldier picked up the cartridges and shrapnel and dumped them into a large bin next to the table.

'Safe travels and I hope you enjoyed your stay in Lebanon,' he said, smiling for the first time.

'It was great, apart from the breakfast situation,' replied Harry.

'You have a beautiful country,' said Chris quickly.

'It was nice to come home,' I said.

And it had been. Very nice indeed.

# Credits

**Song lyrics**

Dry the River, 'Bible Belt'. 2010. Songwriters: Jonathan Warren, Matthew Taylor, Peter Liddle, Scott Miller & William Harvey. (Bible Belt lyrics © Warner/Chappell Music, Inc.)

Duran Duran, 'The Wild Boys'. 1984. Songwriters: Andy Taylor, John Taylor, Nick Rhodes, Roger Taylor & Simon Le Bon. (The Wild Boys lyrics © Sony/ATV Music Publishing LLC)

Duran Duran, 'Hungry Like the Wolf'. 1982. Songwriters: Andy Taylor, John Taylor, Nick Rhodes, Roger Taylor, Simon Le Bon. (Hungry Like the Wolf lyrics © Sony/ATV Music Publishing LLC)

Duran Duran, 'Is There Something I Should Know?'. 1983. Songwriters: Andy Taylor, John Taylor, Nick Rhodes, Roger Taylor & Simon Le Bon. (Is There Something I Should Know? lyrics © Sony/ATV Music Publishing LLC)

Icehouse, 'Uniform'. 1982. Songwriter: Ivor Arthur Davies. (Uniform lyrics © Kobalt Music Publishing Ltd)

Marillion, 'Fugazi'. 1984. Songwriters: Derek Dick, Ian Mosley, Mark Kelly, Pete Trewavas & Steve Rothery. (Fugazi lyrics © Sony/ATV Music Publishing LLC)

Marillion, 'Incubus'. 1984. Songwriters: Derek Dick, Ian Mosley, Mark Kelly, Pete Trewavas & Steve Rothery. (Incubus lyrics © Sony/ATV Music Publishing LLC)

Marillion, 'Script for a Jester's Tear'. 1983. Songwriters: Derek Dick, Ian Mosley, Mark Kelly, Michael Pointer, Pete Trewavas & Steve Rothery. (Script for a Jester's Tear lyrics © Sony/ATV Music Publishing LLC)

Marillion, 'The Web'. 1983. Songwriters: Mark Kelly, Steve Rothery, Peter Trewavas, Michael Pointer & Derek Dick. (The Web lyrics © EMI April Music Inc.)

Nick Cave & the Bad Seeds, 'Magneto'. 2016. Songwriters: Warren Ellis & Nicholas Cave. (Magneto lyrics © Kobalt Music Publishing Ltd)

Nick Cave & The Bad Seeds, 'Jesus Alone'. 2016. Songwriter: Nicholas Cave. (Jesus Alone lyrics © Kobalt Music Publishing Ltd)

The Waterboys, 'Old England'. 1985. Songwriter: Michael Scott. (Old England lyrics © Warner/Chappell Music, Inc.)

## Dramatic works
Abrahams, Jim, Zucker, David & Zucker, Jerry. Airplane!. 1941. USA: Paramount Pictures.

Robinson, Bruce. *Withnail and I*. 1987. UK: HandMade Films.